A Captive of the Caucasus

TRANSLATED BY

SUSAN BROWNSBERGER

Farrar Straus Giroux

NEW YORK

A

CAPTIVE

OF THE

CAUCASUS

———

ANDREI

BITOV

Library of Congress Cataloging-in-Publication Data
Bitov, Andrei.
[Essays. Selections. English]
A captive of the Caucasus / Andrei Bitov ; translated from the
Russian by Susan Brownsberger. — 1st ed.
1. Bitov, Andrei—Journeys. 2. Authors, Russian—20th century—
Journeys. I. Title.
PG3479.4.I8A23   1992   891.78′4403—dc20   [B]   91-40279 CIP

Contents

LESSONS

OF ARMENIA

Journey out of Russia

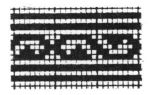

From the Author:
Translating Past to Present

On the first page of this book I was thirty years old, the entire Soviet regime was preparing for its fiftieth anniversary, Russian Christianity had not yet reached its millennium, and Armenian Christianity had already celebrated a millennium and a half. Everything was younger, not only the author but also his century.

Now there have been Karabakh and Sumgait and the earthquake, but in 1967, to the uninitiated eye, nothing of the sort distinguished Armenia from the other republics; written on every store window in Erevan, without comment, in palm branches, was the number "50," the only Armenian character I understood. Apart from the fact that Khrushchev had sold all the cognac spirits for currency, Armenia did not appear to have suffered any upheavals. But the country impressed me as being different, not Russia. I had never been in a different country.

Just the year before, I had been all set to travel to a different country. Even more than the "different," I was looking forward to the country: Japan. Out of the whole unvisited world, and without a solitary chance of visiting it, I had settled my choice irrevocably on two countries, Japan and England—the countries I thought the most civilized, on the one hand, and the most retentive of tradition, on the other. Moreover, both were islands. That was important. But important only to me. No one invited me, no one let me go. I might equally have dreamed of the moon or Mars. All of a sudden, Japan swiftly drew near me; apparently, dreams did indeed come true if they were real, as promised in the songs of my happy Stalinist childhood. And there I was, already rustling my Japanese yen, with a Nakhodka–Yokohama ticket in my pocket. I was on my way to Japan at the invitation of one of their film companies, to write the first Soviet–Japanese film script. The Japanese businessmen were baffled when they met at the dock a translator, a cameraman, and a representative of the film ministry—but not the man they had invited for the job. I was later informed that I'd had an acute liver attack. I have not, thank God, to this day.

Well, about the cognac. I don't know whether I can put this law into words (though I think it has even been expressed mathematically), but . . . quantity is needed for quality. In order to produce, say, a thousand tons of fine cognac, you must have, not that same amount of cognac spirits, but ten times more. Yet this doesn't make sense! To hoard one's gold without any profit, when it could be spent . . . So thought Khrushchev, and I would have thought the same. But the famous Armenian cognac has vanished. Or, rather, it hasn't vanished, but it has deteriorated appreciably. Or, rather, it has vanished in a certain sense. As cognac. But it was still around when I went, with sorrow, to Armenia instead of Japan. Supposedly on assignment, but actually to visit a friend. There was still cognac then: with its real cork corks, before the price increase, before the loss of flavor. It was good cognac. And plentiful.

. . . My friends and I sat under a grapevine. It hung from a wooden trellis, casting shade for us, while all around us the Armenian sun had reached smelting temperatures, and the charcoal in the grill was ripe for the shish kebab.

"You see," my friend said, when, as an appetizer to the shish kebab, some cabbage rolls were served, of a kind I hadn't seen—tiny dark green ones, on which we were supposed to pour yogurt. But the yogurt was matsuni, and the cabbage rolls were dolmas, for they were rolled not in a cabbage leaf but in a grape leaf . . . "You see," he said, "nothing gives of itself so entirely as the grapevine. It can be eaten"—he plucked a grape; "it can be drunk"—he sipped his cognac; "you can sit in its shade, its leaf is used for dolmas, and when it dies it can even be burned."

Around us lay grape firewood, delicate and gnarled. It gives the hottest heat. Which is best for shish kebab.

"Nothing is exploited so fully as the grape," my friend said. "Except perhaps woman, under socialism."

This was a joke. The company was exclusively male.

Cognac, conversation, shish kebab, and song—they followed one after the other, in the leisurely sequence of the south. The eye found repose in the biblical Mediterranean landscape. There was no reason to hurry, no need.

I expected nothing, and everything was a gift.

While one amiable man broiled and served the shish kebab, another gave us music.

He made a bashful entrance, and my Armenian friends welcomed him enthusiastically. From a large case he took a small pipe, longer than a whistle and shorter than a flute. It was entirely covered with gold rings—gifts, it seemed, from admirers. This was the great Rachia! I still wasn't expecting anything.

His pipe was called a *duduk*—as, indeed, it is *dudka* in Russian. And here was the first sound.

This was not a prelude to lament, it was not a lament. It was a postlude to lament. It was like childhood, if you remember, when out of grief comes harmony with the world, and all is clear. This clarity is greater than language. Indeed, it is language. Unspoken, because there's no need. Happiness. Understanding. Belonging and inseparability. The absence of self. Equality with the world. All sorts of things . . . You understand.

I hadn't seen him at first, but behind this small, portly genius who radiated simplicity and goodness there was another man— huge, dark, and savage. Unnoticed, he took out a pipe of the same kind (but without the gold rings) and began steadily blowing on it, playing a single long-drawn-out note on a never-ending breath from his immense chest.

An extraordinary pictorial effect these two created! The huge, menacing man blew his steady ground and background, while his eyes devoured the maestro with somber adoration. Against this background of silver the maestro wove and traced his intricate sky-blue thread. "Cold Days Are Upon Us"* this brilliant music was called, and it drew us in, engulfing our grape arbor, the near distance and far, the grass and the sky, the mountains and the sun and the air. The air was music, the music air—we were breathing them and dying. As though the music, of its own accord, were canceling

---

* I was surprised to discover recently that this music had been used in the scandalous film *The Last Temptation of Christ*, as Jesus' main theme. I did not find our Rachia in the credits.

everything out, even itself, ceasing to be music and becoming music again. I wept.

Evidently my feelings had run away with me. I was in love with the fullness of my own emotion for another people's homeland. Their country belonged to me, far more exactly and profoundly than to them. I had become everything around me. At home I could never achieve this.

The man beside me did not feel so deeply. He sat indifferent and aloof, picking at his meal.

"My God! That's so good!" I exclaimed when the maestro finished, mopping his sweaty brow with a soiled handkerchief and smiling in confusion.

"Why do you believe you're the only one who appreciates this?" my neighbor said to me with inhospitable animosity.

This was sudden and harsh. I wiped away the tears. At the time, I felt hurt.

Now I understand him.

Rapture, too, is aggression. A tank, in its own way.

I was already writing this book.

When the tanks entered Czechoslovakia, I was finishing it.

A year later, the editors ran their caterpillar treads over the text, spilling too much of my ink blood. I don't know whether the fact that I agreed to accept these casualties showed cowardice, or, on the contrary, presence of mind. The book was published twenty years ago.

Ten years passed, fifteen, nineteen . . .

The book did not age, because nothing changed. I alone grew older.

Nothing seemed to be happening—and disaster struck.

When the city collapsed, who among the inhabitants knew that it was not the end of the world?

When the massacre began in Sumgait, who knew what it would be?

What difference does it make whether the official count of the victims is accurate, what difference does it make whether the toll was several dozen or several hundred, if in the nation's memory it is hundreds of thousands?

During the earthquake, they say, a crazed Armenian ran through the crumbling city with a knife, seeking to slaughter the cause of the catastrophe in the form of a Turk.

"If the Last Judgment has begun, why are we first?" That is the feeling of the contemporary Armenian.

In Amsterdam not long ago, on the eve of the chain of Armenian tragedies, at a sophisticated symposium on the boundaries of civilized Europe a highly educated philosopher asked me whether the Armenian alphabet differed greatly from the Russian. He seemed generally surprised that Armenia and Georgia lay within the limits of Europe (at least geographically). I waxed indignant, quite forgetting that I had been little wiser than he until I wrote this book.

This is a book about Armenia as one might have seen it *for the first time.*

Before everything that has happened had come to pass.

Andrei Bitov

June 6, 1989
Zurich

. . . A slender, solitary minaret testifies to the existence of a vanished settlement. It rises gracefully among piles of stones, on the bank of a dried-up stream. The inner staircase has not yet collapsed. I climbed up to the landing, from which the mullah's voice no longer resounds. There I found several unknown names, scratched on the bricks by passing officers. Vanity of vanities! Count*** had followed me. He inscribed on a brick a name dear to him—his wife's, lucky man—and I, my own name.

> *Love thine own self,*
> *My gentle dear reader.*

PUSHKIN, *Journey to Arzrum*

Language Lesson

THE ALPHABET

May Armenia forgive me, but an airplane suits her sky! I stepped out onto the field, and a hot, clean wind struck my face. After yesterday's, it was most welcome. I looked around and glanced up happily. There I saw myself, a few instants before: a plane was banking, coming in for a landing. The sky was Aeroflot's own color, like the stewardess's jacket, and the little plane was like the wings on her collar tab . . . I walked toward the terminal building: EREVAN.

Երևան

Aha, so that thing's an *E*, that's an *R*, and that's the *E* again . . .

Thus the first scene was imprinted in my memory: wind, and sun-faded grass that didn't exactly lie flat in the wind (it was too short for that) but had been combed down by it forever. The wind nudged me toward Erevan. So that's the V, and that's A, and that last one is N. Beautiful.

Then I waited for my suitcase, meditating, out of habit, on whether it was worth it to fly so fast just to wait an equal amount of time for one's luggage. As though my luggage were still in the air, and only I had arrived.

A terminal is no place for a natural man, I am convinced, but this one wasn't quite the same as my previous terminals. It was louder and throatier, in the southern fashion, but at the same time also calmer, for some reason. Of course there was a crush, people were even more temperamental, but somehow no one seemed to be shoving. There was none of the persecuted atmosphere in which every passenger fends for himself, afraid for his suitcase, afraid of being late, afraid of being insulted and duped—which is why he develops a bus-station, air-terminal hardness and tightness, his person assumes the shape and rigidity of his plywood suitcase with the corners that scratch and snag, and his face is like the lock. If such a man brushes you with his shoulder, you'll be black and blue.

Here the crush was different—a gentle, marketplace crowd that stepped over suitcases as if they were watermelons and cantaloupes. And waiting was no tragedy: you could weigh yourself on the Aeroflot scales, beautiful as clocks. People weighed their children, they weighed their grandmothers, they weighed themselves. Strangely, no one chased them away or shouted at them. I had come with the desire to like it here, and I did.

I still weighed the same. Thirty years of age. The scales showed September 7, 1967. I waited for my suitcase to land, and gawked at the scales like a preschool child.

ԱԵՐՈՁԼՈՏԻ ՈՒՂԵՎՈՐՆԵՐԻ ԻՐԱՎՈՒՆՔՆԵՐՆ ՈՒ ՊԱՐՏԱԿԱՆՈՒԹՅՈՒՆՆԵՐԸ.

What could this be, written in letters so beautiful and meaningful in their incomprehensibility? A proverb? A prophecy? A line of immortal verse?

Rights and Responsibilities of the Aeroflot Passenger

those marvelous letters said. Or so claimed a Russian text at the right, which had yielded first place and was subordinate, as is proper for a translation. But if our own familiar "No smoking, no drinking, no exit" was a translation from the Armenian, did this mean that the Armenians were the ones who had introduced it into our Russian usage? Impossible. Thus, what we had here was a rare instance of translation from right to left, or the reconstruction of the original from a word-for-word translation.

Still, respect for the printed word is astonishingly durable—nothing can undermine it. You need only come up against a foreign language to feel as reverent before the mystery of literacy as someone who signs his name with an X. It's hard to believe that foreigners

can write what they please, just as they can say it. Hard to believe
that such wise and perfect letters are indifferent to the words com-
posed of them. Letters . . . Surprise—they have letters, I admon-
ished myself. Except that these are beautiful. Why—are Russian
letters ugly? But write what you please—I don't mind . . . And only
then did I think, Very well, so be it. From Russian to Armenian,
even though from right to left—so be it. But is that really Russian,
that text on the right? And from what wicked language was it translated into Russian?

If you expect a lot from an encounter, you may forget to say
hello. I would never have supposed that letters, after the little sticks
and loops of first grade, could once again become an object of
excitement and even passion. But, if not the first, then the second
question asked of me on Armenian soil was, "Well, how do you
like our alphabet? Very much—isn't that so? Be honest now: which
do you like better, yours or ours?"

May Russia forgive me, but I am ready to agree: our alphabet
does not bear comparison with the Armenian. Our "great, mighty,
truthful, and free" language will be none the worse for this
declaration.

Actually, I had never stopped to reflect on the virtues of our
alphabet, for some reason. Except that I felt it was wrong to typeset
classical authors in the new orthography. After all, they didn't write
in it. I miss the theta in the name Feodor, for example; the Slavonic
"number-ten *I*" in the word *idiot*; and the "hard signs" here and
there at the end of certain words. (Similarly, classical authors were
born not under the New Style calendar but under the Old: they
were accustomed to the month and day of their birth . . . and that
day meant something to them.) We don't rename the cities and
streets in their works according to present-day names, or translate
prices into the new price scale . . . Petty issues like these had come
idly to mind. But I just hadn't paid attention to our alphabet, hadn't
noticed it; I was listening to the language rather than looking
at it.

I reflected on this only after I really looked at the Armenian
alphabet and heard the alien sound of the speech. The greatness of
this alphabet lies in the precision of the match between a sound
and its graphic representation. Everything here is integral, forms
circles. The tenacity of Armenian speech ("The Armenian language
is a wildcat," Mandelstam said) is so well matched to the hammered

look of Armenian letters that the word, when inscribed, clanks like a chain. And I so clearly envision these letters as having been forged in a blacksmith shop: the smooth curve of the metal under the blows of the hammer, a cinder flies off, and what remains is the glimmer of iridescent dark blue that I now see in every Armenian letter. These letters could be used to shoe live horses . . . Or these letters might be hewn from stone, because the stone in Armenia is just as natural as the alphabet, and an Armenian letter, in its smoothness and hardness, is not inconsistent with stone. (Recall the shape of the Armenian crosses, and you will marvel again at this correspondence.) And in its upper curve an Armenian letter is exactly like the shoulder of an ancient Armenian church, or its dome, just as this curve also exists in the contours of the mountains, and as they, in turn, are like the lines of a woman's breast—so universal for Armenia is this amazing conjunction of hardness and softness, harshness and smoothness, masculinity and femininity, in both the landscape and the air, the buildings and the people, the alphabet and the spoken word. An Armenian letter has the greatness of a monument and the gentleness of life, the biblical antiquity of round flat bread and the piquancy of the green comma of a pepper, the lushness and translucency of grapes and the severity and grace of a bottle, the soft curl of the sheep's wool and the sturdiness of the shepherd's crook, and the line of the shepherd's shoulder . . . and the line of the back of his neck . . . And all of these exactly match the sound represented by the line.

I still don't know the Armenian language, but that is precisely why I swear to the truth of my perception. All I had before me was the sound and its representation; the meaning of the spoken word was beyond me.

This alphabet was created by a genius with an astonishing sense of his homeland—it was created once and forever—it is perfect. That man was like God in the days of Creation. When he had created the alphabet, he inscribed the first sentence:

ՃԱՆԱՉԵԼ ՋԻՄԱՍՏՈՒՏԻՒՆ ԵՎ ՋԽՐԱՏ, ԻՄԱՆԱԼ ՋԲԱՆՍ ՀԱՆՃԱՐՈՅ.

This time the sentence had a meaning commensurate with its inscription:

Know wisdom, fathom the words of geniuses.

After inscribing it (not writing it, not drawing it), he discovered that he lacked one letter. Then he created that letter as well. The Armenian alphabet has stood ever since.*

For me, nothing is more convincing than a story like this. You could make up the man, and you could make up the letter, but you couldn't make up the fact that the man lacked one letter. That could only *happen*. So there was such a man. He isn't a legend. He is just as much a fact as the alphabet. His name was Mesrob Mashtots.

If I could, I would erect a monument to Mashtots in the form of that last letter—stone proof of his rightness.

A man endowed with even the slightest feeling and ear for language will never doubt the existence of the Creator . . . A Russian philologist once published an article casting doubt on the real existence of Mashtots, and who noticed it, who read it, apart from a handful of specialists? All Armenia. Echoes of the national storm reached even me, when I arrived a year later. For grown men to be so excited over a few trifling letters . . .

I was surprised and uncomfortable. In just one day I knew more about the history of the Armenian alphabet than of the Russian. I would have to take a closer look at this issue that had never troubled me.

The word is the most precise tool that man has ever possessed. Philology, however, hasn't yet achieved the precision of the correctly intuited word. Humility is in order. Philology has to do with language, but language has nothing to do with philology. Any doubt of Mashtots's existence is an insult to an Armenian. I understand perfectly. In any case, an alphabet like this could not be the fruit of a group effort by linguistic scientists. That much is certain.

The Armenians have preserved their alphabet unchanged for fifteen hundred years. It has the antiquity, history, strength, and spirit of the nation. To this day there is no discrepancy between the handwritten letter and the printed symbol; even in books, the typeface retains the slant of the writer's hand. A manuscript, in becoming

---

* In the years when Soviet Russia was introducing a Cyrillic-based alphabet to all the peoples of the former empire who possessed no written language, such an alphabet was offered to Armenia as well. The Armenians proudly refused it, declaring that they already had their own. The hapless clerk was astonished: When had they found the time? In the fifth century, the Armenians replied. Thus the Armenian alphabet once more stood its ground.

a book, suffers almost no graphic metamorphoses. This, too, is remarkable.

Progress barging into vocabulary and spelling, the unification of rules, the simplification of shapes—these efforts are useful for universal literacy, but not for culture. The protection of language against frugal impulses is just as essential as the preservation of nature and historic monuments. One has only to recall the original Cyrillic alphabet—how much closer it is, in script form, to the Russian landscape, Russian architecture, the Russian character . . .

The celebrated anecdote about the high-school teacher who committed suicide over the abolition of the *yat* (an old Cyrillic letter, dropped in 1917) would not be a success in Armenia. It wouldn't be funny. In Armenia, such a man could only be a national hero.

What amuses me most is that the spelling reform has saved a great deal of paper—in *War and Peace* alone, the abolished "hard signs" at the ends of the words amount to a whole printed page, and on the scale of the state as a whole . . . —yet this economy will never dam the torrent of trashy literature.

PRIMER

Erevan is my alphabet book, my primer, my stone glossary. Armenian on the left, Russian on the right. But the words are out of order. Next to "A for Automat" is "S for Shish kebab." And "B for Bazaar" is on a different street altogether, several pages later.

I riffle the pages of streets, blocks, and squares in search of "E for Editor," "F for Friend," "H for House," and "J for Just in Case." That is my Russian–Armenian dictionary.

Still, if I knew Armenian and could use Erevan as an Armenian–Russian dictionary, things would be no more orderly, of course. This comforts me.

I find my friend, however, and now I have a teacher. He acquires an inept pupil, with a memory enthusiastic and full of holes. But the teacher, it develops, has helpers. I am taken into sweet captivity: at my friend's house are his wife's mother, his brother's wife, his brother's friend, and the friend's brother. I come to know the full strength of Armenian family ties. I am wound about with this chain, and each new hour adds a new coil. I can never be alone anymore . . .

"Andrei, what's *surch?*"

I haven't guessed right even once, and now I say nothing, smiling in confusion.

"Andrei, is *surch* good or bad?"

Everyone laughs affectionately at my embarrassment.

"Andrei, would you like some *surch?*"

"Yes."

"Good job! You get an A."

And they bring me coffee. No one at home makes coffee this good . . .

"Andrei, what's *dzu?*"

"Andrei, is *dzu* good or bad?"

"Andrei, which word do you think is better: our *dzu* or your *iaitso?*"

And I eat *dzu*. Never in my life have I eaten such an omelet. Oh, our wretched fried eggs.

Khorovats, bibar, gini . . . (May the Armenians forgive me for spelling their words in an alien alphabet. But this is a purely technical difficulty.) I eat up my visual aids.

All of them are good. But to eat this much is bad . . .

They teach, and they themselves learn.

"I camed . . . Which is right," my friend says, "camed or came? . . . I camc my sister house . . . Which is right: me sister house?"

When they weary of twisting brain and tongue to translate words so simple and understandable, so beautiful, into a foreign language—mine—when they weary of tangling with Russian cases and genders, all of a sudden they happily slide into their native language and begin to relax in it, among themselves. Meanwhile, I'm eating again, eating still, eating once more, eating for everyone: for my friend's mother and his wife's father, his brother's friend and the friend's brother, except that I don't eat for my friend (he can render me that service). But as long as I eat, they can at least talk in peace.

When they do finally plunge into their tingling mountain river of speech, I suddenly experience the same ease they do—my vague discomfiture falls away, and I am glad to hear foreign conversation. And not merely for the reason mentioned above. Although I don't understand the language, for the first time in my life I find myself hearing something that I never hear in Russian, in speech that I do understand: namely, how people talk. How they fall silent and how they wait their turn, how they put in a word and how they give up the intention of putting it in, how someone says something funny and—this is striking!—people don't laugh right away, they laugh afterwards, and the one who has said something funny endures a kind of pause for the others' laughter; how they wait for an answer to a question and how they search for the answer; at which moment they lower their gaze, and at which they look someone in the eye; at which moment they're talking about you, and you understand nothing . . .

Further, when they're speaking to me—that is, speaking Russian—they never laugh. They have only to switch to Armenian and immediately there's laughter. Are they laughing at you who don't understand? You may well think so, until you realize that people can laugh only in their mother tongue. I had no one to laugh with in Armenia.

If something struck them very funny, they suddenly recollected themselves when they finished laughing. The smile of laughter was replaced by the smile of politeness—the life of the face was subordinated—and they turned to me. The other, involuntary smile didn't fade all at once; the memory of laughter ebbed quietly from their eyes, which, as I saw, reflected me, my presence. Their faces acquired an extremely wise, absorbed expression, as when conversing with foreigners in a poorly spoken language: the sillier the conversation, the more significant the tone of voice, and no amount of effort can check the noddings and yessings. After a conversation like that, your face and neck muscles ache from unaccustomed, unnatural work.

Only in your mother tongue can you sing, write poetry, declare your love . . . In an alien tongue, even with an excellent knowledge of it, you can only teach a language, discuss politics, and order a cutlet. A man has but one tongue.

The more subtle and gifted your poetic and living knowledge of your mother tongue, the more hopeless your knowledge of a foreign one, it seems. The gulf cannot be filled. How witty my friend is, although in Russian he's a somber, almost doleful person. His every phrase in Armenian is greeted with such gleeful, ungoverned laughter . . . "Oh, what a shame you don't understand his Armenian!" What a shame . . . In addition to Armenian, then, there is also *his* Armenian! But in addition to their Russian, after all, there is also, within *our* Russian, *my* Russian . . .

I had no one to laugh with in Armenia. And I was happy when people forgot about me. I was happy in the purl and crackle of Armenian conversation, because I had complete trust in the speakers. Antipathy toward a foreign conversation in your presence is primarily the fear that they're speaking of you, and speaking ill. The source of this fear is another matter. To exchange remarks in a language your companion doesn't know is considered tactless chiefly among people who don't trust each other. Among diplomats, let's say. But we trusted each other. What's more, my friends were so tactful that when I was present they deliberately made arrangements for me in their own unintelligible language, lest I suspect all the burdens of organizing my life: my housing, travel, escort, and itinerary. Again, I'm forgetting that they found it easier to make the arrangements that way.

I listened to the foreign talk and was captivated by it. Truly, what a combination! The harsh, dry, and heat-tempered—and the surprisingly soft, "shentle," as my friend would say. Like the harsh, scorched ground and the lush fruit ripening on it . . . *Khich* is a scattering of small stones, *jur* is the water purling among those stones, *shog* is the heat above the stones and the water, *chanch* is the fly buzzing sharply in that heat. *Khich, jur, shog, chanch*—and suddenly, in the midst of all this, *lolik* is a tomato.

Khich, k'arr'—of course that's not our stone, *kamen'*; it's *their* stone. What is the Russian *kamen'*? Something lying in the road . . . *Jur*—that's *their* water. It's cold, it babbles under those stones, and there's not much of it . . . What does our Russian water, *voda*, mean to them? . . . There is so much water in our *voda*, both above and below the surface . . . *Chanch*—is that really our still-life fly, *mukha*? . . . *Deghdz* is Armenian for peach . . . The skin of the peach is right there in the word—its down, its fuzz . . . And what's the Russian peach? *Persik*—from "Persian" . . . Just a foreign fruit.

"Andrei, which is better: our *kav* or your *glina* [clay]? Our *aragil*, or your *aist* [stork]? Your *zhuravl'*, or our *krrunk'* [crane]?"

Indeed, which is better? Just think, *zhuravl'*! I had never even suspected it was so beautiful. Or *krrunk'* . . . How good!

I'm falling in love with words: with Armenian words thanks to Russian, and with Russian words thanks to Armenian . . .

"Which is better: our *tsov* or your *more*?"

And suddenly I don't feel the sea in the Russian *more*; there's no turbulence, it's a mirror. Suddenly I empathize with the word *tsov*—I see in it an onrushing wave . . . but the wave, it turns out, isn't a *tsov* at all. A wave is an *alik*; it gently licks the shore. Would that *tsov* were merely the sea! But *tsov* is both sea and quietude. *Tsov* is the melancholy in beautiful eyes, or simply "beauty." *Tsov* is the people in a crowd, or simply "many" . . .

CONSONANCES

mayr = Russian *mat'* = mother
sirt = Russian *serdtse* = heart
serm = Russian *semia* = seed
mis = Russian *miaso* = meat
gini = Russian *vino* = wine
. . . = . . . = . . .

But the Armenian *kamar* is not the Russian *komar* [mosquito]; their *kamar* is our *arka*, an arch.

And the Armenian *arka* isn't an arch at all; their *arka* is our *tsar'*, or king.

The Armenian *tsarr* is not a tsar; their *tsarr* is a tree.

par = Russian "steam" = Armenian "folk dance"
gol = Russian "naked" = Armenian "warmth"
tsekh = Russian "factory shop" = Armenian "dirt"
. . . = . . . = . . .

But a folk dance gets up steam. Nakedness and warmth are so close. A tree, of course, is kingly. And all of this is farfetched, but the idea that a factory shop is dirt could not be expressed more neatly.

"You have the word *ataman*," my friend says to me, "and we have *atam*, which means a tooth, a fang. So when I read books as a child, I always thought an ataman was a man with fangs."

"And I thought he was lying on an ottoman," I said.

"You have the word *khmel'* [drunkenness]," my friend explains to me, early in the morning at my first lesson, "and *khmel* in Armenian means 'to drink.' So your word *pokhmel'e* [hangover] has caught on here."

"Andrei, what is *astvats*?" my friend asks sternly.

"Andrei, is *astvats* good or bad?"

"*Astvats* is good," I say. "*Astvats* is Russian *otets*: 'father.' "

"But you're right!" my friend says in surprise. "*Kenats!*"*

DIRECT SPEECH

Ayo is Armenian for "yes." *Che* is Armenian for "no." I don't know why, but everywhere—on the streets, in the stores, on the buses— I more often hear *che* than *ayo*. *Che, che, che*. The usual bus dialogue, it seems to me, goes like this: one person keeps asking, pressing, and the other keeps responding, "*Che, che*." Then they reverse it—the other keeps asking, and the first responds with his "*Che*." So I took it that *che* was Armenian for "yes," and I asked my friend, "What's 'no' in Armenian?" He answered, "*Che*." "*Che?*" I exclaimed. "Then what's 'yes'?" "*Ayo*." So I had been wrong. Now I would get it straight, I thought. But I never heard "*Ayo*," always "*Che*."

My friend's brother is a journalist. He is very fond of me, because I am very fond of his brother. This is natural in Armenia. One time we were walking along the street, and he was terrifyingly, agonizingly silent. He looked at me with such a beseeching gaze that against my will I talked for both of us, without respite. In fact, there was probably no other person in Armenia for whom the Russian language caused so much genuine, even physical, suffering. He spoke to me mainly with his eyes. When he needed to compose a sentence in Russian, his eyes went dumb with effort as the pressure mounted in his brain. His glance became shifty and meek, like that of a ruminating cow, and he did not utter his intended sentence. The problem, apparently, was not that he didn't know enough Russian words but that he couldn't come up with a *single* word of Russian.

So we were walking along the street, and suddenly, from something I said, he grasped that I wasn't here just to visit his brother but on assignment from a newspaper. (I had mentioned this on purpose, knowing he was a journalist.) His face clouded, and suddenly the dam broke. I won't undertake to convey his language exactly—no one would believe me.

"You're going to write about us?" he said.

* *Astvats* means "God." *Kenats* is a salutation, something like "Your health!"

Whereupon he began to converse with me like this: If he saw a truckload of watermelons going by . . .

"That's Armenia watermelons," he said.

If he saw a jackass . . .

"That's Armenia donkey," he said.

"That's Armenia very fat woman. And that's Armenia beer. You want beer? You want watermelon? That's ordinary Armenia taxi. You want we ride?"

First I smiled. Then I decided to take offense, but restrained myself. Then I relaxed: I knew that this would be an Armenian fence, this an Armenian pole, and this an ordinary Armenian policeman. How could he keep it up? I no longer felt offended, but I wondered why he was doing this.

Finally he wearied. "Please," he said, "just don't write that Armenia is a sunny, hospitable land."

He was silent a moment and added, "All these years I've been living here and writing, and still I haven't written what Armenia is like."

"You know," I said sincerely, "I'm bothered by that, too. I don't even think I'll write anything. What will I see in two weeks? What will I understand? I couldn't write anything serious. Yet I'd have to be serious if I wrote about Armenia now . . . Besides, come to think of it, wouldn't I have agreed to make the trip on my own, for my own pleasure? At my own expense? So I'll give back the assignment money and say thanks. Especially since I don't work at the newspaper and don't depend on it."

"But why give it back?" my friend's brother said indignantly. "What do you mean you won't write? . . . Stay a little longer. You'll write," he said, and I did not understand his tone at all. Was "You'll write" good or bad?

And now my trip had ended, here I was at home. I kept agonizing, agonizing, pacing around the table, and finally, despite all, I sat down to write an essay. (I had to give some account of myself—I begrudged the money.)

What was my painstaking first sentence?

"Armenia is a sunny, hospitable land."

And what did I suddenly hear?

"Che, che, che! Che, Andrei, che!"

I flushed. "Yes, but it's true!"

"Che, Andrei, che!"

I made a supreme effort: "Armenia is a hot, long-suffering land."

"*Che.*"

"Well, but what is she, your Armenia!" I flared.

"If I knew, I'd write it myself."

"Well, at least say it better than I did! Look. I said it's a 'hot' land. Is there any other word for it? Armenia *is* 'hot.' Everything's hot: sky, earth, air, sun, people, history, blood. The blood *in* the people and the blood *from* the people."

"*Che,* Andrei."

"Well, say it better! Try!"

"I'll try . . . Armenia is my homeland."

"True. But not mine! I can't write that!"

"Then why write?"

"But I'm writing an essay! Not poems, not stories. An *essay*. Travel notes. Notes by a stranger. Notes by a non-Armenian. An *essay*, see?"

"Do you know what 'essay' is in Armenian?"

"No . . ."

"*Aknark*. And do you know what *aknark* means in Russian?"

????

"A hint."

H I N T

Yes, when I wrote about consonances, I missed one: *ush*. Armenian *ush* is not the Russian *ushi*, "ears." But it's close. *Ush* means "attentive." But *apush* doesn't simply mean "inattentive," which would have been logical. *Apush* means "idiot."

History Lesson

LEO

I can hardly imagine that if I went for a stroll with any of my well-educated acquaintances (my grandfather is no longer alive) I would hear the following:

"This is where they found Rasputin's body."

"And this is where Napoleon stayed."

Or, "See that little hill? Behind it there's a grove of trees, and that's where Denis Davydov came charging out, when we were already retreating, and inspired our exhausted troops with his astounding deeds . . ."

In Armenia, everyone seems to know such things.

The impression is that history had no beginning in Armenia —it has always existed. In the course of its eternity, it has hallowed every stone, every foot of ground. There is probably no village that was not, in days of old, the capital of an ancient state, no hill around which a decisive battle has not raged, no stone not moistened with blood, and no man to whom this is a matter of indifference.

"Andrei, look. That mountain, way over there—do you see it? And the other one beside it. Right between them is where Prince Andranik met and stopped the Turks, and they turned back."

"See that smokestack? And the long building next to it. That's the Central Power Station. Built several years ago. That's where the Molokan sect used to live."

"And this is where Pushkin encountered the cart bearing Griboedov's body . . ."

On and on, without end. I was told these things by taxi drivers and writers, cooks and Party workers, adults and children.

And there was no house where I did not see a certain thick, dark blue book, with three beautiful, confident letters on the cover: LEO. I saw it even in houses where people generally didn't keep books—one or another of the three dark blue volumes by LEO.

Leo was a historian who wrote a three-volume history of Armenia.

As explained to me by specialists, although Leo was a remarkable historian, he was not the best. There have also been scholars more serious than he. But Leo is the most popular. Like our Karamzin or Solovyov.

I ask Russians, "Have you read Karamzin?"

Or, "There was a new edition of Solovyov recently; have you read it?"

We cannot make the excuse that Armenia is small and we're big—that it's easier for them to know their history than for us to know ours. If we multiplied the area of each history by its depth, the volumes, at least, would be equal. And besides, that's not the problem.

I doubt I would find a book by Solovyov in the home of a taxi driver or construction boss. In the homes of writers? One out of ten, at best.

I, for example, have not read him.

But people are always reading Leo. Leo is everywhere. They read as conscientiously as he wrote. He wrote and wrote and knew nothing else in life, wrote from morning to night, every day and all his life. By old age he had gone blind. But he wanted to write his masterpiece, his last. He asked his daughter for pen, paper, and ink.

Blind, he wrote from morning to night.

And finished.

And died.

But the daughter, it turned out, had given the blind man an inkwell without ink, so that he wouldn't make a mess.

He never noticed.

Such is the legend.

Dear God! What did he write?

THE MATENADARAN

If much is considered remarkable in modern Armenian architecture, the Matenadaran is the most remarkable example of the "remarkable." Moreover, it has just been built—and literally in our day, yours and mine.

To begin with, the function of the building is very worthy. This is a depository for ancient manuscripts. Since Armenians have been using their marvelous written language for a very long time, these manuscripts, despite all the national calamities, survive in great quantity. Each is unique and beyond price. This nationalized national treasure must be carefully and fittingly preserved. Of course.

The Matenadaran was built with this purpose. While it fulfills its practical and technical function flawlessly, it was also erected as a monument to a great culture, centuries old.

Everything is so well done that it cannot be faulted. The noble intentions of the builders are visible in every detail; furthermore, those intentions are given full expression. The site, too, is well chosen. The Matenadaran can be seen from afar, nothing blocks your view of it, it has open space on either side and nothing crowding it from behind—at its back are mountains. It drops steeply down those mountains like a severe granite cliff, like a waterfall. Below, where it lands, foaming staircases divide and cascade down into a single main stream at the bottom. Approaching it, you must inevitably sense its lofty mood, and by the time you set foot on the first step you are tingling with awe; as you climb, as the sheer cliff of the Matenadaran draws near and overhangs you more and more loftily and vertically, the tingle becomes a chill down your spine. When you find yourself getting smaller and smaller, while the building above you gets larger and larger, this apparently symbolizes both the greatness and hugeness of human civilization, and your lostness in it. But all is in good taste. Pale gray stone, of the sort that is severe without being gloomy. Lines both straight and soft, in a way that makes explicit both the great tradition of Armenian architecture and a total mastery of all the achievements of modern architecture as well, with its naked function and aestheticized simplicity . . . A wealth of taste. No tastelessness anywhere to be seen. A dreadful vase, for example, could perfectly well stand here at this turn of the stairs, on this pure arc—but it doesn't. A bare spot, a beautiful unblemished surface. There's room for a vase, but no vase.

By now I'm growing angry at this flawlessness, at the fact that the designers were nowhere failed by their taste . . . Or were they failed, perhaps, by the very idea of taste? "This church is tastefully built." Try to speak a sentence like that. Absurd. Or, "A tasteful log cabin." Doesn't sound right either. Meanwhile, both the church and the log cabin are the purest of forms, they fulfill only their function; the more exactly they fulfill it, the more beautiful they are. Suddenly, for the first time, the boundary between old and new architecture is delineated for me. I would never have stopped to think about this—only in Erevan, where there are so many remarkable examples on either side of the boundary.

I climb the stairs and feel no tingle of awe. The heat, indigestion, out of breath. Suddenly there's something enclosed by a blank wooden fence. Rubbish, a trash heap—not everything is quite finished. I peer in. Huge stones stand there in togas. They, too, are very modern and profound in execution. Sometimes the stone preserves its natural fracture: here the human forms grow imperceptibly from random lines of the unworked stone, and here the lines dissolve in the stone's natural integrity. Large men in gracefully draped clothing (what a pleasure, to transmit in stone that large, vertical, full-length fold!). Large faces, their features free of excess commotion and filled with calm, dignified inspiration. There are several of these men. But one is still in scaffolding and one is barely begun, while a third is almost ready. A stone movie about the creation of a single sculpture, faintly reminiscent of the monument to Dzerzhinsky in Moscow (because of his ankle-length greatcoat) or Timiryazev (because of his Oxford gown). But much, much more modern. These great men (apparently their greatness is what has made them so equal and similar), who wrote the great books preserved in this majestic building (such integrity of design!), will stand—aha!—on those landings so beautifully free of vases. But not until somewhat later, when all are ready together, differentiated only by the stone that remains free and unworked as though merging into this ground, with which they are so connected . . . They jut up from this ground as differently, as identically, as they grew from it in their own time. The sort of men who gazed into the future, into our day.

The whole building, indeed, seems to gaze into the radiant future, in accord with the designers' concept of it.

The grandeur of the design achieves its highest point at the entrance (how infinitely the mighty surfaces soar up!) and ends abruptly in the lobby. There is a new order here—noiseless and whispery. Somewhere inside are the thoughtful, bowed heads of our contemporaries, the true owners of these spiritual riches, who are creating a new life on the basis of all the knowledge accumulated by humanity.

With eyes thus narrowed, I found myself in a rectangular hall. Above me was a glass roof, as in a hothouse. The walls were black, with deep shadows. Reaching out of the shadow toward the light were reading desks on delicate legs. Books lay open on the reading desks.

I shook hands with a bored young employee; our names sounded out of place here. With apparent reluctance he led us to one of the reading desks.

This was the biography of Mashtots, written by his pupil. From it had been gleaned the basic information on the life of the great creator of the alphabet.

On the next reading desk lay a diligently copied compendium of botany. The thousand-year-old scholar had drawn flowers in the margins.

A few steps away, stellar spheres whirled, intersecting and scattering in a charming and elegant sketch, while the earth reposed, so comfortably, on something like three whales.

Against his will, surprising even himself, the tour guide came alive for the thousandth time. And, indeed, the crumbling pages even now breathed life, simple and clear. As though all death had departed into the brand-new walls of the Matenadaran.

The Matenadaran goes many stories underground. In its air-conditioned dungeons there are books and more books . . .

"But have they all been read, studied, described?"

"Oh, no! Only an insignificant portion. They haven't even been catalogued. That job will take another ten years."

If you think how much time and patience would be needed to copy someone else's book by hand, what idiot would undertake this in our modern world? Meanwhile, examining the marvelous flower of a capital letter, you realize that the copyist may have been hard put to finish it in a day.

There are tens of thousands of these books.

How much time people had in those times! And how much they managed to do!

They managed to do exactly as much. Or perhaps even more.

They didn't hurry, and their works absorbed time. A man was continued in his sons and in objects he made. The objects have come down to us bereft of their authors' names, but how unmistakably each one was created by a man who once lived!

A book of home cures, a book of medicinal herbs, a book of stars, a prayer book . . .

This kind of herb should be used to treat a person for this kind of illness . . . Both the herb and the illness now have different names, and perhaps they're no longer associated with each other. The same illness under another name is treated with another medicine. But the fact remains that the illness is the same and belongs, in the same way, to a person who must be treated with something.

How much people have always known! How frivolous to suppose that our own century has revealed to man the possibility of using this thing or that, previously unknown to anyone.

What a lot people knew, and what a lot they've forgotten!

They've forgotten as much as they've learned.

And how much they have learned and forgotten in vain!

RUINS (AT ZVARTNOTS)

It's as if my friend found it painful to see. In order to see each successive point of interest, he must make up his mind to it. He forces himself. For me. On my account. This fills me with gratitude and discomfort—although neither he nor I reveal our feelings to each other, and besides, we aren't conscious of them. Before each successive excursion, something in my friend resists. Of course it's not the first time he has seen these things, or even the tenth. Of course—the burdens of hospitality. But these are accustomed burdens. Moreover, the points of interest—again, of course—are such that one can see them countless times; they are inexhaustible and will do him no harm. Furthermore, he can't escape showing them to me, and I can't help loving them. For some reason, however, my friend finds it hard to look again at something beautiful and beloved.

He sets off on the next excursion . . .

And when he sees those stones again, the mask of despondency suddenly breaks up and his face becomes calm and bright. He doesn't quite look at me, and it's not because he wants to hide his feelings. I am suddenly struck that he doesn't want to see in my eyes that I *don't understand*. When our eyes do meet, he looks away again and says: "Andrei, I want—do you understand, I want you to feel very, very tired . . . the sun, all this sun, these stones . . . and you suddenly feel it down your backbone—your backbone, understand?—how tired you are . . ."

"I understand," I said quickly, nodding. "Down my spine . . ."

My friend did not continue. We tossed a piece of burning paper into a sort of well. Certainly the paper never reached the bottom. We inspected stone wine bowls as huge as artillery pillboxes. The custodian who escorted us had the face of a eunuch and an armed guard combined. He was profoundly imbued with his own proximity to greatness, the way the doorkeeper at the Municipal Party Committee is imbued with his governmenthood . . . The idleness of these observations, of this falsely keen eyesight, humiliated me, and suddenly I was so hot, so tired, these stones meant so nearly nothing to me, and I was so ashamed of my insensitivity, that I was surreptitiously fingering the small of my back and almost hoping for that salvific, all-explaining pain down my spine . . . Oh, this gentle violence! How could I force myself to feel anything? My malingering body was almost suggesting that pain to me, when suddenly we were all leaving, we had seen enough, we were already having our pictures taken or eating watermelon. Gladly, with the sensation of a novice, I bit into the cool pulp as soon as my friend indulged. And he indulged then and there, as though his remark about the backbone had been merely figurative.

But a thought did finally visit me. At these ruins—or at others . . . The cathedral had been destroyed in such-and-such a century, then in such-and-such, then yet again, and then again almost in our day. And still, how much remained! When they destroyed it the first time, apparently, they didn't reduce it to ruins; only the third time. Because the stone blocks were, say, two meters square, and so smoothly worked, and so tightly set. And lead had been poured into the heart of each one, to make it lie more heavily and solidly. Men built forever. But later the Turks, or the Arabs, or someone else, needed the lead for bullets—and only then were the blocks finally picked open. Even so, look what greatness!

A simple thought: When we see ancient ruins, the first notion that occurs to us is something romantic and literary about the implacability and might of the physical time that has passed above the work of human hands throughout those centuries. Corrosion, we say. Erosion. The drop weareth away stone. And each day carries off . . . Something more on the brevity of our own life, on transience, on the vanity of our efforts and the insignificance of our deeds. But how false all this is, how wrong!

We only imagine that this is the might of time. Not time but men destroyed the cathedral. They would not live long enough to see time deal with it—at some later date, after they were gone—and they impatiently pulled it down themselves. I suddenly realized that there was no such thing as a ruin caused by time alone . . . "A time to pull down and a time to build up." Even in the Bible, "to pull down" comes first. Time merely succeeds in smoothing the work of human hands, lending to destruction a softened and idyllic appearance that prompts us to reflections on time.

In that form, the ruins stand forever.

CONNECTION OF THE TIMES

I dream of living this moment. In this moment, by this moment alone. I would then be alive, harmonious, and happy. But I live somewhere between the past and the present of my own life, in hope of a future. I want to eliminate the rupture between past and present, because that rupture makes my life unreal, a non-life. I keep hoping that through some miraculous effort I will find myself exclusively in the present, never again to lose hold of it, so that my life will once more acquire continuity from birth to death.

Even within a single life, your relationship with time—physical time—is so complicated. And if you add to that your relationship with the historical time? And if you extend your segment of personal time along a mental dotted line into the past and the future, beyond your temporal boundaries? If you consider your relationship, not with your historical time, but with the time of history? And if you correlate the time of history with the time of eternity?

This is dizzying, of course. But would it be, if nothing connected you with this abyss? What connects the times? And what connects you with the times?

For ease in handling, we connect the times by means of history.

But this is a paper twine, temporary packing. If we reject the idea that progress is governed by laws, history is still entertaining as a collection of instructive anecdotes. If we invent governing laws for these anecdotes, they become simply boring.

Besides, is there any such thing as history? Does it exist, objectively? Or is history our accidental relationship to time? And so on. Once I was visited by thoughts like these . . .

. . . I needed to go to Echmiadzin on Sunday. For the Sunday service. My friend did not go with me; he entrusted me to his brother. True, he had his excuses for this, but something makes me think that his customary resistance to revisiting his beloved Meccas was not a factor here. He simply wasn't interested in going to Echmiadzin.

But I absolutely had to go. The Catholicos would be there. The successor to the great coloratura Goar would sing. And just in general, I wanted to see it.

Hordes of people at the bus stops, all going to Echmiadzin, Echmiadzin. These people, insiders—how many times had they seen and heard it all?—but they were going, and this further convinced me. It was a very intellectual-looking crowd.

A crowd of intellectuals is a type of crowd not often encountered, and rather a surprising sight. Each person believes himself above the laws of the crowd, and yet together they form a crowd. Of all possible crowds, this is the most hypocritical. Though pressed and squeezed on all sides, the intellectual connoisseur nevertheless thinks he still exists in his own personal space. This is very evident on all faces. Their long, tense expression says that it's not they who are being shoved, not they who are sticking their elbows out, sharply and painfully. Even as he submits to the laws of the crowd, the intellectual believes that he alone, in the mindless crowd, has authentic motives. To see so many masks of detachment on faces a few centimeters from each other is peculiar, to say the least. So I, too, wore an expression of detachment from this astonishing observation, until I was calmed by the sight of a remarkably beautiful young woman who wore around her neck a small, plain gold cross, half buried in a wonderful cleavage. I could look at her for as long as I wished—she had nowhere to hide from me in this stifling crush. She was permitted only to look away from me, for as long as she wished.

So the bus coughed us out into bright space at last, and we hastily disengaged ourselves.

But once we were in the open, the glad cries and handshakes began. "All Erevan" was here, and everyone knew my friend's brother. I shook hands as his brother's friend (i.e., as his friend, too), and after the handshake I was already a friend of the person whose hand I had just shaken. This, too, might seem peculiar— the degree to which they had all been unacquainted when packed against each other on the bus, and the suddenness with which they joyfully began recognizing each other as soon as they found an opportunity to see themselves a few meters away from their acquaintance. They recognized each other not on drawing close but on drawing apart—or so it appeared. This was confirmed when we all jammed into the cathedral: if you have ten acquaintances on one square meter, you again cease to be acquainted with them. But here you could privately blame concentration and reverence.

Well, I've peopled that space, and now I can tell what I saw. Or, rather, I have a somewhat different task: to tell how I didn't see.

We walked into a park, and the ancient body of a huge cathedral rose before us. For some reason, it looked as if it had been built toward the end of the last century, not sixteen centuries ago. Perhaps its condition had been maintained so assiduously and for so long, the repairs and renovations had been so thorough, that everything had already been replaced; although the contours were the same, a church couldn't be this new—only dishes are this new. Sudden reality: fresh blood on the wall. Blood does have to be fresh—of course. "What's that?" "They kill doves. Bash their heads against the wall." "Why?" "They bring them as sacrifices." "To whom?" "To God." The little boys suddenly became visible, although they'd been milling around the whole time; they had live doves, in bunches, to sell for offerings—and they were normal little boys, looked their age, neither older nor younger. Then we seemed to be elbowing our way into the church . . . The crowd from the bus— but in the church. The service was under way, the ritual. All was decorous, beautiful. What clothes, what faces! At the right, evidently on a platform, the soloist was singing, singing wonderfully, her voice was marvelous, spellbinding, the music was beyond description—great music.

Suddenly it hit me that this was a scene from a bazaar. In one place they were conducting the service, in another place singing, in another place praying, in yet another just gawking. I couldn't understand the proceedings at all. What was wrong? Why, there were no believers! The church was full, jam-packed, you couldn't breathe, your neck and tiptoes ached, but there were no believers. On the right, the philharmonic. On the left, theater. In the rear, curiosity. And only up front, the kneeling vanity of the habitué. Those who had pushed their way forward had already seen their fill—but they had no way back. The service took its normal course, yet its mystery meant nothing to anyone. People studied the clothes and the faces and sniffed the incense, but ten minutes later the clothes were the same, and so were the faces and the fragrance: there was no clear progress. And I . . . Why did I see it this way? What could I be thinking of! For shame.

Now a child started to cry. He, at least, was sincere—he had lost his mother. Such relief in the faces, this was understandable, a child was crying, their souls even stirred within their bodies, and in an understandable way, in sympathy. I would have been glad to cross myself, at least, from shame, but I couldn't remember which side to start on, or how many fingers to use. "The Catholicos! The Catholicos!" At last the crowd came to life—this was the man they'd been waiting for!

There was a movement to get closer, eddies and whirlpools formed, I was pushed to the exit. But I was even glad. Light, air! Divine space. But all those striving toward the goal had miscalculated: the Catholicos came by a different path, where he wasn't expected. He passed among the gravestones of Catholicoi like himself (he, too, would have a stone here somewhere), and none of the public was there. Only I. He walked through me as if I didn't exist, and stirred up a breeze. I stood petrified, with his breeze blowing on me—and was promptly trampled by the crowd.

I came to in a glade. My friend's brother was by my side, we rejoiced, he introduced me to the soloist, people invited us to sit down on the grass and entertained us so informally, so naturally: Eat, drink! Such excellent people sitting here! While everyone in the church was seeking intellectual diversion and feeling bored, we were eating sacrificial lambs under the open sky: Treat everyone, but don't eat your own sheep . . . Eat, drink, and praise the Lord! We sat on the same ground, under the same sky, shared everything, asked nothing of each other! Peace in our faces, peace in the world. Again we were surrounded by the miracle of life, of people! Over there, someone had brought a small sheep, so touching, with a red ribbon on his neck, and now they would slaughter him . . . And there in the stony gloom, in a flaming and fatty hell, they would make him into shish kebab, and treat you to it . . . Over there, a woman handed a chicken to some poor little old lady; properly, the woman should have cooked it as a treat for her, but she didn't feel like cooking, and it was all right simply to give the chicken away —let the old lady cook it later for herself . . . The main thing is, give away what's yours and don't eat what you're giving away . . . There I sat, my wine in one hand, my lavash-wrapped shish kebab in the other, foreign talk all around me—and suddenly I felt good, so childishly good! For an instant, time disappeared, as probably happens only in prayer and in happiness, when the Lord hears . . . And He was certainly casting an eye upon this glade. This would be His Sunday rest.

We had already been invited to a wedding, and also to visit a certain acquaintance of my friend's brother, and also a certain acquaintance of an acquaintance, and also a certain non-acquaintance. The Lord smiled against His will, out of the corner of His mouth . . .

Well, what can you do? What whirlpool of times had set me spinning? The church is sixteen hundred years old, but it has a one-year-old roof; Christianity is two thousand years old, and the sacrifices are ten thousand; the snob entered the cathedral about ten years ago, yet this isn't the first century in which people have observed custom; the newspaper spread under our feast is yesterday's, but the sky above us is eternal; the Catholicos is sixty, I'm thirty— dear God!—the soloist is twenty-five, and there is someone who hasn't even been born and hasn't yet seen the sky!

What different times they come from, the sacrifices and the slogans, the church service and the philharmonic, the snobs and the populace, the buildings and outbuildings, the text and the singing of it! A hodgepodge, a whirlpool, a rapids of the times, in an instant of time present.

History, in its sequence, is splitting at the seams. Times are connected only by that which has always existed, which does not have time, and which is common to all times. The eternal has no history. History is only for the ephemeral. Biology has a history, but life does not. The state has one, but the people do not. Religion has one, but God does not.

THE BOOK

My friend is an Armenian, and I'm a Russian. We have quite a lot to talk about.

"Oh," my friend said, "if you once show your love, you'll have to answer for it!"

"How do you mean?"

"You'll have to show your love again."

"But if I've ceased to love?"

"Then you've been unfaithful."

"But why?"

"Why did you love before?"

What were we talking about? This . . .

"If I'm an Armenian," he had said, "I'm an Armenian and nothing else. Do I have reason to love any other nation as I love my own? No. But then do I have the right to prefer any one nation to another? Never. You can't be a Judaeophile if you're not Jewish, any more than you can be a Judaeophobe. Now, you've become an Armenophile, and that's not right."

"I've become an Armenophile? Why do you say that?"

"Because. You've already written one article about me, as an Armenian; you praised me and said only good things. There was no particular reason for you to say them. Later you'll write another article, about this trip. Of course you won't speak ill of the Armenians this time, either; you'll say something good again. Then, the third time, you'll be obligated to love us, to insist on it, so as not to be a traitor. You're already an Armenophile."

"Hmm, yes," I said. "I don't like that."

"I don't either," my friend said. "That's exactly why I've promised myself never to say anything, either bad or good, about any other nation."

He was right.

But it's too late for me to follow that principle; I can't retract my many words to avoid being unfaithful.

And now I must confess how I fell captive, how I became an Armenophile. I have no right to discuss what I'm about to discuss, just as, having begun, I will have no right not to discuss it. This statement will soon be clear.

. . . One can become an Armenophile without ever noticing when or how it happened. For example, by opening a certain academic book* at any point and reading any page . . .

In some of the villages the inhabitants were killed, but others were only plundered. Also a substantial number of people, along with their priests, were forcibly converted to Mohammedanism; the churches were turned into mosques.

Most of the villages of Khizan were plundered and subjected to a massacre. Girls and women were raped, and many families were forcibly converted to Mohammedanism. The churches were pillaged, sacred objects were defiled, the priors of the monasteries of Surb Khach and Kamagielya died under dreadful tortures, and the monasteries were pillaged.

The city of Sgerd was subjected to a massacre; the shops and houses were plun . . .

. . . That was the first day of my sojourn in Armenia. I was sitting in the home of my friend's wife's sister, waiting for my friend. I had sampled all the food three times and was listening: my ears were still stopped up after the airplane flight. But my eyes were open. I went out on the balcony.

An unaccustomed scene, which I took to be exotic, unfolded before me. I saw an intersection, and a funeral procession slowly winding across it like a great snake. At home (in my own country) I had long since lost the habit of a ceremonial attitude toward death. Quietly, without darkening my mind, someone bore off my unknown neighbors; I wasn't always aware they had died, any more than I had been aware they were alive.

In the lead, as if to widen the street and cleanse it of activity (and the street did empty), an open Cadillac convertible glided along with unbearable smoothness and slowness. In it, an impassioned man with a red band on his sleeve stood and directed, like a marshal on parade. Next, in the space he had cleared, came a truck: scarlet

* *The Genocide of the Armenians in the Ottoman Empire: A Collection of Documents and Materials.* The Publishing House of the Academy of Sciences of the Armenian Soviet Socialist Republic, 1966.

calico platform, an open coffin in the center, and at the corners, on bended knee, four black-suited men, unnaturally straight and stiff (with wreaths in their hands, I think), staring solemnly ahead, apparently not even blinking. Then came such a quantity of Volgas that I lost count.

The force of the impression was not from death, not from grief, not from solemnity—it penetrated from some other, secret passage. That sun, those sweltering black suits, that inexplicably emptied street, that distressing slowness—I felt the world around me thickening, the air and its clarity becoming material objects. In that vitrifying, condensing, white-hot but already congealing world, pain burdened even the movement of the file of vehicles created for speed. They marched soundlessly, on foot, wading, mired in the air, which fell like snow.

Oppressed, I returned to my chair. I picked up the academic book that I had left face down, and looked back a page to see what the topic was . . .

IX. Bitlis Vilayet. The city of Bitlis was massacred and plundered, together with surrounding villages and districts, which are: (1) Khultik, (2) Muchgoni, (3) Gelnok, (4) . . . (99) Usnus, (100) Kharzet, (101) Agktsop, (102) . . .

What was this? I flipped the pages back . . .

To Our Supreme Patriarch Mkrtich,
Most Holy Catholicos of All Armenians—
Your Holiness, Blessed Hayrik, with tears in our eyes and with sorrowful heart . . .

Who had written this? I turned the page, looked for the signature . . .

. . . That is our fate and lot. We beg you, we implore you with tears, have pity on the handful of the nation who are yet

alive, and if possible do not refuse to cast a handful of water
on the fire consuming them.

Vardapet Hakobyan

I skipped to the end of the book and again opened it "anywhere" . . .

> The policy prescribed on this point by the censorship guide,
> published early in 1917 by the censorship department of the
> military press, was stated as follows:
> "As for the atrocities against the Armenians, one may say
> the following: not only must these issues, which concern in-
> ternal administration, not threaten our friendly relations with
> Turkey, but at the present difficult moment it is also essential
> that we refrain from even examining them. Therefore, it is our
> duty to maintain silence. Later, if foreign countries directly
> accuse Germany of complicity, we shall have to discuss this
> issue, but with the greatest care and restraint, always stating that
> the Turks were dangerously provoked by the Armenians. It is
> best to maintain silence on the Armenian question."

What was this from? I turned the page . . . "Joseph Marquard,
on the Plan to Exterminate the Western Armenians." Who was
Marquard?

A throttled sensation akin to impatience again picked me up
and led me out to the balcony. A new funeral, just as long and
magnificent as the first, was crossing the intersection . . .

Here my device betrays me, although that is exactly the way
it happened: my first day, sunlit and deaf, I wait for my friend and
see a funeral and open a book . . . But by now I don't believe in
this sequence and can't bear it.

All this did happen then, but when I wrote about it later I no
longer had the book at hand. After writing that the book could be
opened anywhere, I left a blank page. My story was finished, but
near the beginning of the manuscript, just about here, the skipped
page was still white: that book had proved to be as hard to obtain
as the Bible.

I am writing these lines at the Leningrad Public Library on
February 18, 1969, in order to fill in the blank. Thus, if we follow
the chronology of my Armenian impressions, the chapter about the

book belongs at this point in my story. But if we follow the chronology of the writing of the story itself, this is definitely the final chapter.

Well, then, I'm sitting in the library, holding that book in my hands again at last. There are five hundred pages in it, I have two hours, and I realize that I will not succeed in selecting the most characteristic, vivid, and impressive passages. And realize, too, that even if I could, it would be false. I resolve to repeat my experiment. I open the volume anywhere, crack it in the middle . . .

Of the 18,000 Armenians exiled from Kharberd and Sebastia, 350 women and children reached Aleppo; of the 19,000 exiled from Arzrum, only 11 people. Muslims who have traveled this road relate that the route is impassable because of the numerous corpses lying there poisoning the air with their stench.

This from the travel notes of a German, an eyewitness to the events in Kilikia.

I turn back a hundred pages.

Madame Doti-Vili writes: "The Turks do not kill the men immediately, and as they welter in blood their wives are raped before their very eyes." Because it is not enough for them to kill. They maim, they torture. "We hear bloodcurdling cries," writes Sister Maria-Sophia, "the howl of unfortunates whose stomachs are being ripped open, who are undergoing torture."

Many witnesses relate that Armenians were bound by both feet, head down, like carcasses at a slaughterhouse, and split with an ax. Others were tied to a wooden bed, which was then set afire; many were nailed alive to the floor, to doors, to tables.

Monstrous pranks are also carried out, sinister games. They seize and bind an Armenian, and on his motionless lap they saw up his children or hack them to pieces. Father Benois, of the French missionaries, reports acts of yet another kind: "The executioners juggled with recently severed heads, and even as the parents watched they tossed up little children and caught them on the tips of their cutlasses."

The tortures are sometimes crude, sometimes skillfully refined. Some victims undergo a whole series of tortures, conducted with flawless art in order to prolong the martyr's life and thereby prolong the amusement: they maim them slowly, at a measured pace, pulling out their nails, breaking their fingers, tattooing the body with a red-hot iron; they remove the scalp from the skull, and toward the end make it into porridge, which they toss to feed the dogs. They break the bones of some, little by little; they crucify others, or set them on fire like a torch. Crowds of people gather around, enjoying the spectacle and applauding the victim's every movement.

At times these are terrifying abominations, the orgies of sadists. They cut off an Armenian's limbs, then compel him to chew pieces of his own flesh. They choke women to death by forcing into their mouths the flesh of their own children. They rip open the stomachs of others and stuff into the gaping wound the quartered body of the child whom the women recently carried in their arms.

I have opened this book in four places. I can't do it again. I feel like a murderer copying these words, and I'm almost peering over my shoulder to be sure no one's looking. About a hundred people are sitting here, and no one knows what I'm doing. They're all quietly writing doctoral dissertations. I'm sure I'm engaged in the most terrible work in this building. I very much want them to believe me: I really didn't select anything, I merely opened the book in four places, any way it opened. I can swear any oath that this is not a device, it's really true. The book has another five hundred pages that I haven't read.

I ran out of black ink when I opened the book the fourth time, and I am forced to write in red pencil. This is neither manipulation nor symbol—it's chance—but my pages are red.

There is enough of everything in this world. If we think that something doesn't exist, that it can't exist, that it's impossible—then it exists. If we but think it, it already exists.

This world has everything, and for everything there is a place. Everything finds room.

I won't open the book again, I'm not going to read it. Back then in Armenia, I think, on my first day, I opened the book to the very passage I last quoted. And down below, a red funeral was passing by . . . It no longer seemed exotic to me: a different sun, a different death, a different attitude toward death.

And now, while I rest and calm down a bit, having resolved not to look into this book again, I can glance at the table of contents before handing the book back to the librarian:

1. The Massacre of the Armenians under Sultan Abdul Gamid (1876–1908)
2. The Mass Slaughter of the Armenians by the Young Turks (1909–1918)

That is the entire table of contents. How neatly 1908 fits next to 1909! As the last page of the first volume fits alongside the first page of the second. A two-volume edition. Early works—the first volume. Posthumous publications—the second.

And a foreword, too . . .

What was the total number of Armenians who perished? A detailed study of the question leaves no doubt that in the years of Sultan Abdul Gamid's supremacy about three hundred thousand people died; in the period of the Young Turks' rule, half a million. Approximately eight hundred thousand refugees found asylum in the Caucasus, the Arabian East, and other countries. It is instructive that if, in the 1870s, more than three million Armenians lived in Western Armenia and throughout the Turkish Empire generally, in 1918 there were only two hundred thousand.*

The Russian for "massacre" is *reznyá*. But my friend says *réz-nya*, with the accent on the root, which is from the verb "to cut." I simply cannot get his pronunciation out of my mind. As though *reznyá* is just people massacring each other somewhere . . . but "*réznya*" is when they're cutting *you*. The taste of your own flesh in your mouth.

---

* After the genocide, half of all Armenians were living abroad as émigrés. But Armenians do not accept the word *émigré*. For them, the word is an insult. To leave your country because of political convictions, or in search of a better life, is one thing; but it's another to save your wife and children from rape and the curved knife.

HISTORY WITH GEOGRAPHY

"You've already seen this, of course," said the history teacher (my friend's wife's sister), taking from the shelf a book as flat as lavash. "What! You *haven't?*"

We sat down on the couch and cracked the atlas in half: one half covered her lap, the other mine. I hadn't seen this kind of atlas since the good old days when I used to cock my head to one side and stick my tongue out as I colored Kievan Russia red.

I looked at these colored maps and caught a melancholy whiff of homework assignments.

The maps are mute for me, Armenian names in the Armenian language. Blue—that's the sea. Armenia is sometimes yellow, sometimes green, depending on the epoch. I am bombarded with names of conquering Armenians and conquerors of Armenia—a forest of centuries and names. My own history seems to me to be sparsely wooded, because, where we have our antiquity in the seventeenth century, theirs is in the seventh, and where we have the seventh, they have the third B.C. We don't even have the third.

Here, green and round, Armenia extends to three seas. Here, to two. Here, to one. And here—not even to one. So swiftly does Armenia diminish from the first map to the last, always remaining a generally round state, that if you riffle quickly through the atlas, it's a movie: it captures the fall of a huge round stone from the altitude of millennia. The stone disappears into the deep, diminishing to a point. But if you riffle the pages from the end to the beginning, it's as if a small pebble has fallen into the water, and historical circles are spreading across the water, ever wider and wider.

My friend came in and saw.

"Ah," he said, "the atlas . . ."

He sat down on the couch, took the atlas on his lap, opened it . . . And disappeared. Became absorbed in it—literally. With each turn or blow of the page he sank into his history up to his knees, his waist, his chest. He went all the way under. Suddenly he surfaced and looked up at me from the depths with faraway eyes, as if holding his head high out of the water. His voice barely reaching me, he shouted: "What I don't like in Armenians, sometimes, is their bellicosity."

"What? What?" I shouted, into the depths of his well. My

voice drifted down and down but seemed never to reach bottom.

Again my friend bent and looked for something at the bottom. He must have lost a ring . . .

Finally he climbed out on the surface of modernity. Before him lay the most recent map, today's Armenia. He drew a line with his fingernail, cutting off a narrow little strip on the east.*

"That will be nice. A nice round republic . . ."

I no longer knew whether to shout to him deep down or high up. I smiled foolishly.

The Armenians are a warlike people. For several thousand years they conquered; for several thousand years they were conquered. Their latest war is the war for their own history. Of this atlas—whose publication, it turns out, was also a struggle—and of the collection of materials on genocide especially, and of the defeat of Klimov, they speak with pride and pain, as one speaks of victory.

. . . My friend's brother came in. The taciturn younger brother. We had been waiting for him to arrive with news: he had taken his wife to the maternity hospital. He walked silently to the couch, lifted the atlas like a burden, and silently sank into it.

He looked through the telescope of his history. He trained reverse binoculars on his country, and there, in the improbable depth, at the bottom, shone the ring of Lake Sevan, and perhaps his future son.

---

* An inside joke. The "strip on the east" divides the Nakhichevan A.S.S.R. from the Nagorno–Karabakh Autonomous Region. Both these regions, with their predominantly Armenian populations, are part of Azerbaijan.

Geography Lesson

PARADIGM

And I pursue that image as a method. With the naked eye I see
nothing—one has to be born here, and live here, in order to see.
Through the binoculars I see large objects, for example, a
watermelon—and nothing but the watermelon. The watermelon
blocks out the world. Or I see my friend—and nothing but my
friend. Or . . . "Armenia donkey, Armenia very fat woman, and
ordinary Armenia policeman . . ." Every time, something blocks
out the world. I reverse the binoculars—the watermelon zooms
away from me, like a nucleus, and disappears over the horizon. In
the unimaginable depth and haze I see a small round country with
one round city, one round lake, and one round mountain, a country
inhabited by my friend alone.*

* This paradigm is legitimate for the further reason that it corresponds to the most
commonly held notions about Armenia. City? Erevan. Lake? Sevan. Mountain? Ararat.
These we know by heart; our knowledge of the rest, to use the language of school, is shaky.
I, for example, was astonished by the following "geographical discoveries":
    1. Armenia does not border Russia, it borders Georgia and Turkey.
    2. Over 95 percent of the republic's population is Armenian. This is the most "ethnic"
of the Soviet republics.
    3. Fewer than half of all Armenians live in the territory of the republic. Nearly two-
thirds are scattered throughout the countries of the world.
    4. Mount Ararat, although represented on the arms of the republic, lies in Turkey.

THE CITY

For me, Armenia began with Erevan. In bygone times, this was obviously impossible. People used to ride into an unfamiliar country. Now they fly. I flew, there was a blanket of cotton batting beneath me, I saw nothing on the ground, and the fact that I arrived in the right place can be explained only by my credulity. If Aeroflot had suddenly developed evil intentions, I might have awakened anywhere at all. Apart from the stewardess, who this time wasn't even pretty, I had no great quantity of travel impressions. By the will of Aeroflot, the country began for me not at the border but in the middle.

This is very important, I think—to cross the border and sense a change of character, even if the change is introduced by you. I should have gone by train. It's very important, I think, to have a beginning, always and in everything, and only then proceed to the end. Books should be read from the first page, or not read at all . . . Somewhere in my disorderly blood the pedantry of my two German grandmothers still makes itself felt. In any case, I have never read a book that didn't need to be read from the very beginning.

This book was opened to me in the middle, and I understood nothing.

And, just as a book that everyone has been talking about too much and too long, but that you haven't read yet, gradually provokes you to an obscure doubt (an awful lot of people, saying an awful lot about it!) and later to indignation (they talk and talk, and you've never read it)—so does this city. But I don't want to read it! you exclaim in the end. I don't want to go to Paris, I never really wanted to.

They deprived me of both the book and Paris. They deprived me of the time of discovery. I haven't yet known love, but they command me to love! I don't want to! I want to assemble the crane from my childhood Constructor Set once more! That's something I know, understand, and can do.

Another way of explaining this is to say that a man wants to be himself and has no desire to submit to the majority. Such is the nature of protest: I don't want to read this dog-eared book, admire this eviscerated splendor, or love a shared belle. To me, I could say, this is cold institutional macaroni. But I don't want to explain it that way.

I had built up too much anticipatory enthusiasm to be able to like the city so suddenly. My enthusiasm was unfocused and imprecise. I didn't trudge into this city dusty and hollow-cheeked, along deserted roads; I flew into it sleek and bloated, from Moscow.

I rode downtown on Lenin Avenue, which had earlier been Stalin Avenue, and, earlier still, Tumanian Avenue . . . There on the left, do you see? That's the Ararat Group. Armenian cognac, you know. And the pedestal in front, do you see? The base of the statue of the former Stalin—that is, the former statue of . . . that is . . .*

Well, how could you see anything here?

Well, Erevan was pink. Pink. Because of the tufa. Yes, they built beautifully, expertly. But I still didn't understand why this was Armenia. Nothing distinctive . . . national traits, socialist in content.

Well, I've mentioned that Erevan was my primer. The language—yes, to be sure, there was a different language here. Armenian. But the part about the primer was just purple prose.

I don't feel this city, I'm not competent in this city. I'm always being led somewhere, insensate.

"Well, shall we go?" my friend says.

"Where?"

"Let's go. You'll see."

We go, and I don't see.

"Let's drop in here," my friend says.

We drop in at an institute. My friend absents himself, forever. I memorize several Erevan wall newspapers. He returns at last, and not alone. Introduces me. The three of us leave together.

"Now let's drop in at one more place." This is half request, half command.

Very busy men we are, very efficient. There's always someplace

---

* The last and therefore the largest Stalin in the Soviet Union was erected in Erevan. It was not superseded, because Stalin soon died. The creators of the monument managed to receive a prize, however—the Stalin Prize.

There is also a story that six workmen perished while placing Stalin on the pedestal, and another six while toppling him from the pedestal. This sepulchral symmetry cannot be comprehended in terms of materialism.

In itself, the pedestal is not devoid of architectural virtues, its heavy lines preserving an ancient, almost Egyptian majesty.

we have to go for something—for what, I don't know, but I believe my friend: we have to.

We become four . . . five . . . six.

"That's everyone," my friend says. "We're off."

Very businesslike, we set off. Six men.

Yet another institute. Almost the same as the last one. In the south, they always seem so accidental and empty! A corridor, then another corridor, three sudden steps down, a little curtain. We pull it aside.

Suddenly we're in a beer hall.

"We just knew you'd be sitting here!" my friends exclaim, and we become seven.

So *this* was our business!

We passed the day in male society. The conversation dragged slowly, kept bogging down. Lots of beer.

I just couldn't believe I didn't see anything; I was ashamed to admit it. My perceptions were forced. I wanted to see Armenia in everything—and didn't see it.

"Well, how do you like it in Armenia?" They looked at me gently and demandingly.

"I like it very much," I said, of course. They looked at me as if I were a failure.

I poured some beer then, and when I set the bottle on the table it had an extraordinary number of slightly convex surfaces bursting in it—subtle, rounded polyhedrons. This was beautiful through the green glass. Suddenly I imagined I saw an Armenian church there, and an idea dawned on me.

"Look," I said. "See! All the surfaces in Armenia are amazing, just like these. Sort of convex . . . Rounded polyhedrons . . ." The accuracy of my observation should remove all doubt as to the sincerity of my delight.

They looked at me blankly. They glanced at my friend, as the interpreter. He started speaking in Armenian. At first he seemed to be explaining the complexity of my image. Then I thought he was just explaining to his friends that I was a good fellow anyway, and they needn't pay any attention to me. But then suddenly I guessed that he couldn't be discussing me at such length—there was nothing to say. And finally I realized that they had been having their own conversation for quite some time, and it bore no relation to me.

I found myself in solitary confinement, as if in a bottle. Its walls were transparent, greenish. Such strange walls, slightly convex, slightly angular, slightly round. They kept bursting, flowing together. Faceted bubbles . . .

My friends suddenly recollected themselves.

"Well, how do you like it?" they asked affectionately.

"Very much."

What else could I say?

"Pretty nice day, wasn't it?" said my friend, who had managed to avoid a trip to Lake Sevan today and was clearly pleased by this.

"Wonderful!"

What else could I say?

For reasons purely private, I had felt imprisoned in my native city and had fled from it. But, having fled, I again found myself in a cell, and moreover an alien one. Despite all, my own had been better.

I needed to find open space, so that I could feel the logic of building a home in that space.

I found space by breaking free of the city. I slammed shut the book that I had opened at the wrong page, and reopened it at the first page.

I still hoped that the book itself, if it really was beautiful, would overcome my prejudice and force me to love it. Love cannot be compelled; I'll never be able to force myself to love anything. It's not within my power. I'm not a saint. But suppose you suddenly exclaim, "My God! Now I see why I didn't trust you. It wasn't you I didn't trust, it was the people who kept telling me how much they loved you. But they loved you the wrong way, not as you should be loved! That's the problem." You are struck by the idea, and you shift the focus of your indignation. "Here's the way all this should be loved!" When I abandoned Erevan, that was how I was hoping to return to it.

We don't care about our beloved's past if we truly love her. (Precisely because all her past men loved her wrong—and were loved wrong?—they don't even exist for us.) Later, perhaps, when love begins to slip away—the ground from under you, like an uncertain foothold—you will need to know the past and to be jealous of it. But it doesn't matter to you now. You love her.

That's how I wanted it to be.

Love for the city could develop only after love for the space that enclosed it. About the city later, then, for I'll have an excellent occasion. First, about space.

SPACE

Space is a national category. A necessary condition for the realization of a nation. When I look at the Soviet map, our scarlet bedsheet, I feel distance—enormous distance—but I still don't feel open space. And if there's a little speck squeezed into a corner somewhere, like a tiny marsh (Estonia) or washtub (Armenia), how could you suspect it had any kind of space? Stand in the center and spin around on your heel, and your eye would demarcate all its boundaries. How could anyone live on a pocket handkerchief like that? Backed by distances so inconceivable, you shrug.

And what foolish surprise overtakes you, when you drive hour upon hour through a miniature (from our point of view) country, and there's no end or limit to it.

There turns out to be a horizon, a skyline, and it sets a boundary to everything. It is also an infinite world. It is what a man can grasp in a single glance, and sigh deeply—it is space and homeland. What lies beyond its boundaries doesn't particularly exist.

I am under the sway of two diametrically opposed impressions.

In Russia, something will always block your view. A fir tree, a fence, a post—your gaze will bump into something. This even seems justifiable or protective, in some measure: to be conscious of such inconceivable distance would be painful, if, in addition, you had boundless open spaces.

Once I was traveling through the Western Siberian lowlands. I woke up and glanced out the window—sparse woods, a swamp, level terrain. A cow standing knee-deep in the swamp and chewing, levelly moving her jaw. I fell asleep, woke up—sparse woods, a swamp; a cow chewing, knee-deep. I woke up the second day—a swamp, a cow. This was not space—it was nightmare.

My other impression is the Charents Arch in Armenia.

The mountain spur crowded close to the road and shouldered it to the right, the road yielded easily and moved aside, but now another thickset shoulder appeared on the right and shoved the road to the left, the road was jammed tight, squeezed, stuck, bogged down among the mountain spurs—the horizon disappeared. And suddenly the road broke free, it sighed—on the right came the sound of sudden light, as though a mountain had collapsed. For an instant something gleamed sky-blue, shone through in the distance, and then a small hill annoyingly blocked everything again. It wouldn't have blocked everything—there might still have been a gleam of blue behind it—except for an odd structure at the summit, hiding the rest of the view. It looked rather clumsy and out of place. We'll be past this in a moment, I thought, angry for some reason at this obstacle to the eye. But we turned sharply off the highway and went grinding up the hill. The arch on the summit grew nearer and at last blocked everything else. We got out.

I looked uncertainly at my friends. Why had we stopped? What was remarkable about this elephantine structure?

"The Charents Arch," they told me. Silently they let me pass ahead.

I sensed a sort of compact; they expected something from me, some sort of display. For all my desire not to offend my friends, I discovered absolutely nothing worth remarking in this arch. They nudged my back, even somewhat harshly. Perplexed and slightly recalcitrant, I walked through the arch and exclaimed.

My God, what space opened up! It blazed forth. Something within me lifted. For the first time in my life I saw the earth as God had created it.

This was a first draft of Creation. The lines were few—a line, a line, another line. No further strokes. The line had been drawn confidently and forever. There could be no corrections. There simply could be no other line. This was the only one, and it was the line that He had drawn. All else, I thought, God had created with a hand either weary or refined or sated. The luxuriant nature of Russia was the Lord's baroque.

"This is the world," I might have said, had I been able.

The dusty green waves of solid ground stretching downward from under my feet made me giddy. This wasn't the giddiness of fear, acrophobia; this was the giddiness of flight. There was a great and majestic footstep in these falling billows. They fell and turned pale blue in the distance, melted in a haze of space, and far away out there, deep blue by now, they ascended just as perfectly, marking the end of the earth and the beginning of the sky. On my right there was a dark rise, on my left a dove-gray drop-off, and I was suddenly aware of standing with my right shoulder slightly raised, as if repeating the shoulder slope of an invisible pair of scales, one pan of which was below me. "This is the music of the spheres," I might have recalled, had I been able. Before me was an unknown effect of distance, a total loss of proportion, an incomprehensible closeness and smallness—and infinity. My own size did not exist. My hand could touch these close, small hills and stroke them, it seemed; I could stand there and turn the pan of these scales in my hands and feel how natural and possible it would be to fashion this world in one day on a potter's wheel. ("What is a master craftsman?" my friend once said to me. "What he creates must be higher than his hands. He takes the clay into his hands—and it flutters out.")

And suddenly this closeness was disappearing. The world below me was becoming so infinite, deep, and immense that I was vanishing above it, and within me was born a sense of flight, of soaring over the world's limitless expanses. "The heavenly flight of angels . . ."

"Masis! You can see Masis!"

I started. What more could one see here?

My friend stretched his hand toward the end of the earth. "Over there, do you see? Just a shade darker? That's the small summit on the left, more clearly visible . . . And the large summit on the right." My friends, vying with each other, sketched the shape in the air. "See? One minute it's gone, the next you see it again."

I strained to see it. Maybe I did, maybe I didn't. After all, I didn't know exactly what I was supposed to see.

"I see it, I see it!" I confirmed ecstatically, as I, too, outlined an invisible something with my hand. (Was there sufficient ecstasy on my Scythian face?) And, indeed, it did suddenly seem that a certain line in the blue sky had darkened faintly, defining itself upward. "I see the large one!" (Or was the strain causing everything to go dark before my eyes?)

"Do you, really?"

I still didn't see Mount Ararat.

"Well, it's time to go," they told me.

Embarrassed, I went back through the arch. My friends walked with light step.

"Oh, if only we'd brought wine!"

"Why is that?"

"We'd have drunk it here, for goodness' sake!"

I took one last look over my shoulder: "This is the world where we did live . . ."

How natural that Noah should have landed precisely here! No, he did not run aground on the rock of Ararat. He moored. He knew no other world, and he sailed back to the same one. Other landscapes simply disappeared behind the stern; he didn't see them, they weren't reflected on his retina. The immigrant erects his new log cabin on the spot where he is able to recognize his homeland.

A man's country is not too small for him if he just once feels its space. How could he suspect the existence of borders, once he had seen this . . . "Here I first saw the world," people say of their homeland.

THE LAKE

From the center of Erevan, where all the buildings seem to have been erected once and forever—where everything is worn smooth and acclimatized, harmonious, solid, and final—we come to the identical pink infancy of the new districts; from there, to a gritty industrial suburb; and then the road sprouts wings. To the left of the road the left wing, to the right the right wing. In the landscape of Armenia, line reigns. The horizon is winged. If the left wing rises, the right dips. If the left turns gold in the sun, the right turns deep blue in shadow. The color changes often and all at once; it is infinite in its nuances, but never dappled—in its every existence it is total, universal.

The last buildings vanish, vineyards appear, chained to concrete columns, a concentration camp of grapevines (how few trees there are in Armenia!), and then the vineyards, too, are gone. Only the road's wings, only line and color, only black puddles of heat rising on the humps of the road. Such authenticity and uniqueness does this country show you, again and again, that by now its authenticity seems redundant. And when an emotion is generated in one person, an identical emotion is generated in someone else, as has always been true. The driver feels the same emotion that I feel and that my friend feels. We have no words to express it. And without words to express it, the emotion resorts to quotation.

"How well Saryan felt this," my friend says. "No one can feel it in a new way. Everyone feels it as he did."

It suddenly occurs to me that the birth of a brilliant painter would be a paradox in this country. Nature here is so exact that it will suffer no transformation by the artistic vision. To remain captive to this absolute exactness of line and color is probably beyond an artist's power; no copy is possible. Ah, well. This earth has already been created once, and there can be no second Creator.

We are climbing into the mountains. They rise up on the horizon, low and smooth; these feminine lines drive me out of my mind. It would never have occurred to me, as a city dweller, that an attraction to the earth was so similar to lust. Without exaggeration, I passionately desire to merge with the earth, even take it by force. The aggressor is wild, unrecognized, but the seed is there. If I have an aggressor in me, here he is . . .

The tension of the mountain road suddenly slackened, the narrowness fell away, the mountains receded, we entered a valley, and for the first time a straight line was marked on the horizon.

Such a road could lead me to Aparan, Byurakan, Geghard. Such an emotion could lead me only to Lake Sevan.

Oh, these famous places! I'm afraid of them. On the way, no matter how skeptically I frame my thoughts, I invariably feel a growing expectation of enthusiasm, discovery, and happiness—but then the place doesn't match. It disappoints and disintegrates. Unless perhaps it regains its life and color in recollection . . . How many different small Meccas I have seen empty, eviscerated, and examined, as if they'd been shot! Not only for men is fame lethal.

Sevan approached me, and I experienced neither shock nor delight. A lake. A beautiful lake. Indeed, very beautiful. But I was listening, instead, to a kind of melancholy and alarm—there was a vague and dangerous commotion rising within me.

Light . . . Too much light.

Now I catch myself: when I said "line and color," I was not being accurate. I was following tradition, rather than my own awareness. I was paying tribute to Saryan, rather than to nature. My habitual affinity for the northern palette may have prevented me from appreciating the harsh authenticity of the colors of the south. In any case, there was nothing original in my awareness of color in Armenia. Although, of course, I can easily credit the authenticity of these southern colors in comparison, for example, with the colors of our artificial Black Sea subtropics . . .

I ought to have said: line and light.

The light in Armenia was perhaps my primary visual impression, my chief physical experience. To say that it was too brilliant and there was too much of it is to say nothing. This was light of a special quality, which I had encountered nowhere before. I remembered the light in the Crimea, in Central Asia, in snowy mountains—in those places there had been a lot of light, brilliant light, blinding, even loud light—but never had I *experienced* it as in Armenia. For the first time it was something just as palpable, perhaps, as water, wind, and grass. There was no shelter from it, no escape, no cover. More than that, I even seemed to want *not* to hide from it, although it caused me true torment: two hours after I woke up, my eyes were aching, sticking shut, going blind, and a peculiar fatigue was transmitted through my eyes to my whole body. I even tucked my dark glasses into the bottom of my suitcase, on the very first day, and not just because I didn't want to stand out among my friends, who didn't wear any. I wanted to experience this inexplicably sweet torture, wanted every last ray of light to pass through me during these two weeks, up to the last day and hour.

And if Armenia is the brightest place in my life, then Lake Sevan is the brightest in Armenia.

There was something unnatural in the fact that I was standing on the shore of Sevan.* There was something dangerous in Sevan itself, in its water, air, and light. Dangerous specifically for me. I sensed this immediately, although I wasn't immediately conscious of it in words.

There was nothing obviously threatening about it. The weather was splendid. Sun, and rich blue skies. The waves were small, quite cozy. All around us were awnings, bathing lockers, wooden lounges, mushroom-roofed pavilions—a beach civilization. Waiting at the pier was a snow-white taxi-launch. Nearby was a restaurant that had an open terrace, with a few people who seemed to have been seated there to create ambiance. The weather slate read "Air temperature 19, water temperature 17."

Still, I shouldn't have gone into that warm water. My unconscious sense of danger, the feeling that I was idle and superfluous

---

* Something unnatural, at least, in the expression "standing on the shore." I was standing not on the shore but on the bottom of Sevan! Much has been written about the catastrophic drop in the level of the lake. The selflessness of the numerous enthusiasts who create schemes for saving and restoring Sevan deserves admiration. But as yet the problem is far from solved. This is not something to write about casually. But at the time I could write about nothing else . . . All the dry land on which I was strolling—on which roads had been laid out and sanatoriums built, and which already gave the impression that it had always existed—all this land was the bottom of Lake Sevan. And the peninsula on which we found ourselves had actually been an island. Just recently.

here, was what drove me to it. Well, why not? What were the awnings and lounges for? And look, people were in swimming. Beachgoers the same as everywhere. That was just the problem— the awnings and lounges did not belong here.

The water stung, owing to properties of its own, independent of temperature. But the sensation was just as painfully pleasurable as the torture by light. The two sensations were very similar. This was not water—it was a second state of sky.

I climbed out of the water a new man. Not renewed, not refreshed—new and different. Perhaps because it's one thing to look at the water from the shore, and another to look at the shore from the water . . . My chill intensified (now I realized that I had been shivering from the outset). My friend looked at me with the mild and distant gaze of a man who has not gone swimming. The steeply rising slope was crowned with a monastery; right there, the rich blue sky began its dome, inverted over Sevan. The emotion that I had glimpsed so obscurely—bleakness, superfluity, danger—turned out to be shame.

I had not done anything sacrilegious. My friend envied me for having gone swimming, when he hadn't; I really don't know what had prevented him. But somehow I dressed with embarrassment and haste, hopping awkwardly about, getting tangled in my trousers and losing my balance.

This defied analysis. There was no one before whom I need be ashamed, nothing to be ashamed of. But shame was shame.

Defensively indifferent now, I stood somewhat apart while the group had a lively argument about the choice of a boat. This was the same happy, marketplace ritual that I had seen many times, preceding any planned event, even the simplest: take a taxi or the bus, go home or to a restaurant, buy plums or a watermelon, and so on. We boarded one launch, then climbed out and argued again. Heat and cold were mysteriously conjoined in the Sevan air, and my intermittent shivers were like the touch of beloved hands—I stood there surrendering to their dangerous caress, and now the argument somehow came to me from afar, like the crackle of a fire in a stove, and the people standing beside me were suddenly swept away into the far distance.

And here I was, touching my foreign heel to the foreign, unsteady body of a launch. The embarrassed faint scorn that I felt and showed toward the launch was supposed to signify that I was not implicated in its artificiality, in the rumble of its motor and the iridescent oil stains on the water. We were equally alien to this light, air, and water, and our equality was something I didn't want to admit.

A magnificent driver? chauffeur? captain? rose lazily and too gracefully from the warm planks, pulled a tight sweater over his bronze splendors, and then, seemingly without a glance at the ladies, walked through us and took his place at the rudder? helm? wheel? Standing statuesque and barefoot on a special cushion, he pressed a small, too simple button—which would have destroyed any notion that his job was difficult, had he not been so magnificent—and shot us all out to the middle of the lake in the frivolous capsule of the launch.

Here we seemed to halt. We ourselves were not racing along —the lake had begun revolving swiftly around us.

The beach, with its small plywood ceremony, was flying away behind us. We wiped it from our faces like an autumn cobweb, and when we took our hands away—

The wind and spray hit us in the face, opaque sapphire waves were battering our white frivolity as if it were a goose feather, and the flock had flown away . . . flown away beyond those green, yellow mountains revolving around us in an arc. We doubled the point, and when it fell in line with the shore, it closed the circle on the bay. We found ourselves on a dark blue plate with a rim as white as sun-bleached bone—the boundary of water and dry land. The low, stout mountains looked cozy and reliable in the sun, but in the shade of the opposite shore they knitted their brows and frowned.

Man could not and did not exist here. To admire Sevan at length is impossible. One can only steal a glance. The ecstasy was akin to the sharp, biting cold of the spray. The water was casting us up as garbage.

I glanced around at my companions—and realized that my face was just like theirs. These faces, undone and ashen with happiness, as naked as the boundary between sunburned and never-tanned skin, were also impossible to look at—and anyway it was time to turn back. We had stolen a glance. Enough.

By the time I set foot on solid ground, I had the full-blown sensation that I was a foreigner, an outlander, an uninvited guest, and a shameful idler.

The beach was now deserted, which always looks rather strange, and in these surroundings, with the bleached grass, the dark blue water and sky, the solitude, and the monastery so silent above, it looked implausible and terrifying, as in a surrealistic painting.

And this unthinkable light, blazing up on the white strip of shoreline! How well I understood the abstract Russian peasant who had been cast here by the fateful hand of a trade union (somewhere nearby was a Holiday Home, inconceivable, equally surrealistic, ostracized by all of nature). Black as a fly, painfully kindred, the peasant detached himself from a little table just at that moment, and as he staggered along that bone-white strip, in that bright, bright, bright light, he struck up an urgent and bloodcurdling refrain, trying to outshout the light: "And da-a-a-a-a-a-ark was the night! . . ."

While we had our snack, I wanted to turn away from Sevan, for some reason, and rest my eyes on a soothingly understandable vendor's booth.

Nothing more, I wanted to see nothing more! The high ringing in my ears kept stretching and breaking, a burning chill ran up and down my spine, and a grasshopper chirred in my nose. I had a tic somewhere in my forehead. We were on our way to the car, trying not to look back at Sevan, when suddenly we turned right, with melancholy and a sense of doom, and started uphill, toward the highest and most exhausting instant.

And there, up above, everything disappeared. Time was gone. The isthmus hid—and the peninsula became an island. The booths and awnings, seen from above, had been cast up on the shore as garbage—again, the work of the sea. The monastery was standing for its second thousand years, just as it had stood here always. The tallish yellow grass forever marked the shape of the wind, which was blowing here for its second thousand years, just as it had blown here always.

Pale now, as if it had emptied toward evening, the sky easily found room for both the wind and the island and Sevan. But as the sky lightened, Sevan was growing dark, and down below us it lay like a pelt stretched to dry, with white petals of shriveled skin curling up along the edges.

This was such a wild, dangerous, tense, ringing, bowstring-taut place on the earth, exposed to the light as to the wind, and to the wind as to the light. A place that might still receive a pilgrim, in order to blow the dust of the roads from him; but the idle visitor was blown away like the dust, and the place remained just as unseen, just as unfrequented, as a thousand years ago, as always. Blinding, like toothache. A place for a homeland . . . It was suited for nothing else. My ears were stopped up, my eyes watered.

"Just such a wind blew in the reign of Rurik, and Ivan the Terrible, and Peter the Great," the weather was just as cold and blue, and the yellow grass lay just as flat, both on the night when Peter denied thrice before the cock crew and when the student in Chekhov's story approached the campfire at the kitchen garden . . .

But no warehouse lock had ever hung on the doors of the monastery; no captain of the Sevan Steamship Line had been buried under an obelisk with a star, between two ancient graves with ornate crosses; the monastery island had not become a peninsula; no highway had been laid along the isthmus up to the very shore of that island (and now up to the foothills of the mountain, where the Holiday Home is); the Komsomol girl in light blue did not stand here with her oar; Lake Sevan was not flowing away like the sand in an hourglass, defining our time, as narrow as the neck of the hourglass, by leaving a dead, bone-white strip between itself and the mountains . . .

It's this bright only when you have a toothache.

My ears are stopped up, my eyes are watering.

"Useless my ears, useless the eyes in my head . . ."

Great poetry is always concrete. And imageless.

THE MOUNTAIN

As well-traveled people had explained to me in Moscow, I was supposed to see Mount Ararat right at the airport. It should be the very first thing I saw.

But it wasn't there.

In Erevan, too, I was supposed to see it but didn't.

It was hidden by the haze. In the direction where Ararat should have been, the haze glowed azure and thickened to a rather turbid deep blue; there appeared to be a sea, out there beyond the city.

I should have seen it from the window of my pied-à-terre in Erevan's new district—the house stood above the city, and nothing impeded the eye. The window was supposed to have an excellent view of Ararat, but the mountain wasn't there.

I should have seen it from the outlook at the Charents Arch, and maybe I did, but maybe I really didn't.

And so on, until the last day.

I was leaving on the first flight and got up at dawn.

Then I saw it.

Both the large summit and the small one.

This proved very unexpected. The mountain wasn't all that integral to the spot where it had sprung up so suddenly in farewell. It seemed like a newcomer.

It turned out to be less resplendent than it is on labels, or in the frescoes at the Ararat Restaurant in Moscow.

A rather morose, frowning mountain, as if displeased by the view revealed to it. A taciturn mountain; yes, it gave me the impression of a vow of silence. Perhaps that's natural for an extinct volcano.

And then—the mountain stared. I at it, it at me. And I felt uncomfortable.

This was probably a one-time chance impression, but I could not understand how the mountain came to be here.

As though Ararat had been forced to rise up and grow against its will, that it might place its shoulder under the Ark.*

---

* Armenian churches are equally unexpected. They have the same cooled volcanic nature. The church appears out of nowhere. On a flat place. Like Ararat. In the opinion of Armenian volcanologists, however, Ararat is not extinct but dormant. There's a difference. Ararat has simply been inactive for a long time; it has not been extinguished.

A Captive
of the Caucasus

———

THESIS

I've been asking myself a question: Where do ideals come from?

Nurture? Environment? Family, school, associates, society? No doubt—yet we soon discover that these aren't the only factors. They don't explain everything. Something remains unclear. But how it stings, how it aches, how it torments us, that something!

Passion. Jealousy. Love. This is the moment when we don't accept life as it is. This is the moment when we don't have the sense to apply sober experience. The moment when suffering appears from out of nowhere, without cause, and yet its objective reality is as obvious as the fact that our body belongs to us. But where have we seen this ideal love? When did we recognize it?

Art? Books? Yes, of course—these are the source of the ideal that we seek later in life and do not find. In memory I begin leafing through the books of my youth, and suddenly, with today's cold and sobered eye, I discover that those books said none of the things I once read in them, like a dream. Those books were written by men just as sober in their time as I am in mine. My youth read in them what it wanted to—what was written in youth itself.

You may grow up an orphan, your family and environment may prove tragically unsuited to the ideal development of childhood and youth, and yet, quite possibly, this very instance will engender dreams of happiness and ideals of the Beautiful, uncorroborated by anything in tender and early experience. All right, then: do these ideals arise merely from opposition, for balance, in accordance with the laws of dialectics?

We know from our school days that a bad environment and society have, with unusual regularity, produced people of luminous character, who calculated their ideals in some manner omitted in the textbook. With mysterious naïveté and obstinacy, they went no further but returned to the same darkness from which they had come, in order to bring their light to people who felt no need of it, people who squinted, fretted, and used very primitive methods to reduce the bearer of enlightenment to nought.

Here again, in my view, not everything tallies.

How does an ideal arise if it hasn't been nurtured in you and if your life experience can't lead you to behold it either? Ideals, after all, do not exist in life. That's why they're ideals.

Are they perhaps innate? And in that case are nurture, environment, life, and experience merely the favorable or unfavorable conditions for revealing them?

The nature of an ideal is exceptionally unclear to a materialist.

It should be acknowledged that the materialization of an ideal is impossible. This is more than obvious, because anything that can materialize is no longer an ideal. An ideal does not exist in the material world.

What triumphs is ideas—not ideals.

And we don't see the ideas triumph, either. Because the most beautiful idea, in triumphing, easily gives rise to evil—turns into its own opposite and proves quite unbeautiful.

But then where is the ideal? What is it that makes me agonize and agitate like a fish in a frying pan? Why don't I accept life as it is—the life that's happening to me? After all, I don't have any paradigm or experience more profound than my own, I don't have anything to compare with, anything to be jealous of. If I haven't seen any other life, don't know any other so well as I know my own, what is the problem? With what imprint, where acquired, am I comparing my life, so that I'm always saying "Wrong, wrong!" and denouncing myself to myself (no one else sees!) so insanely?

We have to admit that there exists within us, and nowhere else, an ideal world inhabited by an ideal man, a world passed down to us at birth (because physically we might have been born anywhere at all). It is revealed in each of us—although with varying degrees of fullness and force—so that we may have something to compare and contrast with our own lives, something with which to torment ourselves and suffer because it's discrepant, unattained, off-limits. What is this torture of being human? What are the pangs of conscience, the agony of shame, the gnawing of melancholy?

Where do they come from?

And where had I acquired, what had generated within me, the image of a certain celestial land, a land of real ideals? That land had always been nearby, wherever I was. Simply, a land where everything was what it was: a stone was a stone, a tree was a tree, water was water, light was light, an animal was an animal, and a person was a person. Where work was work and rest was rest, hunger was hunger and thirst was thirst, a man was a man and a woman was a woman. Where all the stones, herbs, and creatures had their own corresponding purposes and essences, where primordial meanings would be restored to all concepts . . . The land was nearby, and I alone was not in it . . . Under what circumstances had I left this land? How long ago had it happened? I didn't remember. How had I gone on living? I didn't know. I woke up and looked, not out the window, but at the clock—was it morning, evening? I breakfasted without appetite, because one must eat to live. Or perhaps live to eat. I walked outdoors—the traveler went from point A to point B. One has to go somewhere and do something! In the evening I seized a man by the arm—I? seized? a man? by the arm? I looked into his eyes . . . Good God! Who was this? Whose arm had I seized?

It was time for me to return.

I am quite willing to grant that some other country, not Armenia, could have become my promised land. Simply, the time had arrived. But Armenia did become my promised land. She is not to blame. Therefore, this essay is less about her than about what she became for me.

. . . Land with one city, lake, and mountain, land inhabited by my friend! I swallowed the desiccated words in my throat and could not describe you. Stone was stone, light was light . . . I found the word *authentic* and settled on it. I talked with a man who was a man and talked like a man. He and I ate food that was food and drank wine that was wine. Then, in gratitude and still in a frenzy of activity, I absolutely had to hunt up a word to mantle my joy, cover it, clothe it, and I said, "This is a land of concepts . . ."

My convulsive quest for absolutely the one word, the one

definition of this land and this joy—isn't it an oblique proof that there is indeed such a word? that the word for this country exists, if it was so lacking in my vain frenzy?

WEALTH

It was a small black plum; more accurately, a dark blue, ink-colored plum; small not because it was unripe or undersize but because it belonged to a well-known and quite widely available smaller variety, somewhat more prolate than the large plums, rather pointed, somewhat less juicy, on the dry side, in fact, and sweeter.

This was one of Erevan's largest indoor markets. Its architecture, like much in the planning of modern Erevan, should be acknowledged as progressive and felicitous. I especially liked the interior of the market, where function and solution were fully integrated, forming an organic whole. After the light and heat of the outdoors, it had a cool, strangely bright shade and cleanliness, a peculiar stillness. None of the harsh and seething life of the southern open-air bazaar, with its sun, hubbub, crowds, and wasps.

Such loops in time a comparison makes, returning upon itself! If a colony of seabirds is known in Russian as a "bird bazaar," from the comparison with a human bazaar, this is not due primarily to their numerousness but to their sound, in which neither can be compared with anything except the other: the sound of merged voices, merged in such absolute disorder that they already form a harmony. And if a bird colony has no comparison except a bazaar, I have no comparison for the bazaar except a gathering of birds. Thousands of voices, which I could not distinguish or hear, floated up to the high arches, merged there, reverberated, and drifted slowly down. The returned roar was so gentle that I wasn't immediately conscious of it, like the roar of the sea and the roar of a distant bird colony. (The roar of an open-air bazaar is close: as if you had stepped onto the shore, an uninvited guest, and frightened away thousands of your winged hosts all at once.) The lofty vault supported by airy and graceful pointed arches, the diffuse light coming from some unknown source, this soft, gentle booming—all led involuntarily to the thought of a cathedral.

That small plum lay at the apex of a tidily stacked pyramid of plums exactly like it. An elderly woman of neat and dignified appearance had built this pyramid, and now she stood waiting, ma-jestically and modestly. Nearby, superfluous, her homely daughter shifted from foot to foot, with a sort of bored anxiety on her face. Also nearby was a vendor fussing with her herbs, but there was an obvious dividing line between plums and herbs.

They had no customers.

The dignified woman, just at this moment, swiftly caught a plum that was about to roll down. Smoothly and not without grandeur she placed our heroine at the very top, after which, in a somewhat unreasoning and very solicitous gesture, she steadied the whole construction from the side. She let go—and the pyramid froze, unbreathing, obedient to the miraculous laws of friction.

My friend and I had been walking through the market, and my northern heart was staggered, for the umpteenth time, by the abundance of the south. The miracle of the existence of fruit made me slightly giddy. In a way, the fruits were more conspicuous in the indoor market than at a bazaar. The absence of sunlight—the sun being the most oppressive thing at a bazaar—seemed to restore to the fruits their own light (precisely: their light, not their color). They seemed to shine from within, giving back absorbed sunlight; they themselves were small suns. Since my participation in the bargaining, like it or not, was passive, and since I didn't understand my friend's principle of selection or what he was haggling about with his fellow tribesmen, I had abandoned myself entirely to enchantment and contemplation. I began to classify fruits according to the sunniness principle: a tomato is sunnier than a cucumber, and a pear is sunnier than an apple, but the sunniest of all, strangely enough, is an apricot, or so I reasoned. Although the absence of price placards eliminated any opportunity for me to participate in the haggling, their absence pleased me, in and of itself, for it signified a vital, original principle of trade, where a deal is also a sort of alliance, a relationship, a kinship. All the people here seemed to me to be related.

"How beautiful," I said feebly, surveying this magnificence.

"A poor market," my friend said. "But in about two weeks—!"

At this point we drew even with the plum, and my friend undertook to buy it. Perhaps because the dignified woman had not anticipated a customer, our appearance proved too sudden for her; after a momentary confusion, and as if in compensation, she set about the business of bargaining a little too vigorously, though without shedding her dignity in the least. Her abrupt gesture set the topmost plum to swaying. It hesitated very slightly and started to roll. Both the woman and her daughter almost lunged for it, instinctively, but they were already too late to catch it, and apart from the fact that catching one plum would risk dislodging the whole pyramid, this would also be somehow undignified. So the two women froze, arresting their barely noticeable, undeveloped gesture, and watched the plum fall. I, too, stood rooted to the spot for several seconds; an unexpected fall always hypnotizes me. The plum rolled off the pyramid, taking another with it. They bounced from the marble counter to the tiled floor and rolled playfully away, passing each other.

We followed them with our eyes until they came to a full stop. The dignified woman was already weighing out plums for my friend.

The two plums lay not far apart on the rather dirty floor, and people were walking over them. The woman dispatched her work quickly and smoothly, but against her will she cast surreptitious glances at those two orphaned plums. A little boy noticed them, and we looked at him hopefully, but the era of bazaar urchins retrieving things from the floor was long gone. People had grown wealthier. A man nearly stepped on a plum, but at the last moment he jerked his foot clumsily and avoided it. We sighed.

Two small plums of a cheap variety. How can I explain it—in all these emotions, there was neither poverty nor greed! People simply felt bad that the plums had been wasted, that they would be crushed, that no one would eat them.

This pity for the plum was noble. It was respect for the plum. In every drop of respect was the price of land and the price of labor.

There was culture, too.

Culture does not come free. If natives of Leningrad are incapable, even now, of throwing a stale crust in the garbage, it certainly doesn't mean they are close to the land or have respect for the plowman's labor; that is no longer in their blood, perhaps. But if we subtract today's satiety from this never-discarded, always safely stored crust, the difference is the blockade. That deep and distant hunger gives to people who have long forgotten the land an element of peasant culture. And not only is it true that respect for bread is culture, but such culture must also be treated with respect, like bread.

Food is food. Not only a vital function, but also a concept.

For this discovery I am indebted, in many respects, to Armenia. There the culture of food survives, not yet enslaved by the institutional cafeteria.

I close my eyes and see that table . . . Here are tomatoes, so round, so red, so separate from each other. Here is a fist of country cheese, with the netting of the cheesecloth imprinted on it. Here are scallions—long, uncrushed shafts beaded with water. Here are greens—green greens, blue greens, red greens, a whole stack, a whole cartload. These are not food, they are the crystals of food; these are not compounds, they are elements. Gifts from heaven.

And a pile of lavash. Like an ancient, ancient manuscript. Lavash is the first bread, primal bread, the father of bread. Flour and water—so I understand—the crystal of bread. Eternal bread. Here a damp towel has been spread out—and fresh pages of lavash breathe eternal.

It's a clear, clear morning. My friend sits down. I sit down. We tear off a corner of lavash, place scallions, herb stalks, and cheese on it, roll it up tight, lift it unhurriedly to our mouths, take a clean bite, and unhurriedly chew. We are not hasty, we are not greedy, we aren't even playing gourmet—we are eating. We respect the bread, and respect each other, and respect ourselves.

"Lavash is bread," my friend says, tearing off a fresh scrap. "Lavash is a plate," he says, putting greens on the lavash. "Lavash is a napkin," he says, wiping his mouth with lavash . . . and eats the napkin.

In Armenia I saw no dirty plates or unfinished, picked-at dishes. People eat with dignity in Armenia. And it's not a matter of knives and forks, or of napkins. One can eat with the hands, too, it turns out . . . and wipe the plate with the bread, because it's delicious, always delicious. And that's not the only reason.

If I were given the task of defining, in a word, what culture is—not the culture that means higher education and graduate school, for even an educated person can be a churl, but the culture with which even an illiterate person is often endowed—I would define it as the capacity for respect. The capacity for respecting what you do not know, the capacity for respecting bread, earth, nature, history, and culture—and consequently the capacity for self-respect, for dignity. And since I would be dissatisfied with this formulation, since I would feel that it was incomplete, I would add to it the capacity not to make a pig of oneself. He who eats a surfeit and gorges himself is always a pauper, always a slave, regardless of his external property. He gorges himself feasting, gorges himself loving, gorges himself befriending. He throws out his bread, drives away his woman, rejects his friend . . . Filth. A mess. Winded, short of breath. Such a man should have nothing—he should starve. Only while hungry does he still maintain his human image and the capacity for sympathy and understanding. He is a slave. Once sated, he belches, he scorns everything on which he has gorged himself, he takes vengeance on that for which he has thirsted and hungered. This is his imaginary freedom from the mundane, now that he's sated; this, ostensibly, is spirituality. His dull gaze casts about for something more to reject, stain, and break. In making a pig of himself, he has exhausted his hungry striving for freedom. And now his freedom—the next step after satiety—is churlishness. Because, having gotten what he wanted, he again does not have, does not possess, and now, to convince himself of his freedom, he must spit on that for which he has proven so shamefully unprepared: possession.

Only culture can cope with abundance. The uncultured man cannot be rich. Wealth requires culture. The uncultured man will always come to ruin, and then he will wreak ruination.

"Do you like lavash?" my friend asks.

How can I tell him how much I like it! I say, "I wish I could introduce the highest of prizes for poets: if a poet writes a line that is truly beautiful, it will be printed on pages of lavash."

"True, true," my friend says joyfully. "So you, too, have noticed that lavash is like an ancient scroll!"

"Which passage would you choose from your book," I say, as a great admirer of his book, "to be printed on lavash?"

And my friend, who is capable of writing about people guided only by the wind, sun, and clouds; who can write how a man feels hot, just hot—and it makes *you* hot; or how a buffalo cow, in a village where there are no longer any buffalo bulls, leaves her old mistress early one morning and goes wandering through the mountains of Armenia from village to village, where there are no buffalo bulls either, and filled with a mysterious and beautiful melancholy she walks through this beautiful land where there are no buffalo bulls, and all this is done only through her, only through smells, simple scenes, and sounds; and how she finds no buffalo bull and comes home . . . And my friend, who is capable of writing such a thing, says with sincere gravity and sorrow, "To be printed on lavash—no, I don't think I've written anything yet."

Oh, this land, where they ask me, "Andrei-*jan*, which do you want, a peach or a tomato?"

And if I answer correctly, they look at me with love and gratitude, as if I were an initiate.

FAMILY AND MASK

Ultimately, the fruit of love is children. Even to mention this is awkward, somehow. Let's say it for those who, being absorbed in the process, have lost sight of the purpose. Let's remind ourselves. Of course, all parents love their children. It's risky to give preference to any one nationality. We all love our children, but mostly just because we have them. Family feeling has been deadened.

In Armenia, babies seem to be a more conscious decision.

This should be discussed in plain words. "Time to get married," and "Time to start a family." Which comes first, the chicken or the egg, is not a foolish question. Let's put it this way: All my friends married for love. That is, the first love came and went; then came one, two, ten, a hundred more women. This is it, I'm in love, they kept thinking. No, I guess not, it turned out. Finally, by degrees, perhaps even with surprise, they discovered that they loved one of the women, the last, desired to see her more and more often, all the time, always, couldn't bear to lose her, to imagine her with another man, wanted to keep her forever—and got married.

The highest measure, the ultimate. The goal, after all, had been a woman—loved and desired, but just one. Two people, they discovered with surprise, are a family. Children are a fog, sobering and frightening. Their arrival is more often associated with a certain imbalance, the atmosphere is full of conflict and drama. There are so many childless young couples where imbalance, uncertainty, and instability are the source of passion; the length of the marriage . . . And if a baby does arrive, the sensibleness and naturalness of the family again comes as something of a surprise.

They all love their children, of course, once they have them. These are families that just happen, somehow unintentionally, spinelessly, as if in a dream. I'm ready to prefer the peasant's rather crass "I've been knocking around long enough," "Time to have my own place," "Time to start a family." The peasant feels a yearning for his destiny, though he persuades himself by calculating the advantage. There is actually no profit in marriage. But it does have meaning.

We all love our children, of course. Mainly because they're *ours*. A blind feeling. "My child," and not the neighbor's.

How do they love children in Armenia? If it weren't basically absurd to partition an emotion, then in the first place, they generally love children very much; in the second place, because the child is *theirs*; in the third place, because it's a Matevosian, Petrosian, Ionnesian, of the clan of Matevosians, Petrosians, Ionnesians; in the fourth place, because it's an Armenian, one more Armenian, not a Russian, not a Turk, not a Georgian. Here the circle closes—in the first place and in the fourth; the fulfillment of a duty, biological, national, and personal.

To understand, you would need to be slaughtered for millennia by the curved knife: this is your son, he will live on your land and speak your language, he will preserve the land, the language, the faith, the homeland, the clan.

He is not simply your son, not merely your son.

Love for children, like almost everything else in Armenia, is dignified. Intense but not exaggerated, tender but plain. It seemed to me that there was one overall difference between their child-rearing and what I was accustomed to seeing at home. A fundamental difference, I think. Our influence and authority over children are distributed according to decreasing age; theirs, according to increasing age.

A sense of proportion in the display of love is the foundation of nurture. How sensitive children are to this faith, this evenness! Firmness, fidelity, constancy, and calmness evoke trust, above all, in the souls of small conservatives. Effusive affection is probably the equivalent of a shout and a blow. Simply put, in the presence of a child you must keep yourself under constant control—this does not gainsay tenderness. It is a constant effort of will; though difficult, it probably becomes a habit.

From what I have seen of our urban intellectual families, the arrival of a baby is an emergency. Confusion, terror, a love-panic. At some point, everything in life happens to every man for the first time, of course, before he has been armed with this or that experience. Especially his first baby—here we can be very understanding. But in the first place, it's highly debatable whether experience truly arms us; as we go through life, we're always having to act for the first time, and I don't particularly believe that prior experience, especially personal experience, can be applied to a subsequent present instant. In the second place, the birth of a child, even one's first, is something so natural, so true to nature, that the shock of it must have crept in from civilization itself, from the rupture with one's own nature—from a certain biological atrophy.

I arrived at such thoughts by observing and comparing . . .

For example, I was startled that babies had an unthinkable, absolute freedom, such as I had never seen. I walked into my friend's apartment for the first time—his family were at the summer cottage—and began to look around. How well did my friend live? Here was a washing machine. I hadn't seen this kind, and I touched it. The broken lid fell with a crash. "That's Davidik," my friend said with satisfaction. "What?" I said, in surprise. "But he's two years old!" "No, he's not two yet," my friend said. I poked at the typewriter. It clinked dully, like a tin can—it didn't work. "That's Davidik, too?" I joked. "Davidik," my friend said, almost proudly. "Sorry, this is the only cup I have," he said, pouring coffee. "I had twelve. There's one left." "Davidik?" "Davidik." Picturing the perpetrator of the devastation, this young Pantagruel, I felt proud of my friend's pride. "A good name," I said. "Fitting. He'll crush Goliath." But what was my surprise when I met Davidik! He was a very gentle, angel-faced boy with an earache, a little bunny-rabbit angel, weak and sickly, quiet, even sad. It was incredible to me that he could have created this havoc. Then and there, to dispel my doubts, Davidik smashed the last cup on the floor. "Oh, Davidik!" His mother clasped her hands joyfully. "Good for you! That's my Davidik!"

And so they smile to this day, in my mind's eye: Davidik's mama, Davidik's papa, and Davidik himself over the shards, his eyes round, his little arms outflung . . . I smile, too, somehow enviously and happily, and the light of my childhood—the unique light that illumined other rooms, back then—illumines this scene for me.

"V*ah!*" said his mother. "That's the second set he's smashed!" It sounded like "Never mind, we'll buy a third." I should mention they weren't that rich.

But the oldest boy, who wasn't really very big either, might have been taken for a stepchild, they were so strict with him. Their strictness seemed to increase in direct proportion to the awakening of his consciousness. By the age when, in my observation, children in our families are permanently emerging from obedience—and the parents are slipping ever deeper into dependency—in Armenia the strictness of the relationship seemed to have achieved such extremes that there was no longer any need to display strictness. Or perhaps they simply felt it improper for even the smallest feature of the relationship to be noticeable in the presence of a guest . . . The children became invisible, inaudible, so that only in the distance beyond a half-opened door, if a breeze should move the curtain aside, might one notice the shadow of an adolescent. And the shadow might be studied more closely only if the father, during our leisurely conversation, should suddenly take a notion to boast what a fine son or daughter he had. Even then, a light nudge of the father's hand, a parting smile—not a broad one—and the teenager disappeared forever.

In any case, I heard none of what in our families is called "a lively little boy," or "oh, this phase," or "what spontaneity," or "they have so much energy and life"—nothing like that. Or, to end the embarrassment of hasty generalizations, let me say simply that family life, including the children (except for babies), never emerged on the visible surface when I entered a house and the host engaged me in conversation. I left just as uninitiated into family relationships as when I arrived. None of this would seem to be any particular surprise, except, perhaps, the fact that for some time and for some reason I have found the order of things surprising.

The senior in age becomes the senior in position. Why should that be a puzzle? Duties expand much faster than rights.

Sophisticated as I became in my habits of observation, I learned no more about private life than a photographer invited to do a family portrait. Only the frozen facial features, and the make of the living room furniture. Besides, why should I, a stranger, in one hour gain any conception of something that has been taking shape for years? Don't we each have enough with our own family life? In Armenia I didn't need to burden my mind with extraneous knowledge of the psychological patterns, catarrhal sufferings, and sexual tastes of a hospitable family. I will gladly limit my observations on Armenia's family life to this fortunate (and to me, welcome) fact, that it was impossible to penetrate deeper. From what I succeeded in seeing, it appears that I will find no epithets for the family beyond "harmonious, friendly, and strong."

Yet in our language these have long since become clichés: not only are they superficial, they have almost no application to reality.

Gradually I wearied of the absence of indiscipline—there was no place to relax. And I was growing bored. The family cinema here showed only dull, fact-varnishing scenes that bore no comparison with our neorealistic achievements.

I tried to behave properly, of course. If you can't start jabbering in a new language overnight, you should at least take care to avoid accidentally doing something that isn't accepted practice in this country. That is, you have less and less opportunity to be yourself; against your will you become a representative, subordinating yourself more and more to the obtuse logic of representation. For if you, out of ignorance, can think of someone's individual features as ethnic, it is all the more true that your own ways and habits, since you're alone among foreigners, are losing their individuality and suddenly beginning to represent both your group and your nation. At this point the visitor neutralizes himself, on his own initiative . . . More and more often I think of the tourist in the neuter gender. And I'm increasingly alarmed at the thought that I might march around Paris with the vagueness of the neuter sex on my face.

It's easy to behave properly, because to behave improperly is dangerous. Even if it had been my inalienable habit to make the acquaintance of women on the street, I'm sure I would soon have figured out that it wasn't worthwhile in Erevan—there was little likelihood that I would succeed in invading a nocturnal balcony via the downspout. All this, shall we say, was easy to give up. The more so because (and I'll swear to this particular experience) I never once succeeded in meeting the glance (not inviting, not playful—just the ordinary, random glance) of a woman or girl I didn't know. I was allotted no more attention, less, in fact, than any post or fence. I would have believed that such behavior toward me was an unnatural and deliberate undertaking, if the non-meeting of our eyes hadn't come as easily to them as breathing. That was the problem, it cost them no effort. They didn't notice that they didn't notice me. In fact, I wondered how they saw the world around them. Was it true that they didn't see me? Was there some peculiarity in their perception of the spectrum? . . . But suddenly I thought: What of it, actually? Why make a habit of ogling everyone who comes along? What's the point?

Still, it's an odd debate—what is or is not accepted practice. Only when you perceive what's not accepted in this or that alien family, milieu, or country, only when you feel foolishly surprised that "they" don't do everything the right way, do you begin to realize what the accepted practice is in your own family, milieu, or country. Then comes the simple thought: What if your accepted practice— the one you believe to be the uniquely natural and correct way of doing things—is *not* all that natural and correct, but perhaps extremely arbitrary at best?

Well, all right. On the third day I forgot how to ogle women, and the loss was survivable. Ultimately, it even opened up some time for me to notice other objects and consider them. Quite a lot of time, incidentally.

Here I would like to mention a certain remarkable conversation.

One day, in the courtyard of my friend's house, where Davidik was playing, I was introduced to a neighbor, an intellectual-looking young mother in glasses. On her lap she cradled a fat baby, who was clumsily eating matsuni and dribbling it down his mother's front. She was wearing a knit suit, and her prodigality with imported goods startled me, although I had already met Davidik. "As long as he eats," she said calmly, following my gaze and interpreting it correctly. She glanced indifferently at her yogurt-covered bosom and began to inquire about my impressions. After the ordinary questions—how do you like Erevan, and how do you like it in Armenia (very much and very much)—she posed an unexpected one, unique in its way. She blurted, "How do you like Armenian women?"

I was flustered. I said that one encountered astonishingly beautiful faces. I said that in general I hadn't looked too closely.

She was surprised.

I added that I had quickly realized the impossibility of making any contact and had stopped looking.

Again she seemed surprised and uncomprehending. "But would you marry an Armenian woman?"

It was my turn to be surprised again. After stammering that I was married anyway, I said that I doubted I could overcome a certain barrier . . .

We understood each other poorly.

She said, "Don't you wish that you could leave for three years and know for sure that your wife wouldn't be unfaithful?"

"Well, you see," I mumbled, "I trust my wife . . . But after all, if . . . Anything can happen in life . . . The main thing is to avoid falsehood . . ." I stammered something more, and she looked at me as if I were a thing.

This conversation lingered in my mind for a long time, but without giving rise to any definite ideas. Only now, and vaguely at that, do I wonder why I don't so much wish that my wife's fidelity were guaranteed as that I needed the immutability of these concepts: Wife. Family. Fidelity.

AELITA OF APARAN

Certainly, disillusionment stands guard over our hopes. But the skepticism with which we attempt to arm ourselves is one of the flimsiest things in the world—as is any armament in this situation. Essentially, the skeptic is a creature who begs us, one and all, to change his mind about his bitter experience. An Achilles who displays his heel. There is probably no creature more ready than the skeptic to swallow the bait of hope. Or to swallow it so deeply. Later, of course, he may claim that this is the last thing on earth he could have expected of himself; or that he "knew it all along." It's the same, either way.

The first time I saw her . . . But I had no idea that the woman I saw was she.

My friend and I were standing in the middle of a village (this had been an ancient capital of Armenia, of course), in the square, next to a dozing shoeshine man. Just as in Erevan, we were languishing and waiting for someone, I didn't know whom. The sultry heat had jelled in the middle of the road, and a layer of thick, lazy dust had settled to the bottom. Nobody was around. We were standing in shoes especially black from the heat and, moreover, just shined (this errand, too, was finished!); standing unmoving, for the sake of their shine, lest we promptly drown them in puddles of dust; and I was sorrowfully reflecting on the nature of hospitality. What kind of slavery is this? Disrupt the whole course of your life, abandon your family and job, in order to exhaust your guest with wine, meat, and lack of privacy? All this, in order to be obligated at a later date to perform the onerous work of the guest in a return visit . . . Become so entangled in this immutable sequence that you don't know whether you're indulging your guest or taking vengeance on him, showing respect to your host or feeling vexed with him . . .

"Aelita!" my friend called.

A comical young woman came toward us: short, stocky, and red as a tomato, with a carefully arranged beehive hairdo, a black-and-gold taffeta miniskirt, and bare feet. Her knees, also chubby and red, made faces at every step. Aelita was her name, very much in the Armenian fashion. No one, of course, introduced me to her; by now I accepted this as my due, without wondering why. She neither looked at me nor saw me, which didn't surprise me either: could a nice, pure, healthy young girl, defined by the single word *marriageable*, take any notice of me? A marriageable girl must be modest. She listened to what my friend was saying, and only wiggled her toe in the dust.

They talked; not knowing what it was about, I continued my train of thought, for only in my thoughts was I free. How impossible to stray from these paths of refreshment and entertainment! In Russia we dare such expense only in the exceptional instances of births, weddings, and deaths. But just try to deviate from this lavish itinerary! They have plotted it for a guest, not for you—be a guest, not yourself. As if they weren't concerned with you, specifically, in this channeled hospitality—as if they were paying you off. The slightest thought about you yourself, rather than about a guest, was embarrassing. It puzzled, fatigued, and nonplused them. That is, there was no *participation* in the rituals of hospitality. Their worth was defined in terms of energy and resources, the effort and time involved, but they did not have the value of love.

Such were my petty thoughts as I tried to solve an unsolvable problem: we were about to attend another feast, for which earnest, laborious preparations were under way. I wanted to cross the street to the drugstore, but my friend wouldn't let me. He couldn't let me go alone, he said—but neither would he go with me. "Listen, what do you want at the drugstore?" he said, frowning. "You don't need to go to the drugstore." All right: why was it easier to arrange

a feast than to stop at the drugstore with me? I was totally mystified.
    Aelita drew three barefoot crosses and went away.

    Some things they untiringly explained to me ten times over,
and some they never explained . . . It was the simple things they
didn't explain. For example, I had quite a surprise when I returned
to Erevan and found this same Aelita in my friend's apartment,
playing with his children. She, however, wasn't at all surprised by
my arrival, and failed to notice me, as before. Why couldn't they,
I wondered, have explained to me that she was a relative, a niece,
a second cousin? No, it was no use. The firmness and definiteness
with which they decided for me what might be of interest and what
might not—this was the language barrier. By myself, I could catch
hold of nothing except what was offered. I was a crippled deaf-
mute. Only the people closest to me explained themselves and
understood me. Only my friend.
    But my friend was away this evening; he had business he
couldn't postpone. I had already learned not to know, and to wait.
Patiently I sat wearing out the couch and observing Aelita. How
quickly the children had come to love her! They were crawling all
over her, full of tenderness and rapture. Imperturbable, she moved
smoothly and freely in their embraces, like a swimmer. Too bad I
couldn't understand the story she was telling so softly and
dispassionately—but from time to time the children's eyes rounded
and their mouths gaped. She had used up all the candy-bar tinfoil
in the house to make crowns—all three now sat wearing crowns—
and was endlessly drawing beautiful ladies, supposedly for the children, but also for herself, testing styles and fashions on them. The
ladies, all wearing crowns too, were very tall and narrow, unlike
her, with luxuriant loose hair, eyelashes curved like Turkish ya-
taghans, huge eyes amid the eyelashes, and tiny heart-shaped dots
for lips. Embodying Aelita's premonitions of the maxi, they wore
floor-length dresses. Their arms and hands came out worst; not
knowing what to do with them, where to hide them, the ladies had
a thoroughly unrefined way of sticking them out penguin-style.
Aelita kept changing their sleeves, shoulder straps, necklines . . .
Rapturously the children looked back and forth from the drawing
to her, from her to the drawing: it was so much like their beautiful
queen! . . . No, Aelita didn't plan to spend her whole life baby-

sitting!—that was the message of her drawing. I sat and waited for my friend. An hour, another hour. I was a kind of furniture. The children didn't see me because they were absorbed in Aelita; Aelita didn't see me because of her nature; my friend's wife tried to keep out of my sight as much as possible, perhaps because she had absolutely no idea at all how to occupy me. So I sat, and suddenly discovered that, like the children, I was already used to Aelita, the way furniture is used to its owner.

At that point my friend's wife's sister Jacqueline appeared— and the situation was resolved: the burden of my time settled equally on the shoulders of these nice women. We were so immediately gay and informal that I realized, for the first time, that up until now I had been putting my friend's wife in an awkward position. This was another of those simple things that no one explained to me and I myself could not understand. A different country. Had Jacqueline come on her own, to the joy and relief of her sister, or had the latter especially summoned her? Thus, I made faux pas only in the most banal situations. Where understanding was required, I seemed to understand immediately.

Lighthearted now, the three of us decided to go to a movie. My friend's wife was so glad: now at last she had Aelita, now at last she would even go to a movie! But she couldn't have gone with me without her sister, and she wouldn't have let her sister go with me by herself. Give up, we'll never understand, who cares. We were going to the newest, most luxurious super-cinema. All the more wonderful in that we were going to *Fantômas*; because of the southern temperament of the audience, watching the people watch would be still another pleasure.

Everything was settled—and again, not everything. My friend's wife's eyes became sad, her glance brief. A thought, I have absolutely no idea what, had occurred to her—and no, she wouldn't go, she had remembered a certain something . . . But a fresh joy lighted her face: Aelita would go with us! This was Aelita's first time in Erevan, she'd been cooped up for three days—let her see the city.

It was all so complicated! We would never go anywhere, I thought.

But imperturbable Aelita appeared instantly, all set to go—in the same gold dress, but no longer barefoot.

This really was an outstanding movie theater, constructed with such originality that in the evening light I never quite saw how it looked as a whole: it seemed to hover above the earth like a flying saucer coming in for a landing. There was plenty of time before the show started, and we sat in an incorporeal café that consisted of holes, shadows, and quivering suspension brackets. Jacqueline chattered, Aelita was silent. This so astonished me, the fact that she was neither excited nor curious, as any young woman from the Russian provinces would have been in her place, arriving in the big city from the village for the first time in her life; the fact that she had simply sat for three days without leaving the house, and would be sitting there still if we hadn't dragged her out—this so amazed me that I kept watching her. Which was it, obtuseness or singular intelligence? By now I was beginning to think it was intelligence. Moreover, she had come not merely to baby-sit, it turned out, but to enter college. I tried to draw her into conversation—in vain. Then Jacqueline translated my question for her. Aelita listened attentively and replied, although not to me but to Jacqueline. She planned to enter the archaeological institute, she said. I praised the profession and probed deeper . . . Thus we conversed: I asked a question, Jacqueline translated, Aelita gave her answer to Jacqueline, who translated it to me. Aelita looked straight ahead, her eyes level and calm, taking no notice of anything. Her impassivity struck me as abnormal. This was my first time in such a movie theater, too, and I was craning my neck. Her village had just one two-story house. There's no harm in being curious . . . Several young men, drinking their coffee at the counter in an elegant "foreign" pose, were watching us.

"Why are they staring?"

"A Russian comes to the café with two Armenian women?" Jacqueline laughed. "I should think they'd stare!" For one reason or another, she was gratified by their attention.

So one woman's impossible, but two are too many, I thought. It's a movie!

A bell rang, and amid the scrape of chairs being pushed back and the rustle of people getting up, I saw, at last, a semblance of a glance brush one of the boys who had been studying us: a lively darkness seemed to sparkle in the depths of her eyes, and I suspected that perhaps she could *see*, which meant that she could see before, the whole time, and her immobility was rapt and receptive—and who knows how much she saw, or how. Perhaps a lot, and intensely. Or perhaps nothing.

The open-air auditorium reminded me of a Roman forum. Lush southern stars shone above us, as in a planetarium; I had the fantasy that we were in flight, and if I risked walking to the edge and looking down I would see, somewhere far below me, our dear earth, not yet so luxuriantly built up. Profoundly moved, I would read down long poems about the love I had left behind on earth.

I discovered nothing preternatural in the response of the Armenian audience.

Fantômas did his shocking deeds, and the film ended.

We emerged from the theater, and once again the nation's film directors made use of me to complicate someone's existence, in which I did not belong . . . Jacqueline exchanged greetings with someone and became highly embarrassed. She took him aside and made lengthy explanations. He heard her out and left silently. When she returned to us, she had lost a little of her characteristic vivacity. She hesitated slightly. Too straightforward a soul to be able to hide anything, she glanced awkwardly at her watch, feigned a gasp, and exclaimed that she had forgotten to call her mother . . . and now . . . we would find it easy to get home from here, very easy . . . She waved and disappeared.

Thus Aelita and I were left alone together.

I have purposely reported here, more or less in sequence and in detail, the whole system of equations, all the addition and subtraction operations, as a result of which this event proved possible. You may think that I'm talking about something trivial, that I'm being petty and splitting hairs—but this whole system of failures of understanding is intrinsic to the atmosphere of a sojourn in Armenia, and I assure you that such an incident is improbable, impossible, and essentially unencountered in the life of the city of Erevan. That a Russian man should find himself in downtown Erevan, at midnight, with a seventeen-year-old Armenian girl who didn't know a word of Russian—!

There was not a single woman on the streets, even with an Armenian man.

The sky had clouded up during the show, and the stars had gone dark; streetlights burned here and there. Something soft, warm, and furtive had descended upon the earth, like a fog but not a fog, scented with the rare fragrance of some sort of pod. A mysterious narcotic excitement flowered on the street corners, like a nocturnal bud: slender Armenian youths in white shirts flashed noiselessly past, fluttered out of doorways like large night birds. Everything was rushing somewhere. A car would stop, a young man would suddenly detach himself from a wall or post, quietly bend down and have a word with the driver . . . The car would drive away, accelerating abruptly, and then drive up again. A ritual light from the cigarette lighter.

Public transportation suddenly, in one instant—while I was looking for the bus stop that Jacqueline had called out as she fled —ceased to run. I realized that I didn't have even an approximate idea which direction our house was, or how far. I asked Aelita if she knew the way. She shook her head confidently. I would have been curious to know what was going on in her head . . . She was quietly walking a half step behind me, a trifle closer, as I conceived it, than she could allow herself. I glanced at her cautiously, trying to discover signs of excitement, if nothing else. There were none.

We came out on a new street, and it wasn't the street I had planned to come out on. We seemed to be wandering in a different city, a different country, even more "different" than Erevan and Armenia . . . We drifted past the store windows like little fish behind an aquarium wall . . .

The store windows in Erevan look outward in a way that is somehow surprising. Perhaps it's because something remains of the naïveté and straightforwardness of artisans who used to hang a sample of their wares over the workshop entrance (a shoemaker, a shoe; a rug weaver, a rug), but when you're walking through Erevan at night, and the stores and workshops are shining from within, filled with objects that achieve an abstract, alienated meaning in the absence of man, you feel as if the merchandise has come out of the display windows to stand motionless on the deserted pavement. Suddenly, in the middle of the road, there's a bed with nickel-plated knobs. Or a sewing machine—not turning, not whirring . . . As if pop artists had mounted a nighttime exhibit in Erevan.

So we walked among these strange objects, through this deserted exhibit, more and more irresolutely, and at last we stopped. Aelita stood obediently motionless beside me. On a lighted corner—where a nocturnal store gazed out, and its exposed objects, like creatures from another world, made their excursion to the city—a group of young men appeared. They froze like mannequins from the window, silently studying us.

I did not risk asking the way. I may even have been frightened.

But if so, my fear was not for myself. I had suddenly realized that I would be totally happy today if I could deliver Aelita to my friend without adventure. Calmly and faithfully she waited to see what I would do. There was a little more light here, and I could see her face: she was a bit excited after all, I thought. Her face had somehow become thinner, more serious. Prettier, even. Her eyes had grown bigger, it seemed, and were shining a little more intensely, although her gaze still expressed nothing.

"Well," I said, smiling boldly. "We seem to have started in the wrong direction."

She nodded.

I turned, more confidently, and we started in the opposite direction.

She was now walking so close to me that she could barely keep from touching me with her shoulder and the edge of her skirt. I was oddly overwhelmed by her presence, her breathing, her parallel existence—in a youthful, mute, forgotten way . . . Only later, in recollection, did I have the thoughts that might come to a man in such a situation. At the time, I assure you, I was uncontaminated by the smallest design, even in the abstract. Still, her imperturbability was excessive, and perhaps it hurt me . . . Like a shadow, she imitated my every step; there was something of the pack animal in this, something ruminant. What was it? Submissiveness to fate? Submissiveness to *me*? Gullibility, or trust? Whatever it was, wild terror or sleepy fearlessness, she walked beside me as if on a leash, and it did not occur to her to doubt that I would succeed. Although, couldn't she see perfectly well that I didn't dare ask passersby? . . . But if her imperturbability did indeed conceal, or express, some sort of emotion, I flatter myself with the hope that it wasn't because we were lost and in danger but because the two of us had been wandering for an hour through a big city at night. The fact remained, all this was happening to her for the first time in her life! However far I had been from her world yesterday, and however far I might be tomorrow—still, at this moment . . .

"You don't know Russian at all?"

"P-poorly." Her face twisted into a semblance of a smile.

"You aren't afraid?"

She shook her head earnestly.

But I, all of a sudden, became desperately agitated. I started running at cars. I even contrived to halt a bus, but it wasn't going our way. After each attempt, when I returned to Aelita, I found her exactly where I had left her, waiting quietly and patiently. And if I should despair and start following my nose, if should pass the outskirts of the city and emerge in a field, climb a mountain, cross a desert, come out at the sea, and look back—Aelita would be at my shoulder, I needn't look. We could grow old on this march, imperceptibly accumulating children and grandchildren . . . That was how I felt when I failed to flag yet another taxi and discovered that she was *looking* at me. This was a truly Martian gaze, as if from the cover of a science-fiction magazine: the gaze of a truly different creature. It stared out of itself—a different logic, a different world . . . I remember that I was painfully embarrassed to have been grimacing and hopping about, but I could blush freely in this darkness.

At last we managed to hitch a ride on an off-duty bus, and fitted ourselves onto the same seat. Never have I sat so carefully not touching my neighbor! The bus soon filled up, people were crushing me—and I turned to stone, like a caryatid, preserving the clearance between Aelita and me. Let no one (especially her) get any ideas! I had a cramp in my neck, and in the small of my back—but even involuntarily, "under pressure," I didn't touch her. The anxiety for her life had passed; that for her fate remained. Clearly I wasn't myself. Today I see the bridegroom's foolish, bright smile wandering over my face—at the time, I did not.

What about it? I thought. Move to Armenia, marry Aelita, make her a lot of babies, and then leave forever, knowing that she'll never be unfaithful?

We arrived, got out, approached our door—and she walked beside me wherever I went, as trusting as always. Still, it was odd. After all, we weren't lost anymore, no danger threatened us now, I had no place else to take her, we had no place else to go: we were back. I paused and turned to her. She stared straight ahead, her gaze brushing my shoulder and extending into the darkness of the courtyard. So she had stopped and was waiting for me again. But we were standing by our entrance! She was silent—why silent? Waiting—why waiting? Maybe she wanted to say something?

Maybe, I thought sarcastically, I *have* to marry her, now that I've seen her home. I turned cold.

"We're back," I said aloud.

Then and there—it was phenomenal!—the distance between

us became two meters. And it wasn't that she leaped away in fright. It just somehow turned out that way, all at once: two meters. A new status.

We climbed the stairs, maintaining the new distance. Perhaps she hadn't recognized her own house, I thought.

"At *last!*" Kariné, my friend's wife, had been so worried, where had we gone, she'd phoned Jacqueline, they'd been *so* worried . . .

I wonder what worried them so, I thought.

I handed Aelita over to Kariné, safe and sound.

My friend had been delayed. He never did come.

The children slept, I had soup, Kariné waited for her husband. Somewhere in the background, Aelita walked from room to room with pillows. She was unconcerned and regally imperturbable. Nothing had happened. Nothing.

No—I don't have to, I thought with relief and disillusionment.

THE SONG

And there was another incident. Hardly noticeable. So much an "incident in itself" that essentially it didn't even happen. No external events occurred, and the spectator saw nothing, but the internal events were so passionate and powerful that I can't forget them. I remember them ardently.

I have already mentioned that small children in Armenia are given considerable freedom, which a teenager—especially a boy— no longer has. But in childhood, at least, they are allowed to luxuriate in their freedom, storing up a lifetime supply. The same is true of little girls. They, too, are permitted much that is not permitted to young ladies. They may raise their eyes, they have the right to look.

This was the only feminine gaze bestowed upon me in Armenia.

The girl was about ten or eleven. She was a very pretty little girl, a joy to look at. (Thus I determined the boundary when I became "invisible," about fourteen years of age. At ten, curiosity is still allowed.)

Yet another house, my friend's friend's friend's. We were sitting on the veranda, quietly drinking and talking. The little girl ran in, not expecting to see a stranger, and skidded to a halt. Oh, what a look! The father boasted about his young beauty; she gave me another scorching glance, blushed, and ran away. I was embarrassed that I was embarrassed. But really, as we continued our conversation, I did not cease to feel her presence. Shivers ran down my spine, my skin prickled . . . I had trouble forcing myself not to turn my head and look for her. She ran by, somewhere in the recesses of the yard . . . Suddenly appeared from an unexpected door . . . The father grinned in his mustache.

This went on for half an hour. I was extraordinarily upset by her comings and goings. At last she disappeared, for a long time. I had almost forgotten about her, and my embarrassment had passed. When suddenly—not from the side door, not from out back, not in stealth—she walked straight toward us, came right up close, and looked at me point-blank. I could not withstand her gaze. Her cheeks burned, her head was raised boldly, her eyes were frank, and her small figure was so radiant with resolve that I was utterly unnerved. As if she had tested me, she turned away and hotly said something to her father. Her father replied briefly, affectionately, but decisively. The little girl flared up and delivered a whole speech. For the first time, I became aware of all my boundaries at once—I was differentiated almost by the color of my skin, for an instant I almost felt myself to be a Negro—and still I could not raise my eyes. The little girl wasn't asking—she was demanding. Her words were so direct, passionate, and proud that her father gave in, though with obvious displeasure.

"She wants to sing," he said.

I made my face express a pathetic official joy; a momentary scorn appeared in the girl's eyes. But now (I can't help this) she shook her curls, her face lit up, and she started to sing. She had a charming voice, and the ancient song was very beautiful, but now I could look at her without interruption—as if looking not at the girl but at the singer, admiring not the girl but the singing . . . She knew how to sing; this was no kindergarten talent show. Her control of her voice and her melody was so free that she didn't have to control herself. I couldn't understand the words, but how could I fail to understand the gaze! And she was no coquette.

Good heavens, what had she found in me! Perhaps never in my life had I felt so pathetic. I saw, somehow from within, how ugly, old, fat, and unclean I was. I sat like a flaccid sack, and my every gesture struck me as repulsive. My face had forgotten how to shape itself unhesitatingly in surprise, a smile, delight. I tried to remember this procedure and perform it for my face. And made a bad job of it.

My emotion was desperate, hopeless. And what could I have hoped for?

And yet, wretched as I felt, there was happiness in this, the possibility of another life . . .

That happiness ended with the song.

Her voice quavered and stopped. The audience started to applaud, clapping their hands slowly and tenderly. Her passionate gaze turned to me. And now I did a cowardly thing. (Although, what else could I have done?) I looked around—everyone was applauding. Suddenly, in my embarrassment, I awkwardly clapped my alien, stolen hands . . . God, how her eyes changed! What scorn, shame, and hot hatred they proclaimed . . . Her father had been right: it was not worth singing for me.

She dropped her face, covered it with her hands, and exclaimed something several times, something vexed and hurt, which destroyed me forever—she was stamping her foot in time to her wrath. And then she ran away.

Not even once did her swift shadow flash by again, not anywhere, either in the recesses of the yard or from the side door.

I wanted—madly wanted—to ask what she had exclaimed when she covered her face with her hands. Thank God, I didn't dare.

The master of the house offered a toast. I raised my glass. I felt strange . . . I was imprisoned in these walls, I was a captive and would never get out . . . I console myself with the thought that the nice young mother's question no longer seems so frivolous to me.

PARAKEETS (ANTITHESIS)

I'm an inveterate liar. I catch myself at it . . . I'm always catching myself by the arm, but I keep on writing as if uncaught. I steal from myself the impossibility of each next page, in order to write it. And promptly catch myself in a contradiction. I catch and let go—cat and mouse . . . When you write, how can you keep from lying? When you discover a lie, how can you keep from hurling the pen away? (Again. Why did I say "pen"? When it's a typewriter . . .)

But I'm taking refuge in a narrow crevice.

This whole chapter is a series of incoherent and undigested impressions—literally undigested, because nobody could digest that much meat and herbs. Even my teeth constantly ached with fatigue. The digestion, I'm told, is closely linked to the mind. This is apropos of wealth, a topic recently touched upon.

And besides, I had the flu, brought back from Lake Sevan. This is something you can't explain to anyone who hasn't happened to catch cold in the south. Heat, chills; razor-sharp light, and the grating of alien speech . . . What could be more humiliating than to sneeze uncontrollably at a hot, foreign-speaking, sun-drenched bazaar heaped with sunshiny fruit? Where, after all, was my national pride?

It was like the soaked handkerchief in my pocket.

All this was more than enough to make me feel wretched.

Probably nothing so awakens one's sense of homeland as an ordinary head cold in a foreign country. The "nostalgia of the allergic" is an obscene, sensual, lushly blossoming bud . . .

. . . We are invited for watermelon. There was talk of this, I think, as long ago as the day before yesterday. So this is a big event. To test a variety of inferences and surmises, I would very much like to know whether this event would have taken place if I hadn't come to Armenia. That is, would all these people have gathered together for watermelon even without me? Or have they gathered to eat watermelon exclusively for me, or, more accurately, thanks to me? With me, because of me, for me, or thanks to me? Apparently, I'll never find out . . . We have spent the whole day riding around Erevan, from one end to the other, increasing our numbers one by one, in order to settle down together at the home of yet another mutual friend, here on this veranda, overlooking a small courtyard garden. In the garden, right in front of the veranda, stands a huge cage of parakeets, the strange little multicolored birds that people keep because of some secret notion about cloudless happiness and joy.

And here we sit. We've been sitting here for a whole eternity—we've been sitting here always. Backgammon, watermelon, parakeets! I don't know in what sequence to announce you, or what idea to derive from the sequence.

My friend is playing backgammon with the host, and their friends are watching them play. They will never tire of this. I can't say that no one cares about me; but even if they care, no one knows what to do with me. I have refused to try to understand the back-gammon game, or, rather, I've despaired of understanding, and their only alternative is to feed me watermelon. As always—to feed me. What else to do with me?

The next room is piled to the ceiling with watermelons, and my impression is that we've been summoned to finish them all before leaving, because nothing can halt the backgammon game except a lack of watermelons. There are still a lot of them. A watermelon is not a fruit, as everyone thinks, and not a berry, as we were told in school; a watermelon is a measure of time, ap-proximately half an hour. There's a mountain a week high in the next room. Like the striking of a clock with a repeater mechanism, someone rummages through this mountain, lengthily chooses two watermelons—one hour—and then carries them out and loads them into the refrigerator in place of the ones we've eaten.

So, we're playing backgammon and eating watermelon. This is being narrated by turns, but it's happening simultaneously. The watermelons are being chosen, chilled, cut, and eaten. That is, the watermelons being eaten were chilled long ago, so the sequence is different: the watermelons are being cut, eaten, and chilled. Wrong again. Arrange it yourselves.

I'm holding a piece of watermelon in one hand, spitting the seeds genteelly into the other hand, and reaching into my pocket with the third, because sometimes I sneeze. I lay the slice on the railing in such a way that it won't tip over, and it tips over. I thrust the seeds into my pocket to get my handkerchief . . . Oh, this handkerchief with the watermelon seeds stuck all over it! I want to lie right out flat on the floor and have a rooster turned loose on me to peck these germinating weeds . . .

Nevertheless, I still had a lot to learn in this life!

For example, such a quantity of parakeets. I doubt this was typical of Armenia. But what could I do about them? There were fifty of them, no less. They were all raising a racket, and their multicolored noise was dazzling—incomparable in its brightness, loudness, brazenness, and grand detachment from all the rest of the world, which was no concern of theirs. And they were all kissing, with an obscene haste and efficiency. Unburdened by morality and uncomplicated by Freud, their multicolored love triangles and poly-gons developed and disintegrated with the same instantaneousness and ease as in a kaleidoscope: their love was aerial and geometrical.

They were energetic in love, their gyrations had some purpose: apparently, each of them had to exchange kisses with all, so that all could kiss each and then hurry to begin over again, on the next round. As measured by my malice, one of their rounds timed out at one game of backgammon. And while the backgammon stones were being set up for the next game, the host went to the refrigerator, fetched a chilled watermelon, dissected it with stunning grace and dexterity, and handed the onlookers equal red portions, as symmetrical as wax models. I smiled affectionately and accepted the watermelon. "What a racket!" I said, with a nod toward the parakeets. I said it for no particular reason, just out of politeness, lest he think I lacked anything. But one shouldn't be diplomatic! The host took it his own way. "Ah," he said, sorrowfully and guiltily, as if apologizing for their indecent behavior. "Very silly birds!" So saying, he took a hefty stick and whacked it on the railing next to the cage. The blow rang like a shot. The host smiled at me in confusion—so much for that nuisance!—and went off to play backgammon. Can't even talk about parakeets, I thought.

This was dramatic, of course: with a single gesture, to sever the many taut, multidirectional, multicolored threads of their voices, the many translucent ribbons of their movements! It seemed impossible that they could have halted and fallen silent so instantly, simultaneously, one and all. The parakeets had been immobilized in time, not merely in space, I thought. Shock, lethargy, a pillar of salt, a sleepwalker, the seventh seal—I don't know what to compare with the cleanness and absoluteness of their stop. But I, too, had been so unprepared for the blow that I froze like a parakeet.

O Lord! O world! How are we any better? We, too, will stop motionless when the angel takes the seal from the book! Doesn't our globe, painted blue, yellow, and green, hang by a thread somewhere in Thy garden? Is the earth perhaps a watermelon from some tree of Thine in Paradise? Lost in thought over the next move in Thy galactic backgammon game, hast Thou forgotten us? But we've started raising a racket . . . we're better off unremembered. I love Thee, Lord, and I hope it's mutual, as the song goes . . .

The parakeets still hadn't come to their senses. They had frozen so earnestly they'd probably forgotten they were alive and decided they were dead . . . Dear silly birds! How could they help thinking they had utterly vanished—they couldn't see themselves, and they had ceased to reveal themselves through motion and love. (They weren't even blinking. What sort of big blur were they seeing, instead of us?) Fifty little stuffed birds—only now could I begin to make sense of them. Their internal contradictions were not evident, but their external ones were. Trim little bodies—and mysteriously fat cheeks and face. Solidity and decency, even a sense of rank, a Chichikovian countenance—and such frivolity! With that decorous exterior, how could they devote themselves so openly to love? A mystery. As if this were their job. Love in little uniforms . . .

But now the first bird came to life. Adam. He turned his head: no problem. And most important, no one stopped him! He was permitted to live. Then the next bird . . . And slowly the whole cage began waking up, by stages, the way the first standard backgammon moves are played, before a difference is defined and the game begins. Within a few seconds, Adam had generated a new mankind. A shriek, love, betrayals—uproar! The game comes to an end, the host fetches a fresh watermelon and then grasps the stick, and while he's about it, he takes the opportunity to smile at his guest—that is, at me—and . . . Oh, I can't bear it!

Definitely, I do not understand who's spending time with whom. I with them? They with me?

Backgammon, watermelon, parakeets. One hour, another, a third . . . The setting up of the stones, the first moves, the play. Cut a watermelon, hand out portions, finish the watermelon. Birth of parakeets, life of parakeets, death of parakeets. A fourth watermelon, a fifth, a sixth. A watermelon, a smile, a whack. A thought on backgammon, a thought on watermelon, a thought on parakeets. Time, where are you?

I'm locked up, I'm in a cage. Every day they transfer me from cell to cell. The diet is good; they don't beat me. I don't know how long I've been here. The sentence should come soon. I don't know if I'll see you, my darling . . .

I'm in a cage—everyone's looking at me. No. They're the ones looking at me from inside a cage! I'm the one on the outside! I've tricked them all . . .

I'm imprisoned in a hole of time. The little girl with the song is already running down the mountains, bringing me her dipper . . . A captive of the Caucasus. One day the prisoner finds in his pocket a lost watermelon seed. He plants it. He waits for it to sprout. The sprout, again, is a clock: it will put out leaves, ticking up and up.

My time of stagnation has germinated at last. What would I have understood, what would I have seen, if I hadn't been in the cage with the parakeets and grasped the fact that in addition to my time there was a *different* time—theirs? If I hadn't managed to renounce my own time, if I hadn't given up on it, I wouldn't have had *time* in Armenia. There would have been hours, days, kilograms, kilometers of unlived, missed, truly lost time, weighed out on wristwatches, alarm clocks, and the Kremlin chimes.

Only when I lost my alarm clock was I able to live in the present for a few days on alien soil. But if you live uninterruptedly in the present for even a few days, you can remember them for years. Present time seems to be related to ticking time in the same way that time in the cosmos, at a speed close to the speed of light (something from Einstein), is related to time on earth. The present races along at infraluminal speed, leaving behind the past and future, far below it, forever coupled, bound together, so strongly attracted to each other that they have come to a full stop.

I had meant to devote this chapter to a statement of my reservations. In the margins of my manuscript, around the edges of my paeans of praise, I had accumulated birdlike flocks of check marks, asterisks, and *nota benes*. They were quite black and had been ousted from the text. I suddenly saw that they weren't fitting in because I had begun to lie. Because in fact things were by no means as wonderful as I'd been saying. I thought that if I combined my raptures with my dissatisfaction I would achieve truth of narrative.

A shallow, goat-headed idea! Thank God, a different truth from verity's retinue carried me into the present, told me what I didn't know, and asserted itself, against my clumsy will.

And I don't have to sweat and strain over the realism of black pages.

Reservations create reservations primarily about the person who states them.

Yes, I have a head cold, indigestion, and homesickness. And I'm the captive of my own impressions. Neither my rapture nor my dissatisfaction has any independent truth. Nor can I achieve truth by playing at dialectics, crudely adding rapture to dissatisfaction.

Truth is dictated only by truth. And the truth of this book is that I discover, having reached the middle of it, that I'm no longer journeying in Armenia, or in Russia, but in this book of mine. A fantasy land, I grant you, invented by me, from a few comparative impressions. A country of Houyhnhnms. And I myself am a new Gulliver, Lilliputian, giant, and snot-nosed Yahoo, all in one . . .

I feared that I was taking an increasingly lofty and self-assured tone, merely to convince people (or at least myself) that I was still following actual events, when I no longer was. Experience told me that inexactness of speech can be concealed behind modulations of the voice, ignorance behind intonation, uncertainty behind aplomb . . . that a convincing tone is used specifically by liars. Oh, how difficult it is to be objective with my own poor strength!

But is it necessary?

This book, after all, is an act of love . . . With all the clumsiness of love, and all the accuracy of love . . . Who ever said that love was accurate?

So let it remain as written.

Love does not lie. The desire for love lies.

Love does not weigh its declarations on the scales of objectivity, it neither vacillates nor chooses between yes and no, and yet there is a boundary between the two, as between belief and unbelief. The painful effort to be honest, fair, and objective belongs to unlove—love does not have these difficulties. And so:

"Rejoice in the Lord, O ye righteous: for praise is comely for the upright."

Geghard

"What has he seen?" they would ask, meaning me. My friend would recite the list. Everyone, after hearing it, said firmly and always, "He must go to Geghard." The unanimity was tiresome, like a conspiracy. What was Geghard? Where was Geghard? They shrugged. No one tried to explain. You'll see.

To me, Geghard was only a name—an insistent, even a nagging sound. This in itself was a kind of token, as it later turned out.

. . . The open space of Armenia waved its wings and fluttered, like a butterfly, and then, like a butterfly, suddenly folded them. A bronze lion, with more than the usual resemblance to a cat, turned its head to us and lifted a paw, signifying that we had arrived. (A little later, when I saw the same lion on an ancient wall, I recognized the source of the contemporary professional sculptor's genius.)

The lion stood on a beautiful tall column at the throat of a ravine. As we entered the narrowing throat, we seemed to drive faster and faster, accelerating and corkscrewing inward like water in a whirlpool. Suddenly, folding our wings with quiet ease, we found ourselves in the ravine.

Then and there, satiety ended. A shivering, lucid hunger to see . . . The very place was like a temple. In the middle of open space, it was built of open space. Like a temple, it had an entrance (the lion stood at the gates), and only within the gates was the sanctuary revealed, as a sigh and an embarrassed hush.

Here, sight resounded.

A visible sound, extraordinary in its breadth and roundness, was born from the sheer walls of the ravine, where the wind caught like a musician's breath in the mouthpiece of a trumpet and burst out, through the coils of the bell, to wide-open space. We were in a kingdom of no return, although we did not recognize yet that we could never go back, and were therefore unafraid.

For the moment, we breathed rapture—and rapture breathed us. For the moment, it was a frivolous rapture, a tourist's, with no day of reckoning.

At the left rose a choir of cliffs. From the dense, shady, deep sound at the bottom they grew upward in several stages, brightening and thinning, joined by voices ever new, ever higher; the wind-sculpted arrows at the top were like a choir of boys. At the right, like an orchestra shell, the floor of the hollow spiraled downward to a silvery woodwind stream, green leaves lacy as a flute, and the calm, confident brows of the percussion section—the rocks and boulders. The earthly intelligibility of invented instruments, which vanish in the mystery of the human voice like a part in a machine, like a feature in a face, like a plowshare in the earth—the tools of labor, and the object of that labor—all this melted into the chorus of the cliffs. A puff of smoke curled up from the bank of the stream, and dotlike performers swarmed around it: pilgrims broiling shish kebab. An uncommonly red dress among them looked like the first leaf of autumn.

Before us stood a church, harmonious, integral, and no doubt a thousand years old. In this natural temple, the church was like an ancillary structure; it evoked no tingle of awe. Its fresh zinc roof and steeple, and its sturdy walls with their bright rectangles of modern mending, also underscored the impression that it was an outbuilding to the temple. The church was not to blame for this, however, since in all respects it was a masterpiece, and no one—only its natural setting—could have taken that title away from it.

But behind it rose a new choir of cliffs. Nestled at the foot of this vertical sound, the church was but one of the performers of the wondrous music, one of the many and forgotten virtuosi of the past. For what is the performer to the music? A votary, not the creator . . .

The roof of this temple was the sky. Just recently, before the gates, the blue of the sky had been a pale, faded covering for an open expanse, but here, delimited by the choir of cliffs, it acquired an extraordinary intensity, deep and close.

"My God!" we exclaimed. We gazed at this frozen music—frozen at its topmost, highest point—and behind us, like wings, we could feel the upflung arms of its conductor and creator. The eternal, only, premier performance. "My God!" we exclaimed, losing our earthly shame at banality, and shedding the banality along with the shame. "They chose the right place!"

THE ASCENT

Yes, this was a temple readied by nature; understandably, it had become the citadel and cloister of early, persecuted Christianity (the Armenians accepted Christianity long before we did, in the fourth century). This place, so unexpected in Armenia, so unlike anything else in it, this place that simply cannot be (but, since it is, can no longer *not* be), was created in the beginning expressly for this purpose, and then waited its hour, unpeopled, until divined by the first believers . . .

But the place, as it turns out, wasn't yet Geghard. That is, it bore the name, of course, but it was Geghard without an accent on the word, it was just Geghard. And, especially, the thousand-year-old church in this spot couldn't be *the* Geghard.

. . . We climbed up to the ancient cave temples at the first level of the cliff, the bottom line of the stave. We walked in. Time disappeared. The narrow, shallow grottoes, with their rough, smoke-blackened walls, recalled a mine face. As a former mining engineer, I even discovered the traces of blast holes. Crude niches for images, small bowls for offerings, a narrow trough to drain blood, the ancient and no longer smeary soot on the roof—and freshly scratched names, the symbols of a new tourist era, and colorful modern rags (prayers for the cure of relatives), and modern wax from melted candles, the stalactites of these caves. What humility and majesty of faith in these destitute stone chambers!* The temple had been created by nature itself, but the caves were its altars. There had

---

* These caves are the key to the history of the nation. Armenians were slaughtered as "infidels," yet in fact they were annihilated for their fidelity—to the land, to the language, to Christ. They lost their lives, but not their homeland. If they had followed the natural instinct of self-preservation and given up their faith, less blood might have been shed, but the nation would have dissolved and vanished. For Armenians, the word *Geghard* is more than the name of a holy place, it is also a certain figurative concept—Geghard is the stronghold of the faith. The word is pregnant with meaning.

been no disturbance of nature's harmony, no meddling, no modernization of the natural temple. Speak a word, and the cliff would respond in a deep voice, as though you had awakened a musical pitch frozen in the rock. This was a place for prayer; you could never come here in idle curiosity . . .

Squinting shyly, we emerged into the light. We examined the crosses chiseled on the face of the cliff, we ran our hands over them. The ornate Armenian cross! How gradually and beautifully it has acquired its canonical features. Not one cross repeats the lines of another. The proportions change, the round softness disappears, melts away, the crosses become straighter and stricter. But the primary cross is an eight-petaled flower. The petals draw near each other in pairs—a cross with split ends. Did the cross derive from a flower? Or did an artist perhaps liken the symbol to nature and life by first splitting the ends, then spreading them apart to approximate the shape of a flower? No one knows, and there is no one to ask.

We went back down, passed through the gates in the tall church fence—very recent, so extrinsic—and walked toward that strong, harmonious little church with its bucketlike zinc dome. I looked at the church with idle indifference, not really focusing on it. We would be inside in a minute, I thought.

But no, we began to scramble upward again, along a wall where the church grew into the cliff.

"First we go this way," they told me, gently and insistently.

"What's up here?"

"You'll see in a minute."

Oh, that dignified habit of refusing to anticipate my impression with enthusiastic stories! Never once did I have a clear idea where they were taking me, or why; the joys of first encounter were never frittered away in forewarning and preconception. As it turned out, the cave chapels of the first Christians, too, were not *the* Geghard.

The lofty but brief emotion we had felt in the caves did not match the busy urban jauntiness that still clung to us. We talked loudly, not quite looking at each other. Unconscious of our split mood, however, we merely made an instinctive effort to lower the altitude of our momentary blaze of feeling. Our gaze was distracted by details. A tourist's graffito at an unthinkable height. A man selling photographs of General Andranik. A small-minded placard: "Do Not Litter." A bee garden, so suddenly beautiful and natural on the soil of the monastery. Two workmen puttering about near the hives . . . Our emotion was declining, we were feeling better and better. Freed of embarrassment, we became childlike. We turned off the path and went scrambling up the cliff with inappropriate athleticism. Somewhere we had lost our self-possession, and every one of us must have felt somewhat ashamed of our corpulent, winded boyishness. But privately, not together.

And now I think I understand what makes a tourist scratch his name, throw litter, sing songs, and have his picture taken in the most unsuitable places—defile, as it were, the monuments of history and nature. The monument stands high, after all—unbearably, ringingly high!—compared to his ignorant soul. And in that soul, so gauche, untaught, and muffled, it gives rise to an echo, and the echo is a mystery to him. What, if not total disarray in his emotions, could cast him up on a height (physical) so mortally dangerous (physically)? Not just the girl who is waiting down below, after all. (He doesn't climb poles or scale buildings in the city, does he?) I think the sight of true greatness and beauty is as irritating to the unprepared eye as a harsh light or sound. From then on, all reactions are Pavlovian.

Why did the barbarians wreak devastation?

What were we if not spoiled children, in the mature and perfect society of churches and cliffs? . . .

As writers, certainly, we might have thought ourselves better prepared for perfect sight? . . . But no. We have tried for so long to tell the truth to the world, and haven't told the truth to ourselves or to each other. And now we don't tell it—not merely because we're hiding it—but because we no longer know it. We didn't scratch our names (perhaps only because we'd already seen them in print), but in our case the same urge took other forms. Our prosaism, I would even say our "novelism," compulsively sought out the lowest, most earthly details, the ones most safely grounded.

Thus, as we climbed up, we saw an old man, a priest, on a second-story balcony of a residence situated opposite the church. He was seated at a table, looking at a book. A girl came and went in the background, waiting on him. The old man sat perfectly motionless, looking at the book (yes, looking at it, not reading it; his eyes, too, seemed to be motionless, although we couldn't see them from a distance). He was strikingly beautiful, with an aquiline profile, a high, pure brow, white curls, youthful skin, gaunt, pale . . . Oh, how poor are words, compared to a beauty canonical, perfect, and ancient! He was not a work of art, not a beautiful illustration, this old man; he was beautiful in the same sublime, ideal, absolute way as Geghard. And as motionless as its thousand-year-old stones. He had sat down to dine and opened a book, but he had been sitting here forever, eternally—or so I would have thought, looking at him—and even the table of food and drink before him could never make him look earthly . . . My friend and I, glancing at each other, realized that we had seen the old man at the same moment and in the same way. "What a face!" I said tritely. "Yes," said my friend, who is a wise man. "I wonder, now: if I were that handsome, led a holy life, and lived long enough to have hair like that—could I have a face like that? Impossible. Never." Again, this was too exalted for us—everything, absolutely everything here was so beautiful, even the people! . . . My friend's friend, who was walking behind us—an interesting poet, I'm told—demeaned himself by saying, with an ugly smile, "With that face, the funniest thing would be if he were looking at pornographic pictures." "Dreadful!" I said, with a laugh. "The worst of it is, you may well be right." Let him read what he wishes—but oh, if we can even think such thoughts of him, we'll never have a face like his!

Now we had reached our mysterious goal. A small entrance, carved in the cliff, reminded me of the entrances to the ancient chapels we had just visited. Silently my friends let me pass ahead, and I stepped into the darkness of the cavern . . .

Oh, we were bad little boys!

THE SUMMIT

This was Geghard . . . I stood in the center, craning my neck. There, high above me, was a small blue circle—that was where the light came from. That was the sky. "*He* began from there . . . through that opening. He chiseled out the temple . . ." my friend told me in a childish whisper. And although I stood far below, I still see this temple in my mind's eye from the top down, the way *he* must have seen it as he stood there, on the cliff, up above, when there was as yet no temple beneath his feet.

Widening down from the blue round of sky came the bowl of the vault, and when it attained a hemisphere, the dome stopped short, to hang above us in a perfect circle. Tangent to the hemisphere, four columns extended perpendicularly downward, dissolving, when they reached me far below, into the slab on which I stood—and then the dome rested, reposed, on the four columns, which were so graceful and perfect in form that, without expert knowledge, I will not undertake to describe them. From the lower rim of the dome the hollow body of the temple widened to the four sides, from each quarter of the circle, in four rounded petals; out there, in regions far distant from the center, the walls sloped steeply down, projecting the four petals to the base—I was standing on the projection plane. On that plane I recognized, again, the flowerlike Armenian cross.

I was standing at the bottom . . . The arcs of the walls extended into the dusk, and the columns rushed upward to become the dome, from whose summit the round blue eye of the sky gazed at me. All this was inside the cliff, all of one integral stone. The forms were so harmonious, unique, absolute—I had never seen such perfection, and will never see it again. The word *genius* is too low to define what I saw.

He . . . chiseled it out . . . through that opening way up there, from the top down . . . this whole temple . . . Who was he? He has no name, nor can he ever, although he was one man. God, in this nameless man, removed the excess stone from the cliff, and what remained was the temple. This was a man of *faith*, of a faith like God's. Nothing but faith is capable of creating such a thing. An unbeliever would have been unable, and a fanatic would have broken down. A miracle of human faith—that is Geghard.

There was no reinforcement in the temple, of any kind.

The temple was already in the cliff; he had only to extract the stone from it . . . No machines could have done this. Only by hands, only by fingernails could this temple have been scratched out, only one grain of sand at a time. No mistake, no superfluous fracture, could be made in this cliff, because the temple was in it. No blueprint, no calculation, because what was there was *this* temple, these forms and these outlines. He had faith and a single vision, that was all. He did not need to pray, or go to church, or know the word of God—God was in him. He had no blueprint; in his own mind he had vaults so honest and pure that he could transfer them here without error. His mind was the image of the future temple, and the temple was a likeness of God.

Now I'm piecing together the tongue-tied logic of words—I have no other recourse. But at that time I had no words, and couldn't have had, and shouldn't have had—I did not exist. I became like *him*, I now had the same muteness, the same absence of self, the same living faith, because I was contained in his honest and pure mind, in his faith, in his integral and single thought, where no other thought could possibly exist. This was his immortality.

But our imperfect souls couldn't bear this for long. We exchanged glances at last. Then, recalling that as their guest I must be shown everything, my friends left me in the center while they enigmatically dispersed to the sides. Each stopped by a column, and they started to sing. It was an ancient Armenian melody, slow and sorrowful. The echo repeated their voices many times over, the entire cliff responding like a bell. Inside the stone bell, we were the clapper. The polyphony was just as organic and harmonious as the lines of the temple; it could not have been otherwise. Both line and sound obeyed one law here . . . Surely our many-branched knowledge implies that we are bereft of a single-unified law? When that law is gone, of course, we have architecture, blueprints, rules, calculations, physics, acoustics, machines—we work like ants, trying to perfect the fragments of the unified whole that we have lost . . .

The song was beautiful, but when it was finished we were able to carry our weary, burdened souls out into the world.

. . . Simply a cliff, quite undisturbed and ordinary. That same church, the body of it so extrinsic and worldly . . . But when I raised my eyes and saw those beautiful cliffs stretching upward so severely, freezing there like arrows in the deep blue sky, a choir fallen silent on its topmost note, I was even more struck with wonder at the same magnificent resemblance. Now it had been reversed. Those cliffs were now a likeness of the temple from which I had emerged. The temple was more primordial than nature, and nature had come to resemble it. This whole marvelous place and sky were the image of the creation I had just seen, and indeed, they, too, were a creation.

All things here reflected and echoed each other, affirming the harmony and unity of all existing forms. When we attempted to isolate and identify this unity, our gaze slid up and up, seeking something to stop on as the center of the likeness, and could stop on nothing. We had nowhere else to look but the sky . . .

Worship in this temple has never ceased. The candle may be placed on any stone.

ESCAPE

We climbed up still higher. More in fear now than in awe, I peered into the sky-blue opening from which *he* had begun . . . It was a mute black hole. "This," my friend said, peering over my shoulder into the hole, "is why I come so seldom. I wouldn't have come, if it weren't for you . . . How can anyone return from here—go back to the same place, as the same man?" Then, increasingly aware of an empty weariness, we descended a steep, sweeping curve. A Volga stood in the courtyard (it hadn't been there when we climbed up). The driver was tinkering with the engine. Nearby, squatting on his haunches, so that the hem of his black cassock lay on the ground and hid his feet, was the handsome old man we had seen with the book, on the balcony. I saw him up close; I could have touched him. He really did have a splendid face, splendid countenance— we hadn't been imagining things. He had squatted down to examine an automobile spark plug, which he held in front of him with three fingers. His fingers were just as inspired as his face. He was looking at the spark plug in exactly the same way he had looked at the book: just as motionlessly, with the same simple, unworldly, divine grandeur. His eyelids were very slightly lowered, but his pure, marble brow was imperturbable, and as sensitive as an eyelid. Oh, we had been wrong! There was no book, no spark plug! There was nothing anymore.

Down by the stream we glimpsed that same red dress and a curl of blue smoke. A subtle aroma of shish kebab reached us, signifying that hunger, not prayer, was what tormented us. "If only we had a bottle!" the driver said. "We could go down and share in the shish kebab."

How hastily, how willingly the car lurched forward to bear us away from Geghard! As if we had been spat out. No one looked back. When you enter, everything opens up for you, but when you leave, you see only the return road. We glided out from under the lion's paw.

And now, and now, only joys awaited us! We felt better and better, hungrier and hungrier. We stopped and drank water from a stream, we stopped and ate shish kebab and drank vodka, and finally, toward sunset, we reached Garrni. Garrni is the Soviet Union's only pagan temple. The ruins of it. Garrni is splendid.

But here you can eat, drink, dance, sing. It's a pagan temple.

We sat on cyclopean rubble, drank *chacha* obtained from the temple watchman, joked (or tried to) with women in a Polish tour group, winked, chortled, guffawed, whooped, hooted . . . For some reason we passed ourselves off as an all-star soccer team . . . We watched a most amazing sunset, while the ravine below us sank deeper and deeper into darkness.

And at last we were driving back—jolly, boisterous, so happy!—to the city of Erevan, leaving everything behind and taking no note of the transition. Night had already descended; the driver swung the wheel hard as we rounded a bend; moths leaped, a gleam of silver in the headlights; in the back, my friends sang their beautiful songs beautifully, and I was so moved that I almost sang along in my native Armenian tongue. Ahead, the lights of Erevan came in view.

We shook hands and parted.

It was all so simple: the sky had cracked, the earth had split, the ground had quaked, the abyss had opened—just another day lived, so long, see you tomorrow.

Passions
of a City Planner

"THEN AND NOW"

The more natural and profound my experience of Armenia became, the hazier and more distant was my specific purpose in being here. As long as I was adjusting and acclimatizing, as long as I wasn't myself, that purpose survived, perfectly in accord with the general awkwardness of the situation. But the moment I began to *live*, then immediately—as though some dark supreme force, which found my non-life quite convenient, had been vigilantly observing my every step—immediately, retribution poked its head up out of the past and shook its finger at me: Don't live.

The time allotted for my trip was running out, just as inexorably as the per diem runs out when you're still on the road. The day of reckoning was imminent; the pure and honest image of my editor's chief bookkeeper harassed and confounded me.

"Then and Now"—that was my assignment. An impassioned, lyrical report on modern city planning.

Only now was I beginning to perceive the full extent of the frivolity that allows people to move from place to place at their own whim. Temptation is the hope that we won't have to pay. In life, we pay at the exit, not the entrance. And I would have to exit this situation, which I had entered more or less lightly . . . Such were my dwindling thoughts as I gradually brought myself back to the level of journalism.

First, the "Then." I didn't know what the city used to be like. Someone had suggested that I read an essay by M. Koltsov to find out. But even the essay remained unread.

Second, the "Now." It required an unconditionally enthusiastic attitude. This followed from the assignment, it was clear by
the nature of the assignment. There had been more than enough
enthusiasms, yet they all seemed irrelevant. Well, just as in
school—anything but the lessons . . . If only I could paint the fence
for Tom Sawyer.

Schoolboy thoughts before the exam.

I walked around Erevan, looking at its modern architectural
complexes. They were as well executed as if even your enthusiasm
had been allowed for by the architect and channeled in the right
direction. They were constructed in such a way that you couldn't
help noticing them, you were duty-bound to be overcome with
enthusiasm.

Here a dim idea occurs to me. Which is better: a totally *bad*
bad thing, or a slightly better bad thing? A thing that is almost good?
A thing that incriminates itself right away, or is gradually eliminated
by time, or remains useful to this day? Imagining the era when
Lenin Square was built, for example, we can easily grant that it
was an almost impossible extreme of naturalness, taste, and integrated design, for its own era; to bring this concept to realization
required an almost audacious boldness and talent. Its contemporaries felt the breeze of progress on their faces. But something has
happened over these years—and although their time has departed,
the buildings remain. They stand in another time.

Drawing the boundary between "then" and "now" is not so
easy as one might think at first glance. If it were merely a matter
of differentiating recently constructed buildings from buildings constructed long ago, trees recently planted from full-grown trees, and
so on, we would hardly be interested in so formal a problem. Skill
and a clock. But if we seek the boundary between past and present,
this just can't be done, because the boundary slips away with each
second, each instant. Every step, every sigh is irretrievable, every
written line has already been written, is no longer being written . . . In essence, the present *is* the boundary with the past. But
if we draw this boundary at some very important historical dividing
line (as we naturally draw it at 1917), the space between that line
and today is always growing and being filled up with the past. By
now that space can easily accommodate even a man's life and its
personal past . . . as, for example, my life . . . and comparison
becomes increasingly speculative and distant.

So only the "right now," or at most the "just recently"—that is my real material, that's what I can talk about in the present tense before it all hurtles away into the distant past. And is it so important just when a thing was created, if the creation still lives and breathes? If a building erected a thousand years ago and a building finished yesterday stand as neighbors today, they are contemporaries. In this sense, all living things are contemporary. "Now" means the fact that they stand side by side, not merely what didn't exist yesterday. The world is not inhabited by newborns alone.

Thus, no matter what I write about, only the present interests me, only the living: both what has just been born and what has long been alive, both what is emerging and what is departing into the past but hasn't yet departed.

Only the now, I thought, only the now . . .

And could see nothing, after Geghard.

Q U I Z

. . . The next morning came, curtailing my trip by one more day, and I still hadn't attempted any work. But neither could I go on living, enjoying the things I'd enjoyed only yesterday.

This morning I had an appointment with a prominent Erevan official, a moving spirit in modern city planning—a remarkable man in many ways, according to all reports.

I was becoming more and more ashamed at the thought of all the people who had accommodated me: invented a topic so that I could come here, processed the trip authorization, signed for the cash, given me helpful advice, taken an interest in my living arrangements, provided me with a car from the editor's office.

Now they all expected something of me. I must not let them down by making a mess of things.

I strode through the morning city, happily noting that I had been wrong, I was liking the city better and better—I had merely been mired in subjectivity, et cetera, et cetera. And, indeed, the city looked its best in the morning. Clean and not too hot, with its shadows still long, it was quiet and modest. Its pinkish hue was becoming.

"Erevan should be seen very early in the morning"—that was how I would begin my essay. Yes, that's just how I'll begin, I told myself briskly as I crossed the threshold of a large institution.

At three minutes before eleven, gratified by my punctuality, I presented myself to a secretary. She vanished into the office and promptly reappeared: Would I please wait.

Nothing, so far, conflicted with the mental image that I had developed from various people's stories about this man. The stories were never anything but favorable. No one had a hard word for him, despite his exalted position. But always, along with the high praise, a gradual half smile would develop, a little grin, not mocking, not skeptical, more likely good-humored—but not fully intelligible to me. "Yes, yes!" they all said. "Exceptional! Decent! Bright and knowledgeable!" The very unanimity on the subject of this official was exceptional. It certainly couldn't be attributed to fear or caution, which I would have noticed right away. And a decent, knowledgeable man in a position befitting his abilities is a phenomenon that truly deserves all manner of encouragement . . . But . . . now came the half smile. No, no one said "but," I'm the one saying "but"— instead of the "but," there was half of a smile. In some people it was wordless, the end of the matter. One man said, "He loves to play up his resemblance to N.; you'll see." This told me little, inasmuch as I had an even more remote conception of N.'s appearance (he was a remarkable Armenian poet) than of his verse. Another man said, "Oh, he's an actor!" The remark was devoid of sarcasm, however: He's just an actor, that's all . . .

"Ask him how many years since he took a vacation," someone advised, only deepening the mystery.

Something, vague in its features but definite in character, was emerging in my imagination, and I could hardly wait to compare my sketch with the original. So far, everything tallied: both the small, tidy, democratic waiting room—which suggested that the official before me was not one concerned primarily with the impressiveness of his setting, nor was he one who had no time to take care himself—and the secretary, who was neither a beauty nor a former beauty, but just right; neither haughty nor familiar, neither striking nor ugly, as if she were both there and not there . . . Everything, so far, was like a suit from an aristocratic tailor: a superlative fit, but you'd never notice the cut or the fabric.

Just then a petitioner, a venerable highland elder, emerged from the office. He all but wore a felt cloak, all but had a lamb scampering ahead of him. A representative of the people, a plain man . . . The secretary instantly picked up the receiver and asked me to go in. It was eleven o'clock on the dot.

He sat talking on the telephone, at the far end of a large, long office. I paused, shutting the door behind me. Our eyes met, and for some fraction of a second we seesawed, establishing an equilibrium, as if we were on the two ends of a board. Then he tipped the balance: with a precise nod, neither stern nor deliberately courteous, he invited me to approach. My end of the board rose, and I started for his desk easily, as if down an incline. This was time, while I crossed the space between us . . . And it was literally space, because the office had nothing in it but his desk and a pair of armchairs. This, the most glaringly distinctive feature of his office, hadn't even hit me at first. There was neither a *T* nor a *U* in it. That is, no such conference table. No carafe, no glass. There was no television, either. I don't remember for sure whether there was a model sailboat, but I don't think there was any picture above his head. This was an office from which everything had been removed. But . . . how can I say it more precisely? . . . it was not an office which had never had any of the things that weren't in it now. Again, I'm not sure whether there was actually a paler rectangle of parquet, signifying a vanished stick from the letter *T*, or whether there was only a square of less faded wallpaper, signifying a former picture. In any case, such was my impression: that he sat under a picture which did not hang above him, and that I walked around a T-shaped conference table which did not stand before him.

I approached his desk (this was an ordinary small office desk on the site of a previous, oceanic desk, and the desk had nothing on it) at the exact second that he finished his conversation, put down the receiver, stood up from his chair, and proffered his hand. He hadn't hurried to finish the conversation, any more than he had prolonged it until the instant I approached—he had simply managed to finish it by that moment. And he didn't proffer his hand while still talking, or point to a chair while pressing the receiver to his ear with his shoulder, or shrug, or spread his hands, or grimace impatiently at the invisible other party, he didn't fling down the receiver when he finished his conversation. No; he said goodbye to the other party, hung up, turned to me, and extended his hand, without keeping me waiting for even a second. Nevertheless . . . how can I put it more precisely? . . . he had indeed *managed* to get it all done, and his pleasure in this, despite his reserve, was reflected on his face as a sort of bright shadow or highlight. If he didn't look at his watch to make sure that the second hand stood at sixty, it was only because he knew how to control himself.

He was that kind of man.

We seesawed once more in equilibrium, this time up close, on more precise scales—the two ends of a handshake. Both his hand and its grip were irreproachable: the palm was dry but not rough, the grip was confident but not hard, and there was no doubt as to the cleanliness of his hands. He pressed his hand on my pan of the scales—and I sank into a chair.

During the handshake there was a brief and appropriate glance; the pause of it, a certain lengthiness, could hardly even be felt, but it was there. Once again we looked each other in the eye and seemed to understand each other. That is, either we really did understand each other, or each of us understood the other in his own way and resolved to stay within that understanding, drawing strength from it . . . At any rate, the glance signified that in joining the game called "interview" we had both undertaken not to deviate from the rules or go beyond the framework of our chosen convention, whereby each of us clearly saw what we must talk about and how, what to answer and what to ask (in just that sequence: the answer conditions the question). That being the case, it would plainly be unethical to measure him surreptitiously on some other, unstipulated level. Just as unethical as pestering him for an official favor in the sauna.

And that being the case, I am greatly at fault. But I daresay he was left with some secondary impression of me, too.

Well, he looked at me with clear green eyes, which went very well with his irregular features and ivory skin. He tossed his forelock, as if with faint annoyance that this tossing motion, too, suited him very well. And then, with a slight, elusive gesture, he made as if to wipe a cobweb from his face. That gesture . . . I had already seen it.

With sudden and immutable conviction, I realized that this gesture was what belonged to the poet N.—of whom I now had a clearer conception, if only of his appearance. Yes, precisely: I was seeing not my city planner (whose outward appearance had become less clear to me at that moment) but the poet. I was astounded that a similarity is such an independent attribute, even when the object of the comparison is absent from one's field of vision. But that's beside the point.

He was a fine-looking man, very well preserved, and yet without the vulgarity of blooming health or a too youthful face: he was the ideal for his age, and only this idealness made him look a trifle younger. In general, he was a physical aristocrat. His shirt was ideal, as was the shave on his cheeks, and moreover ideal in the marvelous sense that the shirt didn't look as if it had just been taken out of the bureau drawer, just as his cheeks made you think of coffee and fine cigarettes rather than of the shaving brush.

He allowed me to begin. As I felt my way, trying to articulate a topic still vague even to me, he leveled his clear gaze on me, listened attentively, and refrained from comment, but only as a courteous man who knew how to listen without interrupting.

Though I bolstered myself emotionally by making a game of my ineptitude as I went along, the fact remained that I was stammering, drifting, and growing more and more uncomfortable under his wise and attentive gaze.

"You know," I said, the feeble words beginning to flow, "I'm not an expert on city planning at all. And what's more, not a journalist in the literal sense . . ." ("And what's more," I thought for him, "an idiot in the literal sense.") "Let's begin," I said, "with the fact that all I know is, Erevan is famous among other cities for its planning. And that I could hardly," I said, "become deeply acquainted with the subject in a short time, and naturally I don't want to write anything amateurish, and I doubt the reader is interested in coping with statistics . . . All of us, as ordinary people, see from the inside out, from the windows of our apartments and institutions, and our view is partial and fragmented, and what we'd be interested to learn is the opinion of a man who looks from the outside in—that is," I explained, "who doesn't forget the categories of the large and the whole. And what we'd be interested in would be . . ." I was running dry, but he kept listening. Finally—as if glancing at his internal watch, with the crisp, abrupt gesture of a man who wasn't in the habit of wasting time, who had understood me long ago, before I half finished, or even before I opened my mouth, and who had endured my vapid speechifying only out of courtesy—he entered the game.

Irreproachability was his only weakness.

"Architecture as a means for educating man, you say?" (When

had I said that? My mental wheels began to spin.) "Yes, that's true. Positively, man is the primary factor in planning. Not *what* are we building, but *for whom* are we building. His spiritual world, his tomorrow—that's what has to be our first concern, when everything's still on paper, in the blueprints, and not in stone. Not the things we're used to thinking about, not today, not deadlines and growth rates, but what will happen in fifty years!" His voice rang out. "Is this a question we often ask ourselves? We all say we're building in the name of the future—we use these words habitually, without ever probing what they mean. As a rule, we don't think about the future at all, what life will be like for people in the world we have built. When we're bogged down in worries about producing, economizing, and the yearly plan, tomorrow is exactly what we *don't* think about."

A startling word, that *we*!

He spoke as if he himself did the building . . .

He seemed ready for our encounter, more so than I had expected. He was telling me things I hadn't dared hope to hear. He had been ready before I appeared on his horizon. And therefore it would be naïve to suppose that I had somehow steered the conversation. As it turned out, what he was telling me was actually too much what I had wanted to hear from him. He had promptly appropriated even the thought and a half that had occurred to me in spontaneous connection with my assignment, the thoughts that I was already picturing typeset in the form of "A Writer's Reflections." For an accurate reconstruction of the interview—and since this man spoke for himself so completely and sensibly, it seemed appropriate to hold myself to his standard—for that kind of reconstruction, I simply didn't have the journalistic skills. I became slightly panicky, and for a moment I stopped listening to what he was saying. When I discovered this, I became even more flustered. With an inept, uncharacteristic flourish I opened my notebook and wrote down the first statistic, "50." (I would later spend a long time figuring out what it meant.) Like a cheating pupil—the horror of whose position is further multiplied by the fact that even as he copies he doesn't know whether he's copying the right answer, and by now he feels more ashamed to write something laughably stupid than to get a D, as honest and direct as an F—I cupped my hand to hide from him what I had written in my notebook.

None of this escaped him, but neither did he escape.

Perhaps because the pen is mightier than the sword, a normal, healthy person is stupefied and hypnotized by any form of minute-taking. If only in the first instant, the fact that the man opposite you has picked up his pen will give you a chill whiff of dungeons and guards. Even if it doesn't, an accountability-raising reflex will go to work—and you will stumble, tangled up in your grammar. As steam changes to water, and water to ice, a man changes from the state of speaker to answerer, and from the state of answerer to interrogatee.

The interrogatee looked down for a second. Since he allowed himself but few instinctive movements, that glance clattered like a chunk of ice. His speech stopped short. True, the sentence had been completed, and he was able to make this look like a natural pause. All in all, he quickly got control of himself—caught his fall, you might even say—and continued as if nothing had happened. But something, apparently, had. Because, I can't even tell you how, but from that moment on, his speech seemed to have been slightly reorganized, adjusted for the record. And although I was always trying to decide which phrase to record next, and whenever I did decide I totally failed to hear what he was saying, nevertheless, I was twiddling the pencil in my hands . . . My companion did not allow himself to look at the pencil, but his gaze had been tethered by a thread. As I twiddled the pencil, I was twitching that thread.

I understood him better and better, but myself worse and worse. And I was less and less able to listen to what he was saying. I put myself in his shoes and felt embarrassed. Why the devil was I playing tricks on this earnest man? He had enough problems without me. Actually, if I had scribbled without pause, he might have forgotten my dagger. As it was, he had no way of knowing which phrase I would ambush.

"The environment is a means of education . . ." he said, and paused involuntarily for me to write it down. But suddenly I didn't write it down, and he was slightly thrown off. Then, by an effort of will, he banished the hallucination: ". . . to preserve ethnic traditions and create our today!" Still, every time he led up to an exclamation, the distinct apparition of the pencil arose before him, and he dropped his gaze. His speech was sensible and handsome; all the more, then, might he take offense on behalf of each phrase—why hadn't it been recorded?—and likewise feel astonished that another had been. The discrimination inflicted on his speech

by my pencil was totally unjustified and unjust, like all discrimination.

As if honestly, as if absorbed in listening, I laid aside my pencil.
I was so engrossed . . .

This wasn't long in producing an effect.

He told in a businesslike way about prospects for the growth
of the city, and about the current idea of localizing the growth so
that the city wouldn't bulge with irrational, shapeless outlying districts but would find inner resources through reconstruction, re-
planning, and the elimination of districts that were architecturally
backward and unprofitable. He told about the difficulties that still
stood in the way of this idea, about the stagnation in the thinking
of other officials, about their ineradicable loyalty to yesterday, about
administrative inertia and laziness . . .

Easily, without growing short of breath, he climbed the steps
of his words to the very top of the precipice. Together we glanced
back, a bit dizzy, and then slid quickly and smoothly down the
spiral of his speech into the stillness and twilight of a pause, of a
softened glance that lingered in reverie, and after resting there, under
the branching canopy of the last sentence, we began to climb up
again.

He was not the familiar type of orator who takes satisfaction
in a neatly turned phrase, who plunges into his speech with the
courage of a swimmer and spelunker . . . and behold! he finds his
way out of the sentence! At the end of the phrase—a faint light,
like the exit from a cave.

This man didn't crawl into the cave and grope frantically
through the side passages of "which," "what," and "how" in search
of the exit, he didn't get his sandals wet in a puddle of parenthetic
words—he worked in the open air.

"As recently as five years ago the quantities would have seemed
mythical. Every other day, a fifty-apartment building is ready for
occupancy! But we mustn't let the very quantities confuse our
minds, engulfing both our idea and our purpose. We have learned
to pay heed to the exterior of a building, and even to its interde-
pendence with the complex. But the interiors . . . Our task now is
to eliminate this rupture between the room and the façade!"

"Rupture between the room and the façade"—suddenly I
opened my notebook again and transcribed this brave phrase. A
vague idea rose to mind when I was recording the word *rupture*,

which he had spoken as confidently as though it were an established term. Although the phrase was ordinary at first glance, I took it down because I was struck by some elusive incongruity between its meaning and the alien vividness of its form . . . I never did capture the meaning I had paused for, especially as there was no time to delay. My companion, too, had lurched to a halt on this phrase—because my pencil, after a long interruption, had begun to record it, and this implied something—and now he darted aside like a man racing around a sudden obstacle, pretending that this was where he'd been heading. Fertilized by my pencil, the phrase became a flower, an ovary, and here was the fruit, already ripening, swelling. My sudden perplexity over the phrase was immediately answered by an entire speech growing up from it, and that speech explained a great deal to me . . .

"We require of a man that he work better and better with each passing day," he said with ever-increasing animation, as if planting himself more solidly and firmly on ground he had chosen once and for all, "and we take no interest in how he feels as he walks to work and back. We tell him constantly about his obligation and duty to his native city. And no one has yet formulated the question this way: Is the city obligated to the man?" He raised his hand, mildly but expressively, as if to place this phrase just slightly above the level on which I had heard it. Up there, just to one side of the sound source, it took on a nickel-plated shine, like a giant paper clip. "A man is walking to work. What mood comes over him in ugly, squalid, identical streets? Or, on the contrary, are his spirits elevated by the beauty around him, and will he set to work with élan and a surge of strength? Surely it's worth giving thought to a man's route through the city? So that his passage will be orchestrated, as it were, and the city in motion will be exact and well considered, like music? The melody of the street . . ." He fell silent for an instant, as if listening. "This experiment—"

My hand twitched, and in spite of myself I wrote out the word *experiment*. A look of sheer passion appeared on my companion's face. The violin strings of his countenance tautened and began to sound, although without distorting his calm, pleasant pallor.

Just then the telephone rang.

At any rate, my notebook has a little square marked off somewhere near the word *experiment*, and in it is written "tel. conv." Frowning slightly, he listened without interrupting the other party.

Then his face was smoothed by an explosion from within; once again it became calm and decisive.

"I said in the first place that it was an unprofessional sketch. Then I found out." His face froze in a hard smile. "The fact is, he's not even a practicing architect—he's just a dilettante." Something was said to him at the other end. "No, I don't like the method itself," he replied, still maintaining the hard smile. "No, no. What we need here is creative analysis. The main thing is not to hurry . . ."

I was completely bewitched by the words *unprofessional sketch*, *method*, and *analysis* coming from his lips. Even more so because the words were used without special intent—they were spoken in a natural and unforeseen conversation. To stay abreast of a conversation and keep it going in such a way that one could also say something especially for the benefit of a third party who happened to be listening—such a threefold task, thrice interwoven, was beyond the strength of any man, I thought, especially such a nice one.

When he hung up, he again—wonder of wonders!—made no superfluous remarks. No inane apologies for interrupting our conversation, no explanations of the problem discussed on the line, no "Where were we?"—nothing of the sort. He glanced at me briefly and lucidly, as if he hadn't interrupted his speech in midsentence, and the glance said that it was over, he had expressed himself in full on the issue, he couldn't go into particulars, but carry on, ask anything that interests you. Work. You were sent here for a purpose, you know . . . And time is passing, dear comrade.

Much had already become clear to me: the zone of delight and the zone of doubt were increasingly distinct from each other and seemed to be moving apart. The delight, as an emotion, occupied the present; the doubt, as something rational and even bad, required rethinking. It existed rather in the future. There simply wasn't time to interpret the few words and phrases I had tripped over; I had probably just been irritated by the delay, the disruption of the harmony, and by suspicion of my own suspiciousness. I was painfully embarrassed by my own leisure and idleness vis-à-vis this man of affairs. In any case, I had absolutely no idea what else to discuss with him. My main concern was to ask a question that showed at least some intelligence, and to stay more or less on the conversational level he had set. In my considerable distress and confusion, a foggy idea suddenly dawned on me, and I seized on it gladly.

"To be perfectly frank with you," I said, blushing, "I didn't like Erevan very much at first. Of course I couldn't confess this to anyone. It wasn't until I learned a little about the country in which it lies that I began to get used to it. The paradox of Erevan"—in using the word *paradox*, I dropped a curtsy to the words *orchestrated* and *experiment*—"is this: Here you are, celebrating the 2,750th anniversary of its founding, and yet the city has no historical face. The individuality of a city takes shape over centuries. Cities that arise in our time can't even have a face; they can only be more or less in accord with our practical and aesthetic needs." My companion nodded. Encouraged, I promptly lost the thread. "I'm afraid my idea may strike some people as frivolous. But from all we've just said, I believe you will understand me correctly." This was a forbidden ploy. To say such a thing made me narrow my eyes to a slit. For the moment, however, I was alone in thinking myself clever; the gambit merely put my companion on guard. He had not, of course, been born yesterday. "The reason you could conceive a plan for the general reconstruction and rebuilding of the city, including even its central districts, is that none of Erevan's earlier buildings are noteworthy for their architecture. You want your city to look beautiful, you want to give it a unique, individual image . . ." My listener's face softened. He was increasingly ready to agree with me. And although I held the bank, while he was just taking the offered card—and moreover saw that I was cheating, slipping him an ace to go with his ten—he took the card. "But," I said, "however professional or even brilliant the plan, however fine the ideas that guide its creators, you're trying to create this unique new face for the city within a definite time limit. You can't incorporate thousands of years of history into your plan. You can't avoid creating the city in our era. And this imprint, barely visible to us now, will be noticed by succeeding generations. That is, the ancient city of Erevan will be a new city, built all at one time. This temporal monochromaticity—don't you suppose there's a possibility it won't quite suit those succeeding generations, of whom the people of Erevan, in contrast to many other cities, are ever mindful? I can't think of any cities that have managed to acquire vivid, individual architectural features in the space of a few years. As a rule, a city's

individuality is shaped by the labor of time, rather than of its builders. How do you expect to solve this problem without the aid of
time? You don't have time, you know, and your plans are so de-
pendent on principle. Of the examples I'm familiar with, only Peter
the Great succeeded in giving his city a face according to a plan
and in a short time."

At Peter's name his eyes flashed, briefly and profoundly. The
expression was promptly concealed by a timely gesture of weariness,
as if by a theater curtain, but either I had already gained experience
in communicating with him, or I had so much faith in my own
insight that I saw only what I chose to, whether or not it actually
happened—whatever the case, that flash did not escape me.

"Yes," he said. His face paled and lighted up, not in the vulgar
sense of the word, but like a fluorescent lamp, perhaps. "Yes, you're
quite right. You mention Peter the Great with good reason. From
the very beginning, he managed to give his city an inimitable look.
Our department has solved a lot of problems, but we still haven't
worked out the character of the city. Leningrad, Tallin—these are
cities whose mere names call up an immediate image. We want to
achieve the same here in Erevan." He appeared to have missed my
bait about city planning and time, but for some reason he had bitten
where I didn't expect it, on Peter the Great. I grabbed my pencil.
Either his speech was an excited jumble or I took it down feverishly
and mindlessly, but the notes that follow are very incoherent. I've
spent a long time puzzling over them. "For the city to have edu-
cational significance, too . . . Posters, display boards—they're all
so formal, so tasteless. And degrading to the idea itself, as a rule.
Sometimes I just feel like shouting: Why do you pollute the spiritual
world of man?!" (My notes say "spir. wor." It was quite a while
before I understood this phrase, decoding it not as "spiritual world"
but as "spirit of the working man.") "What we've planned is ex-
perimental, of course . . . The ring boulevard, designed in assorted
ethnic architectural styles, will symbolize the friendship of the peoples. Or *** Street, an equally experimental design . . . You haven't
been there? Do go. And do at least notice that there are absolutely
no memorial plaques. So formal—I'm so fed up with them, all
those plaques . . . But suddenly there's a work by a certain talented
young sculptor of ours. No, not a bust—a symbol, conceived in an
elevated, lofty vein . . . Not pasted on the wall like a building

manager's report. Not like something on a bulletin board, 'So-and-so lived here,' 'Human beings lived here.' No! 'Here is something divine!'—that's the idea that should occur to the passerby . . . Monuments like this will inspire respect. They will have an un-witting influence on the thinking of the passerby and serve him inconspicuously as a sublime example of what man can achieve . . . Let's say a father is walking with his son, he's picked him up at kindergarten after work. And suddenly, this sculpture. The father, tired and preoccupied, isn't looking around. But his little son no-tices. He doesn't understand. 'What's this, Daddy?' he asks. And Daddy is forced to explain, or walk over and read it himself, if he doesn't know: 'So-and-so lived and worked here . . .' 'But what did he do? Why did they put this art object here?' And now the father and son are having a conversation."

Somehow, in my delight, I completely missed the rest. Sta-tistics, dimensions, skyscrapers . . . Demolish a million square meters—build a half million . . . Or vice versa. Suddenly I realized that he was silent.

I made as if to write the last phrase, and looked up.

I don't know whether he had glanced at his watch; I didn't see. But after a moment's hesitation he decided to do one more thing. He ran to the next room and brought back a tube.

We bent over the unrolled blueprints, our shoulders touching lightly. These were illustrations out of a science-fiction novel—a swimming pool *cum* aquarium, with a restaurant under the water, an aviary above the water, and fish swimming right toward us into our shot glasses. It would have been hard to believe, if the poolarium hadn't been scheduled to open next year.

I can truthfully swear that he didn't look at his watch at this point. But he froze for an instant, as if listening to it tick, and again swiftly disappeared into the other room. I couldn't quite see it from my chair, but I think it was small and much more cluttered than the one we were in. I even speculated that that was where they had dumped all the things that used to be in our room . . . At last he darted out with several cylindrical paving blocks clutched to his belly. All I could think was: Had there been a sudden explosion? And wasn't he getting his shirt dirty?

"Here." He dropped them on the desk. "Colored asphalt! Ex-perimental samples." Indeed, the blocks were different colors.

"What a boring, tiresome color we have underfoot! But now . . . Not to mention the lowered accident rate . . . Now the driver will never fall asleep at the wheel!"

Here his internal time expired. In such a way that he just managed to get everything done. We shook hands with profound sincerity and not a trace of familiarity.

As I shut the door behind me, I glanced at my watch. Exactly twelve.

BREATH ON STONE

In high spirits, with a sense of easily fulfilled duty, I hurried out of the shady park into the sunlight. During that hour the caressing warmth had become heat; the white-hot air had thickened and solidified in the middle of the street.

I looked at the streets with fresh eyes. Or that was what I should have done, so that my visual impressions could corroborate the propositions just expounded to me. But the day must have grown too hot: nothing looked very different to me.

Then I decided to review these propositions that needed to be corroborated with visual impressions, and realized with horror that I remembered nothing of the interview except for a few gestures. I grabbed my notebook—the precious little it contained made no sense.

I did come across the name of the experimental street in my notes and decided to find it. Luckily, it was not far off. The freshness and briskness inspired by the mere sight of my recent companion had mysteriously vanished. Melting in the heat, I was already wondering whether he existed. Had I invented all this?

I walked along the street, listening attentively for the moment when I would experience the sublime thoughts and the radiant, or at least cheerful, mood which must inevitably be induced by the design of this architectural complex.

The whole street had been built with variety, originality, and taste. Nothing was superfluous—all structures had been planned in relation to their neighbors. Horizontal harmonized with vertical, open space with closed. The visual effect was calm: nothing impeded or arrested the eye. I discovered with surprise that I had been walking for a long time and the street was about to end—as signaled by an ugly building, conspicuously inappropriate on the corner. That building was what I'd been seeing for some time now. I had walked the length of this street, listening to myself in vain: no thought, none at all, had occurred to me. Perhaps the day was too hot. Or perhaps you can't generally expect to have an idea on purpose . . . Here was a café, transparent through and through, and a department store like it, and even if the café had a coffee maker that worked and the department store were piled with jeans, and if, in addition, the department store and the café weren't closed for lunch, even so, everything would remain the same—ready, empty, and waiting. A florist's shop in the shape of a vase; to get to it, you had to hop playfully along flagstones laid at random . . . Although I kept an eye out, I never did see the piece of art about the great man who had lived on this street, the memorial that was supposed to be so eye-catching. Agreeable colors, agreeable combinations of surfaces . . . Suddenly there were golden bubbles rising on one of the surfaces, as though from a water glass, or as though a large carp were breathing below it . . . And now—just like those bubbles, I told myself—a thought rose to my mind. The only one.

Why is this? Why do the planners think for me, why do they plan what and how I'm supposed to think? Which is it, are they thinking as a favor to me, or thinking instead of me? That's the question. In my interest, or at my expense? So that I'll be nice and comfortable—or so that *they* will, in their conception of me? There are a great many services I can dispense with. So far, I don't feel the bleak need to have anyone else think, love, eat, or sleep for me. So far, I'm coping with these things myself, as best I can. What I need is a place, so that none of these things will have to be done for me—neither the thinking nor the loving . . . A place where I can do these things myself.

Such was the resentful thought that came suddenly to mind. I felt almost gleeful when I looked at the undemolished eyesore, epochally conspicuous at the end of the street.

I had an appointment to meet a certain woman, a publisher. Not a business appointment—simply, there were still some things I hadn't had time to see: a park, a fountain, and an art gallery. I had no right to leave without seeing them, so we met. And perhaps I was truly annoyed, or perhaps, having met only my friend's friends for ten days, I missed feminine society and was now exploiting the opportunity, rare in Erevan, to be the escort of an interesting woman who wasn't anyone's relative—but, anyway, I began reporting my architectural tribulations to her with excessive passion. I blossomed with every phrase, I was such a fervent, earnest man . . .

"He totally failed to hear my question, you see. All he heard was Peter the Great. But the point I was making about Peter was a different one, and perhaps not the most flattering. Before leaving on this trip, you see, I visited Peter's house—for the first time, I'm ashamed to say, because after all I'm a native, my grandfather and my father and my great-grandfather all lived in Petersburg. I happened on it by chance. You won't believe this, but for thirty years I had no idea it existed. I thought Peter the Great's house and the Summer Palace were the same thing! But that's not my point. The house is Petersburg's earliest surviving building. I was stunned, overwhelmed. By its very lack of museum atmosphere—by the vividness and unity of the sensation that a man had lived here. This man, Peter. The house is not a palace, you know. In fact, it's a beggarly little house. 'The refuge of the miserable Finn,' as Pushkin said. Apart from its rarity, it has no architectural value for our day, and yet . . . Every object—and the place is modest, very modest! —speaks not of itself but of its owner. Do you understand what I mean? But I hadn't expected anything of the house—that's very important! I hadn't expected anything of Geghard, either. They gave me everything all at once, everything they had . . . And here I'm walking around Erevan, always expecting something . . . Well, about the house. Overwhelmed, I walked out to the Neva—and was stunned all over again. Walking out of Peter's tiny, dark lodge, I saw the Neva, and the Peter and Paul Fortress, and the Summer Garden. And all that lavish beauty suddenly struck me with fresh, unaccustomed force. I tried to understand what had happened, what had given me the strength to *see* it, this beauty a thousand times seen and by now invisible. And suddenly, again, I understood: Peter! That is, I had somehow touched his idea from within, and everything was illumined for me in a new light. The idea was beyond mere words and thoughts: it existed physically! That was the self-evident truth that suddenly came through to me. During his lifetime Peter didn't manage to build all that much, hardly even enough to constitute the face of the city. He built a whole lot more after he died. Historically, Petrine ideas quite soon came to nothing in his successors. Only the idea of Petersburg, the image of it, was powerful enough so that other people's thinking, for a long time, unintentionally followed the course set by Peter. Simply, no other thought occurred to them.

"The builders carried on Peter's work. Amid the forests of completely different, even opposite ideas, no one even suspected that the edifice of this half-forgotten idea was steadily rising. By the time the momentum of Peter's idea was finally spent, Petersburg stood; by its form, integrity, and uniqueness, it dictated the laws of its own continuation. Few things in Russia, perhaps only two, Petersburg and the Soviet regime, originate from a single idea. They have this in common. It may even be that only Petersburg could have become the cradle of the regime. (Only in this city, in this ossified idea, could the idea of a straightforwardly and literally understood order and harmony have been put into practice, as inevitably and unswervingly as its avenues.) And Petersburg, the most un-Russian city, the triumph of Peter's idea, still stands, even in our most naïve of times, stands with its frozen former face, and the new districts separate out from it like oil from water. This is a marvel. A marvel not in the sense of the miraculous but of the phenomenal, for we can still imagine the idea arising in Peter's powerful mind, and yet the fact that the idea was implemented is almost dizzying in its impossibility. Like a centaur or a griffin—and suddenly, look! it's galloping and flying! . . . And the city will go on standing, because Petersburg cannot be changed gradually, it can only be destroyed, destroyed along with the idea that created it. The two of them, the city and the idea, will disappear only together. The other beautiful cities of Russia grew up gradually, without careful planning; they were built by life itself, over the centuries. Their suddenly achieved harmony and charm, unique and elusive, are defenseless in the face of any constructive idea. Thus, Moscow is vanishing. One felled pine does not mean the end of the forest . . . nor the second pine, nor the third . . . and suddenly the forest has been felled, the Arbat district has been cleared . . . And the man who still remembers finding a Boletus mushroom there in his childhood will soon be dead . . . What am I getting at? The word *build* has sounded increasingly proud and elevated, of late. Whereas this is a profession, a job. The builder should not be puffed up with pride. He is building something, and for someone. As long as the builder erects dwelling and temple, temple and dwelling, he builds for himself, and he's outside of time. But as soon as he begins to build for someone else—a palace for a king, a mansion for an aristocrat, a hut for a slave—he belongs only to his own time. No matter how brilliant he is, he will be encircled by time and will build nothing *for the ages*. Only time itself builds for the ages. Time, preserving one thing, burying another, and erecting a third, is what gives a city its unique and beautiful face. It likens the trivial and temporary work of human hands to nature and life itself. The city comes to resemble a grove, its days and nights and seasons are just as natural . . . If we build a city in a period of a few years (we do, and will, have occasion to build in that way), at least we should be cognizant that the work of the centuries is beyond our capabilities, and not flatter ourselves in this regard . . . For, when we proceed from even the most beautiful idea, but only the one, aren't we imposing it, already unwanted and inconvenient, on generations to come? We must not build for the future but for the present, with profound love. It's conceited, to say the least, to fit the voiceless man of the future into our schemes without his by-your-leave. He'll find it far more valuable to see how we lived than to study our naïve, fossilized concepts of how he would live someday after we were gone . . . What's achieved in relation to life is always greater than what's achieved in relation to an idea. Even in the most admirable instance (getting back to Peter), isn't it painful to be forced to live within an alien idea, even if harmoniously and beautifully expressed? The Petersburg melancholy—we have all kinds of literary examples, and, besides, our personal experience is enough. Petersburg is like music, a Petersburg Symphony. Isn't this the same indignation Tolstoy felt whenever he listened to the Kreutzer Sonata—whose creator, although long dead and gone, forced his alien and temporally remote listener into the world of his own passions and feelings, unexplained by anything in the listener's concrete experience? Isn't this the same feeling that will sometimes choke today's Leningrader when he sets foot on some crooked little bridge, looks at the dirty water in the canal, and can't understand what's happening to him? Incidentally, even Pushkin's *Bronze Horseman*. It's not really so much a hymn to Peter and Petersburg, as we were taught in school. Otherwise, why such a sharp boundary between the introduction and the story of poor Yevgeny? That boundary, that contrast, is the very idea of the poem. It's hard to say which is more significant: the poet's admiration for the beauty and might of the city, or his sympathy for Yevgeny, casting about in that beauty—"

Here I felt someone take my hand. My heart leaped. I turned to my companion and caught the exceedingly feminine glance that may equally be understood as doubt or interest, sympathy or mockery . . .

"Come," she said.

I found myself in an old Erevan street at last. *Old* is the wrong word: the street didn't savor of millennia, or of centuries. It may have been a hundred years old. The two- and three-story houses stood close together, with softly defined, rounded windows; they had a half-blind stare, like a nearsighted person without his glasses. Their attempts to be rectilinear, and not made of clay, looked naïve. In olden days, probably, the street hadn't been a poor one—the approaches to the main thoroughfare of a provincial city might have looked like this. The street had no architectural style. The houses reminded me of antique refrigerators, back when there was no electricity and the ice brought by a deliveryman was stored in galvanized boxes . . . The small, deepset windows suggested shadowed rooms and an after-dinner nap. The walls looked puffy. They appeared to have been drawn by a child's hand. Sometimes the line of windows slipped downward, as in the work of a lazy schoolboy . . . There were no passersby.

"Look!"

I stooped slightly to peer under an arch. I needn't have bent down; a man of normal height might perfectly well have walked through standing up. But it didn't look that way. And besides, the place had a logic of peeping and spying . . . as if through a crack, as if through a chink, as if through the optical peephole device in a modern apartment door, where you see your guest in an unthinkable perspective, and he no doubt sees your terrifying eye.

The deep, shady little tunnel with its rounded arch was like a tube and diaphragm, and it gave an implausible, telescopic distinctness to the courtyard beyond. The air is never so clear as it was in that courtyard. In contrast with the entrance, the courtyard was brightly lit, though not, it seemed, by the officious, dull-witted sun that was beating down on our backs in the street. The light was tranquil and even. At the right there was a little stairway—four steep, narrow, hollowed-out steps, and an absurd railing with a curlicue at the end. Beyond, three children were playing a game I had forgotten—the painted knucklebones lay about on the ground . . . Farther beyond, there was a kind of veranda with a lean-to;

grapes hung from a trellis, someone was asleep on a wooden lounge
. . . A drooping tree showed from around a corner on the right
. . . In its small shadow a tiny stove smoked, coals crackled . . . A
black-clad grandmother at the end of the courtyard was gathering
something, or perhaps strewing something on the ground . . .

There are things about which you cannot say that you ever
saw them for the first time—they're in your blood. This was the
first time I had seen such a courtyard, but the phrase is just for the
record. I had always known this courtyard—that would be far more
accurate. Mine was the kind of emotion with which a man returns
to his homeland: One tree has snapped, but that bush—how it's
grown! Everyone has died . . . That can't be Masha, so big! Why,
I used to carry her in my arms! And that barrel, I remember it—
don't tell me it's still around . . . You prostrate yourself on the
ground. Still alive, old fellow!

We walked along, peering into these deep little gates. I had
forgotten about my companion, although there was also some subtle
significance in the fact that she was nearby and knew what she was
showing me: I was not alone with my mute ecstasy.

No courtyard repeated any other, but neither did any differ, it
seemed. None was more beautiful or more interesting than any
other—each was perfect. How had this chaos of lean-tos, cul-de-
sacs, trees, light, and shade developed? It was impossible to retrace
or imagine. Evidently, when life organizes itself according to its
own unpremeditated laws, it cannot create an imperfect form.

Only in the old Dutch masters could I remember such depth
and clarity. A pregnant woman reads a letter by the window . . .
What light! Oh, they understood what it meant to have a frame, a
window! A world that you discover by peering into it, a framed
world, is so much more serious and self-contained than the world
on the street, on the highway, in the field . . . In a frame, it's
already a concept. An idea of the world.

That was how each courtyard looked, framed by the black gate
opening.

This was what it meant to say "Human beings lived here"! And
no abstract "art object" was needed. People lived, loved, gave birth,
got sick, died, were born, grew up, grew old . . . Someone plastered
a wall, someone carried an unneeded three-legged table out of the
house, someone planted flowers, someone tore down a barn and
cleared the site, and someone built a henhouse next to it . . . The

courtyard grew like a tree—old branches died off, new cul-de-sacs grew up—and the branches of a tree are never imperfectly arranged. It's thicker here, thinner there, crooked there, broken there—but it's a tree! Children chirp in its crown, lovers prop up its trunk, and a black-clad grandmother keeps busy at the roots, stooping down, kindling the stove, picking up bits of wood and dropping them. The perspective of the generations, each courtyard like a genealogical tree . . .

The meaning of life, before you and after you, is clear at last.

At each gate, you can't tear yourself away, yet neither can you spy. But the next one, too—when you're walking up to it, you can't believe it might be just as nice . . . but this next one, too, when you look in, is like a sigh, a sigh of relief, a sigh of meeting, a sigh of not parting, and the mysterious sweet faith that even you can have happiness . . .

Neither this street nor these courtyards have any historical or architectural value. They will be demolished. New buildings with all the conveniences will stand here, people will settle in them, they will love, give birth, and die, suffer and rejoice. But I don't know: a hundred years from now, will these walls be so steeped in warmth and love, life and death, that as soon as you turn the corner and take the first step you will feel the same kinship and happiness you feel now, on this blurry clay lane? . . . Or will everything be reflected from surfaces dull and shiny, regular and flat?

We value human labor, and we still value it too little. But do we value that which is even more precious, that which *is*, that which has come about without us, without our participation—the great harmony and art of nature and time? Lumber is more costly than unfelled pine, of course—but in monetary terms! We must not confuse cost with value, expensiveness with preciousness . . . The most brilliant creation of human hands is monosemantic and partial, compared with nature. Nature is a correctly and cleanly struck chord, overheard and borrowed from the absolute harmony and polyphony of life. Harmony cannot be measured by cost. The automobile is in no way more precious than the glade in which we have parked . . . And no effort of ours will ever create the early morning, or fabricate the sunrise, the dew, the blade of grass . . . No artist will ever, by mere force of imagination, be able to scatter the barns and huts as naturally, in relation to river, road, and sky, as they are scattered in any little village; he will never manage to place the lone cow or horse where it belongs, or the haystack or windmill, or to set the jars and earthenware pots in correct sequence on the pickets of the sagging wattle fence. He won't even be able to make the fence sag properly! All he can do is steal a glimpse.

A great textbook of harmony has been given to us by life— free, gratis. And we must remember that if we tear out all the pages, we will have nothing to study from.

Ah, Erevan! Did a bird sketch you? Did a lion
color you like a child with a crayon box?

On this clay lane, when I bent my head and peered into a little courtyard, I saw that Erevan at last. Mandelstam was never inaccurate.

What does a man leave behind in objects? Merely the form he has imparted to them? Or the warmth of his hands, the touch of his glances, the dents from his words? Everything here spoke the language of life, both past and future. Eternal life . . . I dared, I entered the courtyard, and from all the doorways people who loved me came running—great-grandfathers and great-grandmothers, great-grandsons and great-granddaughters . . . People of the past and future embraced me and formed a wordless column, tenderly grieving and nodding, pitying me as I walked past them and wept with sorrow and happiness . . .

The Patriarch

He's the most famous man in Armenia. Although *famous* isn't the right word. Someone may even be more famous now. But that person is famous for the moment, while this one is famous forever. A great son of Armenia.

I was put off by this. I hadn't really planned on visiting him. Unless things just happened to work out . . . My experience of great men had so far been negative. Which isn't to say that I'd been disillusioned by them and discovered they weren't all that great; on the contrary, a great man's small weaknesses had always slaked my skepticism and served to raise my opinion of great men. The problem, unfortunately, lay in me. I ceased to be myself in their presence, I behaved stupidly, and this was unpleasant.

Independently of my wishes, as it turned out, the visit kept being delayed, postponed, until suddenly, on my last day, I was taken there.

We stepped into a quiet lane, which might as well have had a "Do Not Enter" sign. There weren't even any passersby. I thought I remembered having been in this street, having walked through it. Yet no one had mentioned to me that he lived here. At first this struck me as odd.

There's nothing odd about it, however. What's curious is the very nature of his fame. In the first place, even to mention that he lives here is somehow absurd: everyone knows. In the second place, they generally don't talk much about him. Conversation is about more trivial, private, topical matters. And what would they say? It's a fact. He lives. Has *always* lived. Thirty, fifty, seventy years . . . no more rumors, gossip, sensations . . . ninety years. What is there to say? He exists. Always has. They can't imagine life without him.

We turned down that quiet lane . . . Prejudiced though I was against great men, I opened the wicket gate with trepidation. Its soft creak was earsplitting, and the little courtyard seemed lighted by a more brilliant sun. Deep inside I felt an unmistakable, crystal-clear tingle, and I was ready to soak up impressions like a blotter.

But so far there was nothing to soak up. With peculiar caution, I stepped over the snakish coils of a garden hose rolled up in the courtyard. At the left was a pretty little house, and at the right a towering new edifice in the modern style: glass, and that same pink tufa.

I heard an exclamation and tore my gaze from the garden hose. I had felt compelled to stop and ponder whether the hose was a detail, and if so, was it artistic. A gross symptom of the stupefaction that overcomes me in the presence of great men, although the patriarch wasn't even here yet.

I looked up and saw an elderly man with gold-rimmed spectacles and a hereditary air of cultivation. A wave of carefully stifled boredom swept over his face.

Cordially he welcomed my companion, a person of note in intellectual circles in Armenia. It can't be! I thought, in a delayed reaction, and then realized that of course it couldn't be the great man. Introduced, I smiled broadly and vacantly and shook his hand. "Papa!" he called over his shoulder. "Papa! . . . He's in the garden," our new acquaintance said self-effacingly. "Let's go to the studio for the time being."

We walked into the pink house, in the quiet, well-bred single file in which each man gives way to the other, and thus first one and then the other finds himself in front, realizes that he has gotten ahead, hangs back, and so forth, with the conversation continuing the whole time. First in the procession was our new acquaintance, explaining as he went, flapping his arms as if conducting, and all the while contriving not to turn his back on us (except for perhaps an instant, or an imperceptible fraction, to see the path ahead of him). During that instant my first companion would explain his explanations to me in a whisper. Humbled by the effort to act well-bred and yet maintain my dignity, although I no longer had any idea where dignity lay, I moved forward between the two men, listening to both, and simultaneously contriving to turn my back on neither, which was very difficult.

In this fashion we passed through a spacious entrance hall cluttered with unlivable furniture, and through another room, very dark, with drawn blinds, where two beautiful women, one old and one young, were molding dumplings at a large table. They gave us a long, uncomprehending glance from out of this stillness and twilight . . . but we were already parading up a new staircase. And at last we entered a fashionable studio.

Construction had just been completed. Stacked canvases crowded the center of the studio, leaving a narrow path along the walls. A flat light fell from above. The son went out on the balcony. "Papa, Papa!" he shouted down, into the garden. Papa had disappeared somewhere . . .

Now he began to show us his father's canvases, apologizing that he couldn't show them properly: they had just been moved in here . . . He pulled the canvases one by one, as if from a vegetable bed, and inspected them first himself. Meanwhile, I had time to read the date and title on the back. The title wasn't always there, however. You can paint mountains, fruits, and faces all your life, but you can't give every one of them a title. After inspecting the picture and recognizing it with apparent surprise, as if doubting whether the picture was worth it, he would show it to us. Every time, he doubted—and every time, he showed it. There was only one he didn't show. He simply stood it against the wall, with the caption "Spring" and the cord (to hang it by) facing out.

As always, I didn't know whether or not I liked all this. A painting would rise up, bisecting the vacant space of the studio, and I would catch myself feeling glints of admiration for the artist's infinite love of his homeland (an admiration I partly invented), and sincere surprise at his labor: so much fruit, so many mountains, so many faces! Could he possibly have repeated them so many times without ever in his long life doubting the very fact of their existence . . . without ever once wanting that pear to stop being a pear and become the idea of a pear, become a pear with two *p*'s or two *r*'s, a triangle, a sphere? I would have wanted that. But such astonishing good health, which rendered all the realia of this world eternal and eternally worthy of depiction in the long, long time of each day of our instantaneous lives! Such a gift this man had, his innate aware-

ness that for his short lifetime there would be quite enough happiness
in seeing these mountain-shaped, fruit-shaped faces (because of their
multiplicity and the length of the series, it was suddenly becoming
apparent that they had a common character, which also matched
their creator's character)! That awareness, too, can be called by no
other name than health . . . and health, it has seemed to me of
late, is preeminently beautiful.

Tired of showing the pictures, his son called from the balcony
again. "Papa, Papa!"

Papa still wasn't there.

He disliked this new house and preferred the old wing—quite
understandably. The new house was a museum in his own lifetime,
a personal gallery. The reasons for having built the museum while
the old man was still alive were also quite understandable. He had
thousands of visitors like me, and of course it was burdensome—
he was now very old. He was a great man. His days were filled with
ever-greater value and preciousness, it seemed, and required frugal
treatment. All understandable. Even touching. But really, had his
days been this precious when he was young and in love, when he
was a genius? The days of his youth had been worth nothing, but
he had lived, and no one could take that away from him. Now, by
recognizing and worshipping him, they were taking away—what
did the old man have left?—his days. His days did not belong to
him, they had been nationalized. The old man was too alone to
live: isolated by concern and freed from choice. Once, time had
been his, and he had lacked fame; now fame was his, and he lacked
time . . .

Love returns to an old man like infancy. Sunshine, stillness . . .

Quite often he disappeared, escaped gloriously from the house,
with a warm, lively triumph. "Papa, Papa!" But he was already
gone, and his family's carefully concealed displeasure at his escapes
apparently served to awaken the animate life that the old man still
needed as much as the truth, and of which he was still capable,
just as he was capable of painting another few kilos of pears.

These escapes, though not so great as our own great patriarch's,
not so meaningful as his, and yet so kindred, were almost dearer
to my heart. In Tolstoy's escape there was too much drama, role-
playing, and significance; in these, there was far more of the vital
need (like the need to eat, drink, and sleep) to live. And why hadn't

Tolstoy escaped long before? After all, his brilliant mind had seen the issue clearly for quite some time . . .

. . . When he succeeded in wandering away, he would sit in the sunshine with the old men and chat, unrecognized by them, equal at last, free, not alone . . . The family would find him and reinstall the great man in his place, cozy and cared for, a relic and national pride. The pearl would repose in the crimson velvet of its cushion until it disappeared again. But they always found it.

No one here should be ridiculed—neither they nor he. There is nothing to correct. And nothing to criticize.

Papa had disappeared again. For some reason I wanted this very much.

We went back downstairs the way we had come. The women were not in the darkened room—they had finished making their monuments to dumplings. An enormous dog whose paws were smeared with brilliant green ointment clacked his claws across the parquet and sniffed us unwillingly at the threshold of the bright entrance hall.

"Papa, where have you been?" I heard.

I was caught by surprise. The patriarch was sitting in an armchair and reading a newspaper, without glasses. He still has all his teeth, I reflected. He laid the paper aside and studied us, calmly waiting.

There was no longer any chance of escape.

We started to smile.

. . . He was sitting in a square armchair. His wide black smock (it matched the chair) draped as loosely as if there were nothing under it, no body. His head seemed to exist separately. It was much handsomer than in portraits, even self-portraits. In portraits his face looked a bit womanish and too old. Here, he was younger, wiser, and more courageous.

We were smiling.

"This, Papa," the son said, pointing at my companion to forestall any misunderstanding, "this, you know, is So-and-so So-and-so (So Sososian), our famous director from ArmenFilm. You know him well."

The father looked at So Sososian with bright, cordial, unrecognizing eyes.

"And this is"—the son pointed at me and paused to be prompted—"our guest . . ." He glanced at Sososian.

"A poet from Leningrad," Sososian supplied.

I do have a name, and I'm not a poet, but now suddenly—and it was almost a revelation to me—I discovered that this did not, in fact, matter. Compared to his name, my name equaled zero; compared to his life, if only in length, my life equaled the moment of conception; compared to the quantity of people who had passed through his life, my quantity equaled just one distant acquaintance, that acquaintance being myself. Well, what difference does it make, I thought, if I'm the prose writer Bitov and not the nameless poet "Their Name Is Legion"? This was a useful experience. I suddenly realized that my name *was* legion, that the word *poet* and the word *Leningrad* told far more about me than did my name. I sensed that I was a part of history. I lost myself in it easily. "What's in a name . . ." "Exhibits no historical value, has no independent significance . . ." I was a representative of an epoch. Between us lay an epoch. I couldn't imagine that he knew me. I might as well hope that Lev Tolstoy would wish me good luck in the *Literary Gazette*. This was a meeting in time, à la Bradbury.

The patriarch looked at me with an interest that I obviously did not merit. Had I been sitting in his place, at any rate, I would have looked upon the poet from Leningrad with ennui.

"From Leningrad?" he asked, brilliantly attaching no importance to the word *poet*.

I nodded with relief.

He extended his hand to me. It reached out from the void of the chair, inordinately long. Only old men have these beautiful hands like autumn branches, and (so much!) like their faces. Only old men who have done a great deal of work. Timorously I enclosed his ancient branch in my fleshy hand, and he shook it boldly.

"What's your name? I didn't catch it."

I began trying to remember my name. The patriarch glanced impatiently at his son.

"Vítor," Sososian prompted.

The patriarch looked at me. "Is that right?"

"It's Bitov. Andrei Bitov!" I exclaimed in despair.

"Bitov . . . Bitov . . ." The patriarch shook his head doubtfully. "Are you Russian?" he asked, suddenly intent.

"Yes," I replied uncertainly.

He sharpened his question: "Russian–Russian?"

At this point, I somehow began to think.

"Russian–Russian," I said crisply, casting aside my two German grandmothers.

"Because," he said thoughtfully, and his hand flew up, far up, and from there began slowly falling, like a leaf. "Poles, Frenchmen, Germans . . . but where are the Russians?" he asked, again in a rush.

"Yes, yes . . . Where?" I repeated, blinking.

Poles? Germans? What about them, I wondered, in extreme perplexity. But wasn't it lucky I'd betrayed my German grandmothers so deftly!

We sat down in the chairs offered to us.

A strange and untimely delight overwhelmed me. So this was what I'd been thinking about, constantly, agonizingly, ever since I first set foot in Armenia! This was it! This was what had made me so anxious. The land of Armenia exists—I wander through it, here it is. The Armenians live in it. Here they are. The Armenians are Armenians. The Armenians exist. But who am I? A Russian? Why, yes. I had never stopped to think about this . . . The contrast— that was what tormented me, that was it. How had I failed to guess! To the very end, I had never understood what it was that bothered me so much about seeing another country. And wouldn't you know, the first words I heard from the patriarch addressed this very issue. He was the first to say them to me. A truly great old man.

Stop! I've been carried away . . . "Poles, Frenchmen . . ." What did he mean, "Germans"? There was no genius, not even a hint of genius, in his question. Why was I all excited? Russian, non-Russian . . . Stop.

Now is the time to impart the following thought: We could certainly use a few lessons on the proper treatment of our own history, character, and traditions. These are matters of shared culture. But the principle of our ethnic existence is different from that of the Armenians; our ethnic self-consciousness is structured according to other laws. The main factor in this distinction is the arithmetic. Everything rests on the numbers. We are many. We have no reason to prove that we exist, and no one to prove it to. Everyone knows it, except us. What can we do about this? . . . That which is splendid in a small country, that which is noble and admirable, cannot apply in equal measure or with the same logic to a large country.

This panicky idea came to me at the feet of the patriarch. If he didn't suggest it to me, it wafted from him, even though un-intentionally. I am grateful to him that the idea has stuck in my mind. I am also prepared to attribute to his greatness—though perhaps this wasn't his doing either—the fact that my mind some-how started working especially well in his presence.

Such plain, direct, final (or first?) accuracy is the destiny only of great men (and it doesn't matter what kind of painter he was). How absurd of me, to have painted a mental image of the great man on the basis of my own experience! I had put myself in his place . . . That is always a vain undertaking. You can't put anyone in anyone else's place. Each has his own. A great man, especially, has his own—his is completely unique. How could I imagine great-ness, when I'm not great? Only by magnifying myself severalfold. By magnifying a small thing, I can create something cumbersome, perhaps, but not great. There are other laws and categories here, unknown to me, never knowable. In any case, a great man is a different person. At the very least, he's not you. With a little imag-ination you can picture yourself in his place. But this will be you in a place that is someone else's, not yours; you will take an im-mediate dislike to your weary, indifferent, surfeited self and feel antipathy to the great man in advance. As though greatness were the goal of even one truly great man! When I pictured the great man, I had forgotten to take into account one trifling fact: that he is great. Not installed above me, not appointed from on high, not promoted by society like a village elder. Greatness is his essential quality. He is interested in my name precisely because my name and membership in the human race are all I have, whatever may be said of me and whatever I may think of myself. He is interested in my face and voice and gesture. He is interested in *me*. Because he knows me, and has for a long time. He doesn't need to learn about me. He can say something to me, specifically to me, because to someone else he would say something else.

My skepticism came tumbling down, covering me with the dust of my own senility. The patriarch was younger than I, and that was why he had lived so long.

The dog clacked across the floor and lay down at the patriarch's feet, spreading his green paws and oversized male pouch on the parquet. The old man gave this monster an affectionate look.

"He's old already?" I asked, with false sympathy.

"No, he's quite young," the old man replied, and then I saw

that the dog was, indeed, still quite young. Simply, the old man was so old that even his dog seemed old.

The patriarch's son said goodbye and went off to the Institute, where he seemed to be a dean. Such a nice, well-bred son, old already, with his touchingly battered black briefcase . . . The father frowned and did not watch him go.

"I can't understand the young folks today," the father said sorrowfully. "Now, where did he go? Back to work? What do they do there? What does everybody do? What the peasant does, I can understand. What the artist does, I can understand. What he does"—the patriarch pointed to the window, where a workman suspended in a cage basket was finishing painting the new palace —"I can understand that, too, though not completely. But what *they* do, the physicists, capitalists, Chinese, Fascists . . . Who are they? What do they do? What do they share? They eat, drink, go, argue, have meetings, get paid—and what do they leave behind them? You've heard about the atom bomb?" he asked in an anxious whisper, leaning toward me. (Sososian grinned with one corner of his mouth.) "Why, it's terrible! So terrible! Believe me, a man who knows was just telling me, such things they've invented now! Gas . . . Can you imagine? Killing all the people—by gas!"

It occurred to me that this old man, though we might think of him as uninformed, was again more accurate than all of us who are up to date. We're inured. The threat is so close to us, and has been for so long, and is so well known, that it's not even a threat anymore, it's a wearisome noise, preventing us, the busy people, from doing our work . . . But what are we doing? What is our work? We should wake up . . . How old he is! But still he remembers that this is the earth, that people live on it, that nothing is more beautiful than life, or more sacred, and that life must be preserved. He remembers the final (or first?) truth, the essential truth. And speaks his last simple words, not many, a few, but each of them in its most primordial, vital, and direct meaning, on a ninety-year-old pillar of life. Behind each of these last words lies a guarantee so golden—the dignity of a life spent in labor—that we cannot disbelieve them, which means these are the truest words in the world. Dear God, the very same words, repeated over and over to the point of incomprehension—and suddenly they come back to life, glide past like silver fishes into the scum-choked pond, to struggle there, alive . . .

"There's one way out, just one," the patriarch was saying. "Space!" And again his hand flew up, very high. The gesture especially captivated me because the swift flutter of the long wooden hands occurred relative to a body absolutely motionless and absent under the smock. He needn't even have spoken the word *space*, so precisely did his hand convey the concept. And now I realized something I had never understood about painting: painting is motion. Only a painter (not an actor, not a pianist) could make such a gesture at the word *space*. I see the dried painting, static on the wall, and everything in it has hardened. I think of it as depicted, but it was *painted*. Painting is the trail of a movement—that is the secret, I suspect. A wave of the hand, a trail of paint. If the painting is beautiful, then the gesture was beautiful. Rather, if the gesture is beautiful, then the painting will be beautiful. Painting is motion, I thought.

"Space," the patriarch was saying (a wave of the hand, a trail of paint). "The earth has become so small. No, I'm not speaking figuratively. This is actually, physically true. In my lifetime the earth has grown several sizes smaller. This may be caused by overpopulation, or communications. Radio and what have you. Airplanes, rockets . . . It's tiny, our earth. This is a signal, this shrinkage. We just have to interpret it. The earth used to be huge, difficult, forbidding—now I sometimes think it would fit in my courtyard . . . With the earth shrinking so, how can we fail to see that this is a summons to space! The earth is just a launching pad. The cosmos—that's the future of mankind. Space . . ." A wave, an upward flight, a dab. "It's man's destiny! We must all understand this, here and now. Space is very, very difficult to conquer! And unless we all unite for this goal, nothing will come of it. We'll perish. Everything that has happened is pre-history; we have lived our few thousand years in order to face this task. This, after all, has been the goal of humanity—space! Don't forget," he said, seeing Sososian stand up (he had managed to whisper to me that it was time we left, or else the old man would tire himself out with his talk), "don't forget, then, I'll think of you as my missionaries." He smiled apologetically. "Explain to everyone that our goal is space! This is our divine destiny."

. . . We walked for some time in silence. Sososian irritated me; I wanted to be alone with my thoughts, which had been so strangely stirred. Besides, I was afraid Sososian would start snickering at the old man to show that he was far too sophisticated to be moved by this chatter about peace and the cosmos.

I flinched when he opened his mouth, but this is what he said: "Oh, what would become of us if he weren't there? I can't imagine. It would be as if we didn't exist."

THE END (THE BELL)

Day has begun to dawn. I am straining toward my goal, after almost losing sight of it. By now, my only goal is to finish. Toward morning my typewriter pounds like my heart, and in rhythm with it. More and more briskly and inaccurately, irregularly. It pings when it bumps into the end of the line.

Essay, *aknark*, hint . . .

The essay has been hinted at, essayed.

O Lord, holdest Thou my right hand?

I have tried. I've attempted to be honest, I've attempted to be accurate. And I no longer have the strength to try to be understandable as well. I risk being misunderstood by both Russians and Armenians. Who am I, to take it upon myself to do all this talking? Why, nobody. But nobody speaks for me, either. I risk being misunderstood, my address is ambiguous and imprecise. My material may seem interesting to a Russian, since he knows Armenia as poorly as I do, or even worse; I'll get by with my ignorance and the naïveté of a first view. But my emotion—it is riper in me—may be easier for Armenians to understand than for Russians . . .

I know Armenia very little, and I don't claim to know it. Hence the form of my book: elementary-school lessons, a primer of sorts. The only picture I could create with any objectivity or accuracy was a picture of my own emotion. I would call my essay "Armenian Illusions," if I hadn't already given it a different title and structure. I have painted, with love and idealism, a country foreign to me, and yet I love not Armenia but Russia—"my reason cannot conquer this strange love."

I do know my own homeland, at least to the extent that I was born there and have lived there as long as I've lived in this world. How could I know any other country better? In point of fact, this Armenia of mine was written about Russia. Because what comparison does the traveler make, what does he marvel at? He compares with his homeland, he marvels at the dissimilarity: the things he doesn't have, the things he lacks, the things he has but not enough of, not enough. Only after this does he marvel at the things that are the same, that are similar.

But what a debt I owe to Armenia! And if I have returned even a drop of the love (though not the hospitality—of course not!) that Armenia so insistently taught me, namely, the love of my homeland, then I have fulfilled at least my first, though not my final, task. At any rate, if I should be born anew, born an Armenian on your soil, I would love you madly, my homeland . . . In some ways, that would be easier than our "strange" Russian love.

"I have promised myself," my friend told me once, "that I will never say anything, either bad or good, about any other nation."

And how strongly I agreed with you!

And nevertheless—I sin, I sin . . .

But I've tried to be accurate. The only accuracy I can claim is that everything did happen to me in this way. And in this very sequence. Even when editing I didn't rearrange things in time, relative to my actual stay in Armenia. Or rather, no such editing was required. Events gathered momentum in just this way and this sequence: at first I didn't like Erevan very much (if not for my friend, I wouldn't have liked it at all), then my strongest physical impression was Sevan (I got sick), my strongest spiritual impression Geghard; just after Geghard I listened to the lecture on progressive city planning, just before I left I visited the patriarch, and after that visit it was already time to return home. Suddenly, events acquired their finished state.

They could have been even more finished. Had I lingered for a day, I would have gone to Byurakan, where I would have visited an observatory for the first time in my life. Then I would have been indebted to Armenia for the stars as well. How neatly that would fit here, right after the patriarch and his farewell words sending us into the cosmos! My narrative would overcome the earth's gravity. The last cosmic chord would long resound in the reader's ears, even after he had closed this primer and laid it aside. And he would long gaze after my rocket . . .

There are a great many things I didn't have time to see in Armenia. What can you manage in ten days? I didn't visit the laboratories and institutes, didn't get to the pastures and vineyards, the factories and mills, famous throughout the Union. For that matter, I didn't even get to do any tasting in the cellars of the great

Ararat Trust! Many of the things Armenia takes pride in, I didn't see. The distance between my notes and an encyclopedic essay is vast. For an encyclopedic essay, however, it's just as far to my notes! The truth and harmony of a first impression are given to a man once in his lifetime. This is wealth that can and should be shared, because beyond the first impression lies such a sea of knowledge that you can sail away and lose sight of all shores . . .

I have lived in this book far longer than I did in Armenia, and that is the book's subject. I spent ten days in Armenia and have been writing it for over a year—I have lived nearly two years in Armenia.

Each day added so much to me that I needed a month to describe it. From whom could I have borrowed that much time?

Yes, if I had lingered in Armenia even one more day, you would now be reading an "Astronomy Lesson"! But life dictated its own accuracy. That's just the point, life has but one accuracy—the accuracy that happens. All else is inaccuracy.

I cut my last class and missed astronomy.

I came home from school an hour early and found people who perhaps had been planning to leave the house at that very moment. Had I come home an hour later, I wouldn't have caught them. And this event has an accuracy of its own.

VIGNETTE

And how did I ever get so homesick in those few days? As if I'd been gone a century . . . I remember meeting Rogozhin on Arbat Street, but after that, nothing . . .

I woke up and thought I was in Armenia. But when I looked it was some strange shed, I was wearing my clothes and my shoes, and instead of a clean and careful bed prepared by the hands of my friend's wife or her sister, I was lying on a cot under a prison blanket. I looked out the window: a little meadow, birches—I was home! Thank God! The only place you can get properly drunk is your homeland—that was my first and fully patriotic thought.

I took off my shoes and went wandering on the wet grass—so fresh—what happiness! My headache eased a little. Who could have thought that even your heels were connected to your head? I discovered my friends, two at once, asleep in another shed, but Rogozhin wasn't with them. Their names were Goncharov and

Chudakov. "How did you get here?" "How did *you* get here?" they replied.

And from out of nowhere—Rogozhin. Good man. Explained everything. We weren't just anywhere, this was his country place. We had slept in the sheds, he in the house with his wife and baby daughter. Now we scrounged in our pockets: a kopeck here, a kopeck there, and we had a ruble. Rogozhin collected some returnable bottles. Chudakov being the youngest, we loaded him up and put him on a bicycle. He rode crookedly out the gate to the highway and was gone, I thought, forever.

I caught sight of Rogozhin's wife—she had come out on the porch, her daughter in her arms. I was glad to see her, and started smiling and waving.

"I don't even want to look at you!" she told me, but she gave me a whole pot of cabbage soup. Cabbage soup, as sober as yesterday, is the only possible food in the morning.

Now, luckily, Chudakov came wobbling back on his bicycle. True, he'd smashed the headlight. But he himself was unhurt—and so were the bottles.

Who needed a headlight, anyway? It was daytime.

There we sat, the four of us—such a fine morning!—drinking fortified rosé and eating cabbage soup right out of the pot, from the ladle. Little by little the conversation got going. Armenia was an ache in my heart. I looked at my friends and wept with love.

"Where are the Russians, indeed! Then who are we? Here we are!"

And really, who sat before me? Goncharov, Chudakov, and Rogozhin. So very Russian, couldn't be more so. Their hair a light brown, uncombed. Their eyes all a matching blue, slightly red from hangover, like rabbit eyes. Snub noses. Stubbly red beards. Such handsome men—not dark. Blond. And they all had the faces of children. Suddenly I was struck with wonder by a forgotten word: adolescent! These were adolescents! One was past thirty, one past forty, but all had adolescent faces, utterly untouched. Untempered by manly experience. Even the stubbly beards looked like first fuzz.

"We're adolescent boys!" I shouted. "Russia has no men. Never did have. Only invaders. Mad-dog knights and Varangians and filthy Frenchmen! We still had patriarchs, but they're gone. Now we have old men. It used to be boys and patriarchs—now it's boys and old men. *That's* the problem!"

They looked into each other's faces, as if into mirrors.
"Why, it's true!" they said.
Rogozhin took up his guitar.

> *Russia is lost*
> *Among tribes of the plains.*
> *And men walk that road,*
> *Men in chains.*

There was nothing left of me—just happiness! I was the one "in chains," I would "slit someone's throat," though I was "pure in heart" . . . I shed tears in the cabbage soup.
Or:

> *My chamber is bright*
> *With the evening star . . .*

Such a fabulous language this damp earth has brought forth! The Russian man—he's right there in the language. Completely revealed in the language. Words are a great comfort, and a great misfortune. You listen to a song, to words of genius, and you grow, you expand, the genius is yours now, as if the great words were coming from you. You are great—truly great! The song breaks off—you plop to the ground. Dull, stupid, slack-jawed. How about a drink?
Is there any language like it! This *language* is our homeland. What stupid questions.

> *Splendidly pure, she keeps silence,*
> *The garden's young mistress:*
> *Only the song needs beauty,*
> *Beauty has no need of songs.*

How beautifully Rogozhin sings today!
"Hogwash!" I shout. "Who cares whether we exist or not! We'll always come back!" I shout. "They just don't have any more history. But we still do have history!"
That morning is vivid to me even now. On my lap I have a pot of cabbage soup, my tears are dripping into the soup. Three fair-haired adolescent boys sit before me. Outside the window is a

little meadow with birch trees, very white, very tall, the sky above them is high as can be, and the patriarchal church on the hill sparkles in the sun's early rays "like decorated gingerbread" . . . Words of genius—and their genius audience.

The word is my homeland.

After Class

———

RECESS

I wrote it all. I even drew a vignette at the end, in the form of a first Russian impression. We had arrived, as it were. *Finis*, I thought. Not so. Here's where it all begins.

I had to strike out my "vignette."

But that was the way it happened! The minute I landed I found myself in their embrace, we got gloriously drunk, and we talked in our native language at last. And I still agree with my own exclamation about our Russian homeland, the word. Yet I shouldn't have drawn that vignette. I shouldn't have gotten involved!

It would have been wrong to say nothing about my return, but saying too little proved still worse, and if more needs to be said, how much more? And why just that much? You can't write it all. And if you did, how would it be relevant to Armenia?

All at once I needed to qualify even that little scene, then amplify the qualification, and add another scene to explain the amplification. Retouch, supplement, amplify. And again explain, qualify, justify. Like a mad tea party: "Another cup of tea?" "I don't care for any more." "Oh, you want less?" "No." "So you want more?"

Then suddenly, all at once, my eye couldn't take it in, my mind couldn't grasp it, there was such a lot . . . What should I begin with? This? That? But why that?

Too little is bad, but a lot is even less.

Muteness sets in. This is my homeland . . .

Even to describe events merely as they happened, merely in

time's natural sequence, proved impossible on my native soil. And wrong. Almost a lie. As if everything you saw here and now were a random and meaningless chain. As though perhaps none of these visible things existed, and yet something did exist, primary and remote, not visible, and you had to *catch sight* of it. And when you did, it would be the truth, you had only to write it! Homeland. Muteness.

I had been too intoxicated with the natural accuracy and logic of the way my impressions built up in Armenia; I had been too convinced of my method. All you had to do, it seemed, was to keep going, day after day, on the momentum of your accumulated emotion and thought, just keep from losing altitude, and you would climb ever higher and higher, and your graceful trail, nowhere bending or breaking, would lose itself in the clouds . . . But no, here was a stop and a precipice. At the edge of the precipice stood my ancestral home. This was no longer a journey in which the integrity and accuracy of the scenes were bound up with ephemerality, and the insight with ignorance . . . Your very life moves right in close—and you can see nothing. Like it or not, you must look into life's familiar and eternal, hateful and beloved face. The view from the window will not shift, your name will not change, you will always have the same mother and father, who will call you by your name, and your years on this earth will be added to, not diminished. There is a different logic here, a different method, a different flow of speech. In motion, where would fantasy come from? You have impressions. But as soon as you pause and stand in your own courtyard for a moment, your imagination goes to work. For what can be more fantastic than the everyday, or more banal than new impressions? At home there is another dimension of love and pain, another dimension of knowledge, and how can you reveal what your land is, your house, your language—what you are—in ephemeral little scenes? Here you falter, words fail you, and you begin to stammer, your head turning in dumb, bovine torment, your eyes red and meek with love. You come up against a fence. Homeland. Muteness.

But perhaps my fortunate, easy method was inaccurate when applied to Armenia, too, if it's inaccurate when applied to my homeland? I was in Armenia ten days—and wrote a book. In the ten thousand days of my sojourn in Russia, I've written nothing of the sort.

But here I'm attempting too much, a 101 percent accuracy, so to speak. I'm not an Armenian, to experience *his* muteness. That's my first qualifying remark. There are multitudes of them.

Here is another . . .

THE NEW BOOK

Living prose breaks through your personal time and anticipates your experience in many ways. Not only is the new book your life while you're writing it, not only is it the previous life experience that's included in it, but it's also your fate, your future. If you were merely narrating for the reader, it would be sheer boredom, and when you're bored, what can you write? The fact is that if a man writes, he himself comes to know things he didn't know before. Writing is his method of cognition. Geniuses, perhaps, come to know things that no one knew before them. Others rediscover: for themselves, for people like them, for their time. Strictly speaking, a man gives the world nothing new. When he suddenly discovers that there are things in this world he didn't know before, he believes they're new . . . but if he has found them, they already existed. He just didn't know it. New and old do not exist in the world, because everything in it is *now*.

And so, having written a book, the author inevitably ends up in a discovered world. In the process of writing, while he's still discovering this world, he thinks it's the product of his authorial will, insight, and fantasy, of his personality, rather than a real likeness of the legitimate world. This illusion is called inspiration and exists so that the book will get written. But as soon as the finishing touch is put on, as soon as the door is opened, the author finds himself in the very world he has described (if he's really an author, and if it's a real book).

At first he finds this flattering. Then he is overwhelmed by the universality and prevalence of his "discovered" laws; he must learn to live by these laws in his discovered, once so secret world. Romance ends and fear begins. He finds himself surrounded and blockaded by the creations of his own mind. He has known all along that some of his phenomena, events, and heroes existed in this world, and he is impressed that they proliferated dreadfully while he was writing. But he is shocked to find that the others, the ones he fabricated, also exist in reality. He will have to see for himself that this is true, he must begin to suspect that it was true all along, because otherwise he may lapse into mysticism. And when the author has made the acquaintance of everyone he created, when events that occurred only in his book and not in his life have begun to happen to him, he will cast about in search of an exit—and that will be his new book.

(Thank goodness I noticed this a long time ago. I have tried not to resort unnecessarily to acute turns of plot: imprisonment, war, the death of loved ones, and other literary murders.)

Something similar happened even with this book. In Armenia I lived almost exclusively in the present—neither recalling the past nor peering into the future—for ten days, and they proved to be a lot, because at home we rarely succeed in living for the moment. Insolently I saddled those ten days and drove them straight ahead like an eternity. At first I didn't want to dismount; later I couldn't. A whole world of scenes and problems opened up to me. In the beginning it was rather remote from my personal torment, and I could enjoy immersing myself in it, literally, as in a bath. I saw Armenia as an example of an authentically national existence, I became imbued with concepts of homeland and clan, tradition and heritage. (They would sustain me for some time.) I discovered with pain that these concepts are often forgotten in Russia, and that I must dedicate myself to reminding people. I raced along, I looked ahead with great expectation . . .

> Bored with posing as a Melmoth
> And sporting various other masks,
> He awoke one day a patriot
> In a dull and rainy season.

And just as I came to the end of the book, rubbing my hands in satisfaction; just as I was finishing the last chapter, namely, the passage where the patriarch says "Where are the Russians?" (curiously enough, this was on Christmas Eve)—I heard a knock on the door. In walked a Russian, my Moscow acquaintance S., and straightaway asked whether I was Russian. Somewhat taken aback at seeing my images materialize so literally, I managed to answer yes. He shook his head doubtfully: "But why?" "What do you mean, why?" I asked in surprise. "Why are you Russian?" "By blood," I answered, with rising anger. My reply, I must say, startled S. "By blood . . . Unbelievable! No one's ever answered me that way." "What have you been doing, asking everybody?" "They all say the birches, the language, the homeland," he said.

Two days later I found myself surrounded by a crowd of people interested in problems of nationality, perhaps because I had begun to notice such people as a result of writing this book, or perhaps because S. had told them about me . . . That is, it turned out I had opened a door into a world settled ages and ages ago. Somewhat shocked that the world I had thought of as so much "my own" belonged to everyone, and suffering some disappointment over my loss of precedence, I began to acquaint myself with the aborigines of that world, at first simply by shaking hands . . .

Many too many hands!

But stop! I don't have time for this here. Again, I must say either too much or nothing. I had better conclude the series for now. I had better postpone, promise. Without fail, later, separately . . . No, I can't follow the facts straightforwardly anymore—I must either ignore or interpret them. And to interpret them will take a lifetime. Muteness is guaranteed.

Moreover, what with all these encounters, people, conversations, and facts, the whole particular world into which I was inevitably plunged after writing about Armenia has now expanded so greatly, has so obscured Armenia, has so totally destroyed my expectations, and has accumulated so painful a burden of experience, that I can cope with it all only in a new book.

1967–69

CHOOSING
A LOCATION
Georgian Album

I traveled by post-chaise from Tiflis. My entire baggage consisted of one small suitcase, which was half stuffed with travel notes on Georgia. Most of them, happily for you, were lost, while the suitcase and the rest of my belongings, happily for me, survived intact.

LERMONTOV

The Phenomenon

of the Norm

When you try to prove that something is something,
you lose it completely.

The plot of a book possesses the peculiarity that it must be concluded. Having entered into it, you cannot exit via some other
labyrinth. Do a thing once, and you've gained experience; gain
experience, and it immediately proves unusable, but you'll be
drafted as a witness, if not as a specialist: "You were there when
Ivanov died? Well, Sidorov isn't feeling good." In this sense, to
specialize is to submit to the first opportunity: you no sooner say
"one" than you're required to count to three.

The decision is no sooner made than everything falls into
place . . .

I had no sooner admired the new Georgian cinema, no sooner
attempted to analyze the sources of such success, if only in one
example, than my analysis struck me as too limited. I jettisoned
almost all of it. I would have to start over, in order to check and
make sure I was right.

The chance to do so arose suddenly and of its own accord. I
availed myself of a tempting invitation to go to Georgia to "choose
a location." In shooting a film, there is no happier time than the
choice of the natural setting! The anxieties of launching the production are behind you, the bitterness of defeat is yet to come. You
enjoy the rights of a man for whom there is every expectation of
success. Ahead, you have only prospects like the view unfolding

from the window of the truck. The windshield is a scene from the film. (Yet another farcical film, unfolding against such a marvelous background!—the memory of the high emotion you began with . . .)

"You shall see the Georgia I have here!" My friend thumps his chest, enticing me to come. So he's inviting me to look into his heart—this is too much. You win, you win.

All right, I'll come.

In excuse for the randomness of these notes, it may be said not only that they were lost (but along with my suitcase), not only that they hadn't even been written, but also that they couldn't have been written. Here are my recollections . . .

. . . I was ready to part with life. The reason no longer mattered to me. Its intolerability had still been life, and I had not been ready. Now the intolerability, too, was gone. I had no illusion. Time had sifted through my fingers, and out of the whole thirty-three years, with the possible exception of infancy, this was what I had left in my hand . . . The sand grains were silent. I kept trying to pick open these condensed knots of silence—I supposed it my mission. A duel of this sort may even have appealed to me, and for the very reason that it was doomed. Of all the functions of language, what fascinated me was to conquer the truth. I thought I might not return. I kept returning from those ravines—lacerated, but without having entered them. For, stronger than the fear of death (I thought I no longer feared it), stronger than the thirst for truth (I thought I thirsted for it), was my fear of falling silent. No, I didn't want to understand! I didn't want to die.

In Georgia I wrote about Russia, in Russia about Georgia . . . To reevoke my intoxication with springtime in the Georgian town of Signakhi, I gazed at a crooked Finnish birch frozen into the swamp of my native Toksovo; to relieve my homesickness for that same swamp in Toksovo, I tramped alpine meadows. The seasons and locales and descriptions became confused and conflated in my mind, obliterating reality . . . The village of Goluzino in the Kostroma region, or the Moscow suburb of Golitsyno—why did I have to be overwhelmed with visions of Tbilisi in these places, only to write about the Leningrad Zoo when I found myself at last in Tbilisi? I don't know. But for the same reason, in Georgia's legendary Vardzia I dreamed about the birds of the Kurisches in Lithuania . . .

The traveler's empire is another planet. A different sun illumines the parent state and the province. The dual sun blinded me in either direction; I cast two shadows. And whenever I finally blinked away this blindness and corruption, I submitted. The happiness of conformity possessed me for a moment, while I renounced my own sense of homeland and abandoned myself to that of another people. Spy and invader! I wanted to carry home with me something they still had: the sense of belonging to oneself. No such luck! Only from there could I see my home, only from there could I feel that I was in it. At home I began to pine because I had lost this feeling. In truth, only in Russia can one feel homesick without leaving one's country. A great advantage!

Having invaded, I kept finding myself trapped. This traditional Russian capacity to be penetrated by an alien way of life (Pushkin, Lermontov, Tolstoy . . .) proved Russian, came full circle . . . With what military sub-unit can A *Captive of the Caucasus* or *Hadji Murad* be equated? The essential thing is impeccability of artistic form—to carry on the standard . . . It's hard to claim that they wrote badly. We can write something down, no matter what our topic . . . but strength of spirit cannot be borrowed from a neighbor: the spirit fills with strength only on its own soil, poor though that soil may be.

I didn't want to understand. I wanted to seize. Anything added to someone's fame (even by me), any recognition (however well deserved!) from an outsider, is a portent of the end. An invasion and appropriation. For some reason, love is acknowledged to have an incontestable right. But, in fact, the person we love should be asked whether he needs this, whether he is flattered by our unrequited right to him . . . The rights of the loved one are neglected. He is a victim of our passion.

Then again, there's no need to exaggerate. No one asks *us*. Not even our parents ask us. Midwives, in some sense, bring a man closer to death, which is the norm of life. Its normal absurdity.

The word *norm* has been spoken. I will take advantage of it to say something about the norm. The norm that is as beautiful, desired, and long awaited as water and air—air and water being in short supply.

In my childhood, I remember, this was a normal word, almost slang, almost from backwardness and poverty of vocabulary, but whatever the reason, this was the word: "a normal fellow," "a normal movie"—with an exclamation mark, as the superlative degree. The "normal" was surrounded by the "not normal," which was expressed with more variety: "He's a crank. Not normal. Backward." Or, "Lies, foolishness." In short, "To hell with him!" It is common knowledge that children, like dogs, have an aversion to abnormality—to freaks, drunks, fakes. In this they are categorical and severe. Their sense of the norm is keen. Devoid of humanism.

After the "bread norm," in a less hungry time, the popular meaning of *norm* became more condescending: normal in the sense of "not bad, but nothing special either." Still later, nearer to the present, it was even disdainful: in the sense of "merely," in the sense of "and nothing more." As though we ourselves were indisputably above normal. As though we had surpassed the norm and were accustomed to turn our gaze only upon the truly exceptional . . .

That is how the word developed, at least around me, along with me. Until there came a day, just recently, when I saw in the word *norm* a glimmer of possibility that it could almost regain its former, childhood life.

You're always rushing somewhere, it seems. Always rushing, rushing, always somewhere and somewhere. Onward and upward. Suddenly you're gasping for breath, you're either going to drop with fatigue or grow old running. Look around: does anything still comfortably serve its intended purpose? Yes. And no: things are somehow askew, slapdash, done on the fly, not quite finished, not even quite begun . . .

Here's an image for you: a beautiful capital lying around without a column—as if the Coliseum and the Parthenon were being created directly as ruins, bypassing their intended purpose. The seductive economy of abbreviating the technological process—and right away the product: *nothing*. Worse and worse: the macaroni factory accidentally turns out matches, the caramel factory cigarettes . . . Sit down for a moment, please. Light up. Think: while you're running so fast that you already view the "norm" as something lower than "our" (your, my) norm (nowadays, instead of *norm*, the word is *level*: a thing elusively in the vanguard, always fleeing frontally, a thing to be overtaken and achieved—a category instead of a reality)—while we're racing along like this, will much remain when we're gone?

How to arrange it . . . so that the chair can be sat in, the window seen through, the train ridden, the bread eaten, the water drunk, the air breathed, the word spoken . . . So that objects have names and functions that correspond to them, and do not cease to be what they're meant to be—like meeting place, observation slit, means of transportation, food product, culture park, and recreation area . . . Social norms.

But one day, on hearing through the din of my frenzied activity the music of Mozart, how astonished I was, as I listened and judged, to find that I felt satisfied with everything, at last. It was a long time since I had felt satisfied with everything. Not that I hadn't heard any good music . . . But somehow it had all been limited, now in one way, now in another; it had no fullness. But this music did. And not because it was better than the rest in any one respect— the way something is always better than something, progressing posthaste—but because it was whole. It was complete, everything in it was *correct, everything* corresponded, everything was *normal*. There was neither limitation nor error. This was the *divine norm*. The same norm as in nature—the Norm of *Creation*.

"God grant I shall not lose my mind . . ." What constitutes normality in this world is quite unclear. Ideally, it would seem to be a total correspondence, an involvement with us personally. Because if a thing is capable of corresponding to us, this is evidence, first and foremost, of our norm. Here we discover how unsure we are of this—of our own norm—we don't know where it lies. We're holding on with our last strength, keeping up appearances. I'm not talking about those who have so much self-confidence that life belongs to them. I'm not talking about the obtuse norm, the nor- mality of insensitivity. I mean the norm of feeling—the higher, palpitating norm, the delicate balance, the pause in flight, when the joy of life is not yet lost, and at the same time you are capable of losing it at any moment, but you go on living and living in this unstable and dynamic equilibrium. The form of feeling in which you almost lose your senses. Happiness.

Recollection

of Haghartsin

(in Anticipation of Zedazeni)

——————

Beyond Pushkin Pass, where the biblical landscape of Armenia begins to give way to the warm, moist breath of Georgia, and everything so smoothly and swiftly becomes different—the lines of the mountains, the crowns of the trees, the fruitfulness of the fields, the color of the grasses, the murmur of little rivers—we turned off the highway into closing depths of verdure.* Along a narrower road, we drove for some time up a little ravine, deeper and deeper into the moist twilight of the forest. On the right, a cliff hung over us, exposing fine yellowish-green layers; on the left, a thick, leafy forest dropped steeply downward, and at the bottom of it a stream tinkled, silvery as a fish. By now the foliage was so dense it was

* I suppose I must have thought of Pushkin (both when traveling and when writing). But in setting my style I did not make a point of looking into Pushkin, did not refresh my memory. And what was my surprise when I stumbled across a half-forgotten text!

I began to ascend Bezobdal, the mountain dividing Georgia from ancient Armenia. The wide road, shaded by trees, twists around the mountain . . . There appeared before me new mountains, a new horizon; stretching below me were lush green fields. I glanced once more at scorched Georgia and began to descend the gentle mountain slope to the fresh plains of Armenia. With indescribable pleasure I noticed that the sultry heat had suddenly diminished, the climate was already different.

Journey to Arzrum

Everything the same—but exactly reversed. A negative and a positive. Pushkin's, we must assume, was the positive.

hardly green. The scent rising from the bottom of the ravine—water, cliffs, and leaves—cheered the soul. With difficulty, a ray of sunlight broke through the overarching trees and flickered on the road.

The car stopped before a small footbridge over a dry tributary. The bridge was half dismantled. We got out. The tributary parted the forest, and as we crossed the bridge we could see the bottom of our ravine through the missing planks. White water seethed over the rusty frame of a wrecked car.

The road grew still narrower, becoming a path, and went more and more steeply uphill and to the right. For some time we climbed single file in this steep green corridor. The trees lost their lushness (showing the effects of altitude) and changed to shrubs, they opened up the sky overhead, they alternated with cliff and gave way to cliff.

We had only sky above us now, but for some reason the vista was narrowing rather than widening, constricted by the fortress line of the crag to which the path was leading us, and the sky was just a bright little patch. I was in a hurry to surmount this rise and see over the cliff. Our excursion had a pleasant frivolity and unconstraint, as though crawling up the mountain were not obligatory or difficult for us, and my northern heart was gladdened by the freshness of living nature, green at last, and not scorching; it was easy to breathe, and I felt like someone in an engraving, in a cloak and broad-brimmed hat, with a tall alpine walking stick, as though I were a whole century younger than my real self.

Still in my broad-brimmed hat, I crested the slope at last and found myself on a small bluff, from which was revealed to me, with some suddenness, the goal of our excursion. This was a monastery. It rose up on the path to meet me, like a man coming around a bend.

Small, modest, cozy—nothing majestic or oppressive. It had a lived-in look. And if it blocked my path with the suddenness of a live creature, as though the curiosity were its and not ours, the creature was benevolent. There was nothing special about it, to make it worth such a climb, but neither was there anything to disappoint us. I looked back and smiled at my hastening companions; except for them, I saw nothing below. The cliff, the path, the monastery wall . . . This peaceful village didn't even have a view.

There was indeed a village here. The monastery had not functioned for a long time, of course; the family of watchmen, made gracious by peace and health, had established themselves here with a cow, a calf, sheep, bees, a grandmother, and children. These people and their bashful smiles were redolent of something warm and milky, fresh from the cow.

We visited the refectory, which they showed us with what seemed to be greater liking and special good humor: "Now here's where they had their meals . . ." This was surprising and understandable. We lighted our faint candle in the chapel and lingered aimlessly in the dusty twilight of a small church, which had gathered the monastery outbuildings around it like a brood hen. The watchman's family stood apart, a bit shy in our presence. Everything here was very scrupulous, plain, and so tranquil—there was nothing to excite us, and we felt sleepy. After all, it had been rather a long climb, compared to how fast everything had appeared before us, been toured, and in fact was over. Stretching and limbering up as after a nap, we walked out of the church and took a few last untrodden steps along a narrow passage between the church and chapel . . . This short lane immediately ended, bringing us to a small glade or yard. A spreading hollow tree took up almost all of it. Under the tree a bench and a small table had been set into the ground. The tree blocked our view—we wanted to look and see what was there, beyond the yard. We walked around the tree and . . .

O God! We were *found*.

Again I can think of no other verb. We were found. But no, nothing supernatural. We found ourselves in the place where we had lived our whole lives, where *we*, and no one else in our stead, had lived. We found ourselves in the world we lived in. But this whole world, all of it, was placed within our view, as if we had just arrived in it, as if we had appeared from out of the blue. Had flown here, had been exiled . . . As though we had just been led here by the hand and told, "Be fruitful and multiply."

Abashed, I lowered my eyes. I dug at a pebble with the toe of my shoe. The pebble started to roll, drawing its brother after it . . . Only by watching it go was I able gradually to raise my eyes again. The world flowed out from under my feet like a little brook, a stream . . . It widened as fast as if it were flying . . . A river—a sea—an element . . .

This world of deep blue-gray was not yet peopled. Neither roof nor smoke, as far as the eye could see. Or could not see—everything was so distant and unending. I was standing at the throat of a funnel.

It was narrow here. The gates of the ravine came right up close, drawing together directly behind me. But ahead the ravine widened, awoke, stretched, came to life, lived, bloomed, expanded, unfolded, and flowed as from the horn of plenty. In its shape, in its flare and curve, the whole valley spreading out below me seemed to resemble that horn. As though the horn had been dropped on the ground, and its upper arc had become transparent, like the sky. I had been put into the very bottom of the horn, and spilling out from under me were all the riches that filled my view.

The earth was gentle, fruitful, calm. Beyond the azure alpine meadow rose huge blue spruces; a white brook or river parted them, drove them on, pressing now from the left, now from the right, as if herding this spruce flock downhill: the bleak forest became rounded and lush, spilling into a gently rippling leafy sea. At the very bottom lay the deep, sapphire basin of the valley, quiet and massive, and beyond it, just as slowly discovered, stood the mountains. My heart thudded sweetly, following the curve of my gaze as I tracked the world flowing forth from my lookout point and returned through the thoughtless sky, back to myself. I could not see myself. And then, with surprise, I looked at my hand to make sure. A hand. It had not yet touched this world. It had done nothing in this world. It had not yet known work. My hand wiggled its fingers like a baby, staring at the world that lay in store for it.

As if I had been brought here, led here by the hand . . . I looked, exclaimed—but when I remembered and glanced back, He was already gone. Only my empty hand still preserved the touch of Him who had led us. My hand was empty.

. . . In my lifetime I had seen several churches that struck my imagination. Imagination in the ancient meaning of the word, when it had not been divorced from reality and still represented speed of ideation. Not fantasy, but the formation of images. The image of a church would appear before me.

This sight had always put me in my place, so to speak; that is, I shed whatever I had ascribed to myself in vanity. This effect was not lasting. I could not prolong the mood when the church was out of sight. Such a church was always located in the background, an organic part of nature, and not blocked from view by man and his handiwork. By now I understood that the choice of a location for a church was almost its main architectural idea. Just as, in the infinity of the taiga, you will suddenly encounter a small gray

triangle—a triangulation point, the site of a topographical survey
—so a church, built uniquely and correctly *there*, had always struck
me as a sort of witness point for man, not on the earth's surface
this time, but in the universe. It would, if he lifted his eyes from
his daily bread, remind man where he was. The churches were
majestic and grand. They oppressed or disconcerted the soul, opened
it up or exalted it, showing it now a place below God, now near
God. The builder was fully embodied in his creation, in a way that
no secular architect has ever managed. There were different approaches a builder could take in erecting his church: God and I, I
and God, God alone . . . But never had I encountered a church
so subordinated to the idea of dissolving in Creation. A church so
absent. As calmly, as inconspicuously as possible . . . in a whisper
. . . the builder led his lines away from our eye, led our eye away,
so that we would not see the church—no, this is a trivial human
affair, a building. So that where the church stood, where we lived,
we would see God's face reflected in His own creation. For what
better reflected it?

Think of it—such care had been taken, just for me! So that I
walked uphill for a long time, on an artfully chosen path; so that
the view was more and more curtailed, and my soothed eye saw
less and less; so that I reached my goal just where the vista was
completely cut off; so that the buildings, while neither irritating nor
captivating my eye, continued to hide the distance; so that nowhere,
looking back, was I able to see more than I had just seen; so that
my attention and expectation were lulled, and I was led by the hand,
like a little child, to exactly the place from which . . . at exactly
the time when.

A man's place can be shown (taught) to him only by one who
himself knows his own place. There was not, could not have been,
a more brilliant architectural idea than to entrust to the Creator
himself the erection of the temple . . .

So I stood clenching and unclenching my hand, as if it were
covered with resin, and I could not comprehend that which had
been familiar to me since my first breath: my world.

Lord! Here it is . . .

No, not in the church, *this* was where I could fall on my knees.
I didn't make that gesture, didn't make a display to anyone . . . but
even so, I was on my knees at this moment—exalted and meek,
humbled and grateful.

I had no words. They were gone without a trace.

Here we had to learn language anew, generate it, barely unstick our lips—with the same effort, full of courage, with which I had dared to open my eyes—and pronounce a first word, one word, to name what we saw: *world*. And then along the syllables, in the toddling steps of the primer, clinging to the edges of the page: This . . . is . . . the . . . world. The whole world. This is all. All is before me. The world is all. The world opened before me. I stopped on the threshold. Stood still in the doorway. The gateway to the world. Gates of the world. I stand on the threshold. It is I who stand here. It is I.

The Last Bear

*On April 8, 1944, Hero of the Soviet Union Lieuten-
ant Lapshin and his rifle platoon, in a sudden attack
from two sides, took the bridge in the zoo, killing 30
Nazis and capturing 195. This decided the outcome
of the battle for the zoo.*

*Inscription on a monument
at the Kaliningrad Zoo*

I live God knows where. Occasionally I return home. My little
daughter reddens and says obliquely, "Remember, Papa? Last time
you came, you said we'd . . . go . . . *somewhere?*" That's it, that's
the whole point—which words she speaks loudly and which softly.
It makes me feel bad that she knows, already knows from experience,
that once again we will not go. "Somewhere" (which is whispered)
means, I remember, *to a castle.* A castle-in-general.

Suddenly, decisively, with the ruined dignity of a man who
has known success and lost it, I stand up and say, "Let's go." This
is hardly less humiliating than to say again, "Next time." I say "Let's
go," and hate myself—but she believes me. She knows much more,
however, than is generally assumed (for the comfort of grownups)
to be known by children, as it were, of her age, as it were. She is
not horrified by this; I am. She seems satisfied by my consent, taking
it exactly as intended—with no romantic "scarlet sails."

We go. We walk out, and now we discover that it's a beautiful
day. So sudden—it has the taste of some other life that is passing
you by, the remorse and intolerability of a yesterday that has already

happened to you . . . The lid has been lifted from our narrow courtyard, and we smile at the sky, smile inwardly, like corpses. Even the vicious old yard-ladies are like watered flowers behind their washed windows. Someone forgets caution and suddenly greets me, dooming us both to the necessity of greeting each other from now on.

But it's time to cross the courtyard and get down to business.

So I walk out, squinting shyly, holding her sweaty, obedient little hand in mine, unsure that this is me walking out, that these are my footsteps and my daughter, that I wasn't captured in advance on all that film I watched in the interminable class periods back in school . . . Think of it—experiencing the world, day in and day out, just to be reduced to such unreality! The weather stretches out around me—it alone is reality—such a beautiful day. Let's leave individuality for cloudy days. As Edik K., of fond memory, once remarked, "Would I drink, if I could order up a half hour of sunshine instead?"

"The weather's so nice," I say wickedly, "let's go to a castle another time." It is not despair, not resentment when my daughter complies, but resignation, a knowledge of life: no matter what, we won't go. She hasn't lived long enough to appreciate good weather.

We go neither to a castle nor to the circus. We go to the zoo. Old devil that I am . . .

After the trampled bare areas before and after the turnstile (servicemen and schoolchildren, 10 kopecks), after the plywood fairyland of ticket offices, signboards with maps and rules, ice-cream vendors' carts, and mobile eighteenth-century laboratory contrivances for making carbonated soft drinks, you naturally expect plywood animals as well, with a little white circle to hit, where the right profile has given the artist more trouble than the left . . . This is why the first animal is so unexpected.

Granted, an elephant. You still don't believe in him. Then again, elephants are generally hard to believe in. But all right. An elephant it is. Mostly you look at the attendant, who is sitting right there. Either he's making sure that no one gives the elephant totally inedible rubbish, or he's just for comparison. It is instructive to contemplate the elephant's attendant: through the legs of his large friend he actually sees the clock tower, where the hands are implacably, but too slowly, approaching the vodka hour . . .

The elephant knows all, and to keep from going mad the elephant serves, just like his servant. You walk on, without quite registering him.

You come to the hoofed-and-horned section. Unlikely cows, colorless and matted. Reindeer, too; you pass their cages especially fast. Somehow a reindeer is no novelty to you. Then a few gnus and a llama. Something that has never crawled out of the darkness of its room—let's say, a bison. You leave this cheerless barn quickly—almost without noting the unexpected unimpressiveness of the deer and the roebucks, without ever shifting your thoughts to the savannas and rain forests.

There is a puddle here, with something pathetic and dreamlike, but not horrible—a hippopotamus flank. And a breakfast roll disintegrating as it floats. You don't wait for the hippo to show any life.

You marvel at the tapir. All sleek and new—synthetic. The little girl says, "You can tell right off, it's American." The average man reads the plaque to his pregnant wife: " 'Has no commercial value . . .' Aha, then it's just for show." The wife stares with unseeing eyes, as hard as two boiled eggs—and sees her belly, one more proof that the earth is round. Why do people always bring pregnant women to the zoo? Have you noticed?

There are too many birds to make sense of. They are mostly black, and by the look of them they all eat carrion. Up at the top is a stuffed vulture. Thinking about this, you look closely at a sparrow. A positively stunning little bird. It is free.

The sparrow is king of the beasts.

The monkeys are closed for repair . . . The chimpanzee is exhibited separately. He's sad: he has the prospect of humanity ahead of him. By delaying, he fills us, for the umpteenth time, with astonishment that he is human. He picks and looks, scratches and looks. He is surprised by his hands: nothing in them, it turns out. Empty. Absence.

Unaccountably, you become sad and bored. Your hypocritical desire to be revived through the help of your child—to look at everything through picture-book eyes—is also futile. Children are merely intent. Their eyes verge on terror. Terror not before the scariness of the animal—how could it be scary, poor creature? in its cage?—but before life itself. The children are *pre-*; you are *post-*. You cannot share the holiday feast of their vision. The morning after? . . .

I should add here, again, that the sun is out. The city is so unused to it, was deprived of color so long ago. The colors here reveal themselves only in gray light. Like the skin of a blind man . . . Nothing is illumined: a sunlit space is a thing in itself, squeezed in between the objects, not touching them, not brushing against them, not sticking to them. So, too, the animals are colorless, or they're the color of khaki, earth, and spring. A trashy array of plywood, fences, and pelts. The light has taken all things by surprise, not one has had time to acquire color, all are bewildered, illumined, and blinded, there's nothing to hide behind.

A blue dome over a dump.

Until you come to the predators. Only the predators have color. Only they, strictly speaking, are even animals. This is true in terms of their audience success, at any rate. There is quite a crowd here—liveliness, conversation, spontaneity. Yes, extreme spontaneity is what you see on the average man's face, as at an accident or someone else's funeral.

It's time to shift from "you" to "I."

BEAR, it said on the cage. So, this was the bear. I met his eyes.

And, all at once, all the animals I had seen here looked at me. This was quite odd. One and the same creature can look at you in various ways. But to imagine that creatures so numerous and distinct from each other would give you, at various times, one and the same look, can mean only one thing: either you are mad or they are. The metallic noonday of madness was in the bear's eyes. Not horror, not fury, not fear, not ferocity, not melancholy—madness . . . This was a bear who had lost his mind. He was eating and eating candy, just as it came, without opening the wrappers—indifferent to his audience, himself, and even the candy. Wearily and dependably, he would catch a piece if it flew conveniently to his mouth; if not, he didn't catch it. Then the piece of candy thumped against him as if he weren't alive, and fell. So he sat in a circle of candy, and there were so many pieces that he must have been sitting like that for a long time, not stepping over them.

The steady, unwavering madness in his eyes could simply have been blindness, if he hadn't been opening his mouth in time for the candy; that is, it wasn't blindness. One might propose the image of an ancient toothache, pain since birth, pain as the only known state of the world, pain unbearable if absent for even a minute, even once in his whole life, and bearable because it had always existed; pain of such constancy and intensity that he indifferently put candy on it like twigs on a campfire—piece after piece, right into the cavity. If not blind, the bear could have been mute. Then his gaze would be a silent howl. But in that case he wouldn't be catching candy; he would understand pain, if he were howling . . . That is, this wasn't muteness, either.

But all these theories—which are merely approximations, intended somehow to define, to delimit by a circle of comparisons (with a radius as yet too large and variable), a new (to me) concept of *madness*, and specifically this madness—all these proposed analogies are irritatingly inexact. At the center of this ungainly and overlarge circle of comparisons, his gaze still burns dull and steady, heedless of my attempts to define it.

Well, first the bear, and then all the animals I had passed in a careless hurry, glanced at me with the same unseeing, mad eyes. (Except for a goat of some kind, who looked at me with the lively cunning of a schizophrenic who knows all about the world and continues to have insights as he watches you; that is, the goat alone was familiar to me in his type of madness.) Thinking along conventional lines, I might have supposed that the animals had been driven mad by lack of freedom, by life in the zoo, by prison. But no. If indeed that was true, something further had happened here. And that *further* was more central, more terrible, and newer for man.

With suddenness and heartache, I realized that the bear in front of me did not exist. Worse than that—he *could not* exist. If modern man did not ascribe and appropriate unto himself all things—to such an extent that even an opinion on some object in the outside world is no longer seen as characterizing that object, but rather the man speaking of the object—then the famous anecdote about a certain personage who saw a hippopotamus and said, "It can't be!" would not be about him, ultimately, but about the hippopotamus.

The hippopotamus, indeed, cannot be.

No, I did not pity the animal in the cage; I all but thanked the zoo for still having the bear who no longer existed. Otherwise, how would I have learned of this? He was a miraculously spared bear, the *last* bear, as all the other animals were also the last; he himself did not seem to believe he still existed. Again, I am describing a circle of approximations to the center of his madness, and getting no closer. I am convinced, however, that the look in his eyes was precisely this—the madness of the one left last. The problem may have been that the bear had given up on life; but this bear specifically (personally) was not the one who had surrendered. The bear-in-general in him had surrendered. He did not have enough vital energy left to *be a bear*. And indeed, if animals— whose instincts, in contrast to man's, are as yet undivorced from the logic of Creation and the Creator—have not lost their accurate sense of impending death (when the animal hides, crawls away, and so on), then why couldn't the bear have sensed death more globally: the species, the genus, life itself? The animals of Noah's Ark had a better chance of survival among the terrors of the elements than did these animals in the absolute safety of the zoo—a safety like that of condemned men between sentencing and execution. Here, they were no longer the clean and the unclean. They were all the last, sky-blue, in a haze of farewell.

I wanted to go running back to the elephant, I wanted time to look at them all through these suddenly opened eyes, to peer into their last, kindred eyes and feel guilt and brotherhood, the brotherhood of all living things on earth in the face of death. Indeed, why not embrace that gnu as a sister, why not say: I've been found, your brother who was missing in Progress! I am he, still alive, and have not forgotten you . . .

If anyone should say that I've forgotten about my daughter in this story—no, I picked her up in front of each cage where she had trouble seeing. She experienced everything intensely, that is, silently, and did not hinder me in the mute experience that I have just tried to convey. But—and here's another problem—she was experiencing something *different*, though I can't say for sure what it was. In any case, if these same animals, which for me, by virtue of my sudden discovery that they bore the stamp of being last, were beginning, amid the plywood, the peddlers' trays, the fences, and the cages, to merge as one in their conventionality, like their lopsided tin fellows from the firing range—if these same animals were implausible to her, it was because of their very reality and life. And when, not far from the carousel, I saw a pitiful threadbare pony, hardly distinguishable from a papier-mâché carousel horse, and said to my daughter, doubtfully, as if apologizing for the pony, for the way he looked, "Do you want a pony ride?"—she suddenly nodded so deeply and laboriously, turned so red with passion, that I realized the living world still existed in earnest.

Isn't this strange, that we produce more and more storybooks with pictures of rabbits, wolves, and foxes, inflate more and more little fishes, bear cubs, and deer, made of rubber, plastics, and stuffing . . . And our children already live in a world where toy animals are thousands of times more numerous than animal-animals. These toys are no longer the subject of our first acquaintance with, and knowledge of, the things with which we will spend our lives. They are the subject of mythology. And the day is not far off when the fabulousness of the beast of fable—the rabbit, the wolf, the bear—will outgrow allegory and acquire the dimensions of the fantastic: dragons and griffins. And this is as it should be. Objectively speaking, a rabbit is no easier to make than a griffin, if the rabbit no longer exists . . . It is eerie to think that all our toys and fairy tales are merely a vestige of another, departed epoch, when kindly old-maid teachers supposed that games and amusements like these would plant in a child's soul the first seeds of love for his neighbor.

The City

Look—the city! It is both large and small. This perhaps constitutes its principal charm. On the one hand, it has everything you find in an octopus-city: a million inhabitants, a subway, traffic, industrial outskirts, and a climate that is not, strangely enough for such a promised land, the very best, with a certain perniciousness to the air. On the other hand, it has none of these. You turn . . .

And around the corner, this city is like a tree, a nest, a beehive, a vineyard, an étagère, a wall twined all over with ivy. It suggests a house overgrown with floors, wings, superstructures, and galleries—just as its every house is a city, in a way. Its every twig is unfinished, in the same sense as a living branch that has a bud and is growing. You can't be sure the house will not have another little balcony added to it, or another stairway, or another attic on top of the attic: either you didn't notice it yesterday, or they'll build it tomorrow. And if you hail your friend from the courtyard and he answers "I'm coming!" he vanishes and reappears three times, you see him first on the left, then on the right, then on the stairway, then again on a little balcony, before he finally gets all the way down, stands before you, and shakes your hand, most probably suspecting that you don't need anything from him. And if two liters of white wine take the place of your night vision, you will surely get lost on these branches, realizing that you were supposed to climb, not that stairway, but the one that twines around it like a vine but takes you to some other window. Oh, pardon, *kolbatono*, I'm looking for someone else. Pardon, pardon, I'm dreaming you: these

stairs don't stop short, entangling yours—they simply lead to someone else.

Here, behind a tall and narrow grille, on an area the size of
a man's footprint, a vineyard grew up, as if from under the house,
breaking through the asphalt, parting the stones. It stretched up its
trunk, mighty but incapable of standing alone; it reached to the
cornice, caught hold, and spread to the sides; covered the wall,
covered the windows, covered the balcony; its tendrils repeated the
curlicues of the balcony grille; it wound all over the balcony, all
over the woman who came out on the balcony to water her flower,
it twined about the teapot tilted in her hand; it caught time in its
twists and turns as in a net—time was entangled, halted, stuck; so
was the nineteenth century, and the houses in it, and the people
in the houses; the darkened rooms, and those who wander about
quietly indoors in the cool and do not lean out . . . And by now
it's not that the grapevine has overgrown the house, not that the
grapevine is clutching at these doomed walls, but rather that the
walls are suspended from its mighty degeneration, they are held
together only by the fact that they once supported it, and by the
memory of those who once lived inside them, for within their fragile
shell they contain the image of the love that is called homeland.

The water cascaded past the flower in a slender stream, it
crossed the street—and around the corner came three carefree
gentlemen: one was tall and narrow-faced, with a mustache and a
cap; another wore a quilted jacket and looked like Pushkin; the third
was a crow in a suit coat . . . They walked through me, quite
unsurprised that I was not such as they, and for a long time their
unsteady, faintly merry song zigzagged down the hill. I was just
thinking it had run dry, when suddenly, thanks to a new bend in
the street, it reached me again.

Should I perhaps hail them, stop them? Because if they walked
another half kilometer or so, they would suddenly burst out on an
asphalted street with fluorescent lamps. They would be blinded, get
hit by a trolley bus, anything could happen . . .

Or perhaps they themselves would turn the corner in good
time; a *dukhan*, of its own accord, would bring its insidious doorstairs
to their feet, it would suck them in and not let them out again.
Because, where had they appeared from, just now on my path,
where had they crawled out from, into the light, if not from yes-

terday, having overslept their century? Positively, they would not get as far as the street named after the great poet, they would not spend a long time bargaining and choosing, they would content themselves with whatever Chance might afford them, a few steps away.

You will always round the corner just in time for such an impression, which may even overwhelm you with its persuasiveness or logic. Scarcely anywhere else can the frayed or worn psyche find such comfortable transitions as in this city. You won't lose your mind here, your lunacy will fit in. This city still has room for the urban lunatic, indulged as a universal favorite.

This enormous city will endlessly come true for you. It will keep coming true—like a wish, like a dream—around every little bend. You are always finding yourself in a small and cozy space, only to look back and see distance and mountains. This constant discovery of a space that is new, and yet slightly the same, will calm, comfort, and tranquilize you.

The city clings like a bird's nest to the perpendicular left bank of the wide soapy river: beams and balconies stick out over the edge like nest twigs. It creeps smoothly and eternally up the gentle incline of the right bank, it entwines the near slopes like a grapevine, with some leaves growing large, dark, and coarse, some turning yellow, some red, and some a fresh green—and this whole carpet is the city. From above, it presents the appearance of an étagère, an overgrown matchbox: little shelves, terraces, stairways, and galleries seem to join house to house, they are all fastened together, perhaps by a shared tree growing in one courtyard and drooping over another, or by a shared grapevine flung from the balcony of one house to the balcony of the next . . . Everything has spread, tangled, grown together—all of it is alive.

You wander around in it, expecting nothing, as in the forest. Monotony and constant change, obscurely determined: a tree. And this unwearisome monotony, inconspicuous variety, this living rhythm—the city—begins to conform to your breathing, your pulse, the small whisper of your blood. But if you are able to wish for anything more from life (as, in an excess of love, one can want more love, even within mutuality), then even a whim may come true in this city, here and now, around the bend . . .

We turned out of a lane that we had failed to get into, as it were . . . how can I explain? . . . My friend wanted to show me a painting by a certain artist, and I stood scrutinizing the little house beyond the grille, the garden overgrown with burdocks of some sort, the lopsided dry bowl of an inoperative fountain buried in the grass . . . I stood shifting from foot to foot while my friend disappeared inside, trying to arrange a visit. But at last he emerged, distressed: the artist's widow was ill and could not receive us. Failures of this sort inspire me—we turned out of the lane we hadn't seen, and found ourselves in a lane still more surprising and unseen. From where we stood it swept upward and to the left, pointing, exactly as if with a hand gesture. Cobblestones; grass between them; a little house with a stairway running up the middle to the second story; a man carrying a bundle of twigs . . . Everything here was as well ordered as a righteous day of rest in a pure soul. Only the plaque with the street name struck me as somehow superfluous. A cast plaque, the kind that is tastefully modern, with explanatory text. Though the letters were Georgian, the dates were mine. "Only this plaque is out of place," I told my friend, enchanted. "Remove it, and no time has gone by." Just then a morose, unshaven man came out, leaving his fat wife at the window with an expression as if she had just shouted. He positioned himself, yanked the plaque down with a nail-puller, and vanished into the house with the plaque under his arm. The wife shouted something after us. My friend laughed. "There, you see . . ." "Really?!" I said. "She's sick of people peering in her windows," he replied.

That is the city. That's the way it grew, that's the way it was, until now. Is everything satisfactory with regard to its public utilities? Are there sufficient heated bathrooms and hot water? Is it safe, shall we say, fire-preventionwise? No, no, a thousand times no. It needs to be all torn down, to its foundations, and then . . . There's no other remedy.

If you want to see the city as it always was, you can do so today from just three vantage points.

One good way is to stay at the high-rise downtown hotel, which is too visible from everywhere else, but wonderfully invisible from its own upper floors. The city straggles around the hotel like a goat around the meadow—to the length of the rope. You see the stake from everywhere, as soon as you walk out of the hotel and look back.

Another good way is to view the city from above, by climbing a mountain on which stands a Teutonic aluminum mother with a sword. You see this marvelous city spilling out from under you in a bluish tobacco haze. From here, so far above, even the high-rise hotel won't seem all that large. In an excess of emotion you tip your head back and see above you the riveted nostrils of the aluminum woman; crossing the sky directly above her is the jet trail left by a TU-104, her brother, her equal in size.

It would also be good to try one more vantage point, although I myself did not have time. You should cross to the high left bank, climb up the cliff to the monastery overhanging the river, stand below it near a recently erected horse on which rides yet another of the city's founders, even more ancient than the last, his arm outstretched—again, with a sword—and look down at the site where the malignant slums have at last been demolished, where there will be a park and a Young Pioneer swimming pool. This view of the city will be one that takes in everything but the horse. I didn't see it. I wandered around down below, through the demolished chicken coop, the junk heap of bricks, rags, and tin cans. I kicked aside a worn-out shoe with the toe of my own shoe, wandered through the contemporary cultural layer, as the archaeologists would put it, and listened to the story of the languages, trades, and peoples who had quite recently lived together here in harmony, in this small local Babel. What a fantastic and incomparable little whirlpool of language—a philological flower, a tangle of dialects, unique, irrecoverable. A dialect is alive as long as people speak it. It is spoken as long as they have someone to speak it with, as long as they are together. Now this language is gone; it has been resettled, with conveniences. This was strange to imagine. A stratum of human speech demolished by bulldozers, a language layer scraped off. I did not climb up to the level of the horse, but I could see her well: as I looked around, stumbling along on this junk heap where "the city shall be and the garden must bloom," I kept seeing her triumphant hoof raised over me. This mare is unique in her architectural vanity. In order for her to be located next to the adornment that had dominated the city for centuries, it was necessary to "trim" (blast) the cliff on which the monastery stood, because there was no place for the horse on that perpendicular line. But he who had chosen this particular spot, so much to the sculptor's envy, had seen precisely that line of the cliff; he had made his edifice grow up from it like a cultivated branch grafted to a wilding. You will never see again that overall line of monastery and cliff: the horse stands there, stands deliberately in your line of vision, so that when you look up from below, she is always trying to block the church with her massive croup.

This integral rock of a city, this living body, has had three precise wedges driven into it, as in an ancient slave quarry. The fissures widen with every night. Soon, very soon, the city will fall apart, crack into three sections, and then it will be a quick and easy job to splinter each segment with infinitesimal little wedges.

All of this is reasonable and expedient, though at times uneconomical, like the mare. But, somehow, my heart aches unreasonably. Let them live out their lives! The alive . . . let it live. Soon, all too soon, it will die of itself.

Here is a fact about this city, a fact about its people: the city is living but not surviving, its people do not seem tenacious. You can survive only in a new self, but your former self is your soul, and you do not have another. Fidelity is doomed to die; betrayal, to live. And if people cannot live differently, they disappear, they fail to stand firm within changed values, for they do not want to change them. Perhaps they think of change as laziness, a lack of hardiness. Yet is it hardiness to die out as you were born? They brag to their neighbors—who are tragically dispersed around the world, but surviving everywhere—that they have no emigration, that they cannot live anywhere else. They cannot live anywhere else, but even here they are becoming fewer and fewer. For anything that does not want to betray itself will die out. Its blood will turn blue, and fail to clot, and flow out, drop by drop, from faint scratches inflicted almost accidentally . . .

Who will explain to me where all the étagères have gone? What explanation will I believe? . . . If the bamboo étagère in our house survived even the blockade, apparently because everyone clearly saw that it would blaze up and promptly burn out, giving no more heat than a match . . . if it outlived even the blockade . . . where did its incorporeal yellow skeleton later disappear to, leaving me to remember all my life the way it creaked and wobbled when I was assigned to dust it? . . . Who, one day, became fed up with dusting it, who couldn't bear the fact that there was nothing to put on it, and what, after all, had they put on the étagère during the étagère period? And if, for decades, the need to dust it had surprised no one, on what morning did this suddenly become so irritating? At what instant did we realize that if, all our lives, we omitted to dust it, then the dusting time multiplied by the number of rags would equal a sideboard? Where were we going in such haste that we began snagging our pockets on its absurd little shelves and sticks, cursing as we ran? When did our alarm clocks begin their nervous tick, overriding the measured movement of the almost motionless pendulum, which did not hurry the clock hands? When did I replace visits with letters, letters with postcards, postcards with phone calls, and disconnect the phone? And why do I now recall that silly étagère with tenderness, when even I can see that the étagère was in fact an extraordinarily inconvenient, ridiculous, and useless thing, which not only had lost its function but had never even had one? . . . Tears on a trash heap! Don't mope, it's not worth it.

That's what they'll tell me . . .

What is alive will survive, what is weak will die out. Why this strange passion for the doomed? As though anything good were doomed, and everything doomed were good. It's not so. Not worth it. Nothing to cry about.

But it's a shame.

People can live here, though you do not. Even an ill-tempered man will adapt to living here, sullenly, doing evil to no one. People settle down here.

. . . It's as though you had lived once before . . . Such peaceful and loving recognition in everything, as if you'd been given permission to make one more visit, a short one . . . And you go to the office where you used to work, you move official papers from place to place, blow the dust off the desk, call someone to the phone: "One moment . . ." The day is over. Heading home . . . You meet an old friend, he remembers you, hugs you, timidly claps you on the wing, he's going your way . . . you have a drink or two, gather up a few more friends, start off for another place, where they're "really looking forward" to seeing all of you, together . . . and suddenly your friends have scattered somewhere, fallen like leaves, and you are walking alone—up the rising street, along the sparkling stones, along which hooves no longer clatter and no phaeton rolls toward you . . . the last spark has congealed as a single star. The wind brings now the warmth from a stagnant lane, now the freshness of the hills. Around one more corner, and there's your house . . . In your arms, like a bouquet of roses, you carry an enormous paper bag, it has cookies and macaroni in it, and two pomegranates on top—you can't arrive at the house empty-handed . . . But who knew you'd be going home: once again you found yourself without a shopping bag, without a carryall, without the mesh tote that has spread from here throughout the whole immense land. Somehow a man is uncomfortable with a shopping bag . . . Your stairs are rather noisy and full of holes . . . Oh, don't bark, for goodness' sake! What an old fool you've become, you don't recognize me, my friend . . . but I'm home. There is even a window alight—yours . . . Your wife plucks at her old-womanish braid . . . She gives you a look of fond displeasure—either you haven't been home in ten years, or you've stayed out late again, like last night . . . good heavens, this woman's a typical woman: she imagines you're her husband . . . no need to upset her, she's probably a good woman, thinks she's your wife, let her believe it if she wants . . . she thinks you're alive . . . well, she's irrational, of course . . . why supper? you don't need any, where you've returned from they don't eat anything, I've already had mine, thanks . . . and now—clasping a straw mattress as though you were going up to sleep on the roof, as though you wanted to look at the star—go ever so quietly away, steal away forever, while your wife breathes heavily, and your daughter breathes heavily, and your son has unscrewed the light bulb under his covers . . . ever so quietly, knocking over basins and potted ficus trees and entangling yourself in thickets of laundry, across the balcony, over the fire escape, go up there to the attic, where the brown onions hang in the brown little window, in defiance of art . . . You go up and away forever, until tomorrow, when you will have to lug it back here—the ugly spilling paper bag, God knows where it came from—clasping it to your ever-larger belly . . .

You go away forever, you always come back.

You turn the corner. Oh, the nineteenth century was such a short time ago! You could accidentally get stuck in it and settle down. Or rather, what I mean is that you feel like settling down in this city. But immediately you realize that you can't. Because it's not the nineteenth century. Or rather, the city is, but it's not for you.

How strange to realize that this is someone else's affair, not yours . . . You've come to have such a feeling for it, such love, such understanding! But this is envy.

You are so selflessly, so wholeheartedly enchanted that people begin looking at you askance and suspecting you of a hidden motive. But how could it be hidden, when it's out in front and you're driving it ahead of you, afraid of falling behind. Oh, this international vulgarity—the sense of shame for your native home . . .

But you don't admit to yourself that you have any motive, not even one . . . You are so successful at being enchanted, at loving everything foreign, that you don't see yourself as an invader. You do not demand for your own homeland the same love that you exude for someone else's; the authenticity of your enchantment will be more than sufficient atonement, in your opinion, because you are no longer responsible for either family or fatherland. They're not your fault. For this very reason, you see yourself as worthy of a reciprocating love. The superannuated agent of the empire comes forward as myrrh-bearer, utterly unaware that he is master and host; he accepts everything unthinkingly, by right. Everyone knows he's collecting a tax—he alone remains modestly ignorant on this score. As if out of shyness, just to keep from violating custom and offending his hosts, he allows them to propose a toast to him and pay for his dinner.

Spit out the chunk of innocent lamb, belch up the surplus years of the cognac, say who you are, and, in the end, violate the custom you misunderstood—even if they kill you . . . Walk away from the hospitable table, smearing tears of injustice on your face as if they were someone else's . . . You turn the corner.

You turn the corner, having paid three times too much for diluted beer and poisoned train-station dumplings; you are utterly alone, the young women don't look at you, your razor is too dull to shave your stubble, your shoes are chafing, and there's a sharp, sour pain in your belly. You turn the corner.

And you're happy . . . The street glitters with uneven cobble-stones, it climbs up and to the right, and at the end of the street, through the warm black air, shines a single star.

There the city ends. Its upper stories, the mountains, have gone dark; in the morning they will be the first to grow pink.

How light it is in this darkness!

What unthinking power an inborn image has . . . As though when a man is born he records on his infant retina his first impression, once and for all, and that is why he later weaves one particular kind of rug, builds his house in one particular way, forges one particular kind of grille, receives one particular kind of cemetery cross. This integrity is taut in your soul, it sings like a violin string: you hear your native song, and its words are you.

Fate

—

Among the evolved characters which frequently occur in the self-replicating systems we call living organisms is the termination of the individual. This "natural death" of the living units which carry for a time the unbroken line of descent from the first primordial origin of life is of little consequence to the vast majority of living things, for the places of those that die are soon occupied by other individuals.

BERNARD STREHLER,
Time, Cells, and Aging

THE PEASANT

I am walking to the store, to the post office, and nowhere in particular . . . Don't forget to buy butter and soap powder, don't forget to call my editor in the city, but if he's not there . . . forget to buy a chocolate bar for my daughter and forget to drop my mother-in-law's letter in the mailbox (I keep touching it in my pocket, so as not to forget, but then I pull my hand out of my pocket); be sure, on my way to get butter, not to forget to think about my article, an extremely vital one on the state of contemporary criticism, so that I can sit right down to it when I get back, and send it off tomorrow to Moscow, where for some reason (nothing better to do!) they are eagerly looking forward to it. (Even now, a month later, I won't have sent it off, for which I'll be cursing myself roundly, instead of praising and encouraging my not quite extinct punctuality and membership in life.)

So I walk, and some of my urgently pressing errands I'll remember, but some I'll forget. I won't forget and will forget butter, nails, milk, soap powder, and kerosene, one phone call, two visits, and three farewells . . . yet I will surely forget that life is going on around me, with weather, passersby, and clouds; that I myself am being swept along in this torrent, which is illumined by the sun for my eyes; that I will someday "suffer agonies over the aimlessly lived" moment, *this* moment—because, whether I do forget or don't forget one or another little twist of my duty (imposed by whom?), I am nevertheless preoccupied with *not forgetting*, rather than with the present instant, which in the meantime has inevitably gone by and is now irretrievable. Forever.

My brain is a saturated solution. The poisons and salts of memory have eaten spongy passages in it, and the tremulous liquid of life is visibly departing through them; the surface of the cortex is holey and dry. But I am still alive, or at least I still have a necrosis-free toe I can wiggle, and the corn on it still hurts. And since I'm still alive, I can't pass life by altogether. No, no! She will touch me. Granted, she won't cling to me, won't embrace me; but, for no special reason, not noticing me in her animated reverie, in which there is still no canker of articulated thought, she, like a young woman going to a rendezvous—not with me but with some other lucky man, handsome and strong—will brush against me, in the aisle of the bus, with the edge of her cloud of health and clean-washed youth. And although I'm no longer one of life's immediate relatives, I, too, sometimes go, nameless, to her name-day celebration, and an added place is made for me, with a peripheral snack. So I don't always pass life by, carrying in my arms an awkward, shameful, ripping, newspaper-wrapped parcel of errands resembling undiscarded mayonnaise lids, and duties reminiscent of unwashed socks and unpublished manuscripts; and even though I don't throw away this parcel, with its two passport photos, a few buttons, corks, and pre-reform kopecks, and a great many small coils of old string . . . it has a tack in it, too . . . and a telephone number, I forget whose, written on the top . . . even so, the newspaper is bursting and ripping, and I'm one week short of thirty-three, I can't get home and can't ever forget it, can't lose my home or my parcel either . . . it keeps spilling things out. And now, when it spills just one thing more, I suddenly experience—after the horror of loss—the relaxation of freedom; and then I see the corner of a mouth, a rim

of water, a patch of sky; all at once there is a blossoming field, and
no one has noticed me going there (not going there), no one has
challenged me, no one will . . . and then, to an empty place in
the wretched parcel, a place where there had been only a tack,
crooked and rusty, or a dried-out cork—to that place will come a
forest, a cliff, a bird . . . Despite all, it's impossible to walk past
life, accidentally lift my eyes to her, and not immediately forget at
least something! Blessed be all that I have neglected, omitted,
dropped, lost, let go, forgiven, and been forgiven. Blessed be my
laziness. Cursed be my greed, that I have never thrown anything
out, flung it away, shoved it aside, but have kept waiting for this
mercy, the chance to lose something.

So I come bursting into this narrative flushed and sweaty, in
my arms I have a bundle, I clasp it to my belly, my neck is pierced
by the wire from a champagne cork (for some reason, that is what
has poked the uppermost hole), clinging to my trouser legs are candy
wrappers and someone else's confetti, lucky streetcar and lottery
tickets, no-lose store receipts for two rubles eighty-seven kopecks
each to even things up, and here's a ticket to the American *Porgy
and Bess*, which was given on New Year's Eve of a year new fifteen
years ago, and in my watch pocket I have a cloakroom check accurately indicating, without clock hands, perhaps the day, perhaps
the year, perhaps the hour when all this happened . . . I hold in
my hand several exam cards on botany, the constitution, and explosives; the elevator's not working, my feet are burning, my heart
is thumping against the parcel; I also contrive to take from my back
pocket a rusty bunch of keys for long-vanished locks, in order to
open the window of the bus as it plunges off the bridge . . . This
is the state in which I encounter my love, and as luck would have
it, there's no place to put the parcel down so that I can throw my
arms around her neck, besides which I can't put it down, even if
there were a place, because I'm still holding it together, and it would
immediately come unwrapped in plain view of my beloved, which
would be quite unseemly. And how can I throw my arms around
her neck if, before that, I neatly set my bundle aside? That's dis-
honest. I fall to my knees on the deserted stair landing, the bundle
is in front of me, a fresh scratch from the champagne is bleeding
on my neck, and I genuflect to the garbage pail . . . But what I
wanted to say is that if life does, through some misunderstanding,
come visit my cell, it means I have lost my memory for some snippet

of past life. For, as in a saturated solution, the addition of salt, even with constant stirring, causes the precipitation of a like amount of salt, which is crystallized out, then and there.

So this is the unreal being who goes wandering like a ghost among real shrubs and grasses, where real birds chirp and real bugs crawl, to buy butter and soap powder at the village general store. But actually he doesn't do even that, not only because the paper clips and thumbtacks of his errands prevent him from looking about and finding himself in a sudden reality (sudden for him, though always there in his absence), but also because the butter and . . . what was it? . . . the soap . . . are not realities for him, either. On the contrary, they, too, are alien, crude things, rejected by his soul and not perceived as real. In this breach of reality—in the breach itself, with the fibers and shaggy little threads of its edges on the right and left—in this dead zone—the shade of my being wanders, he crosses a putrid little brook that climbs uphill, he finds himself in a bright corridor of fences and birches, and at the end of it, between pines now, he sees a blue gap . . . The soap and butter slip his mind, and suddenly I feel a sharp pang of happiness. The sky is inverted over me, uncommonly blue and bright—it's a long time since we've had such a lovely day!—the leaves begin rustling, a child shouts, a swallow dives right by my feet, and a ladybug lights on my finger . . .

Ladybug, ladybug flew away home, and from the sky three apples fell: one for me, one for you, and one for the storyteller . . . The blue gap opened wide between two infinite pines—it was a lake. I was cast up out of this narrow, tense corridor of light to sprawl flat on the shore. Weakly, I tried to recall the faded words: plucked out at random, one by one, they no longer meant anything. They dried and turned gray, like pebbles from the sea . . . Besides, how can you catch the delicate, breaking thread of a poetic "high" without debasing its subject—which, it must be said, gets along just fine without you?

I sat on the shore of my lake. No better than others I had seen or not seen, it was "my" lake because it was the one that always appeared in my mind's eye at the word *lake*. A generic lake. With boats, black and half submerged, or buoyant and colored, just barely rocking, like fishing-rod floats. With a sandy precipice on the right, and above it a railroad train flashing through the pines, stitching cliff to forest; a carpet of swamp on the left, with a spruce-covered promontory, usually likened to a bear at a watering hole; and hills over there in the distance, on the other shore, where at the very summit, indistinguishable from the trees and continuous with them, against a background of sky, stood a grove that looked like a ruined castle. Floating in front of me was a small island with sparse, crooked pines, and the carpet of swamp came right up to it. Peculiar swamp flowers or bolls of some sort, gradually blending together in a dense white, shone on the island like decadent little lamps. The sun was sinking into the swamp, turning an ever-richer crimson, and although the water at my feet was a soft gray, just in front of me it flared mother-of-pearl, then lilac, then gold, scarlet, and deep blue, and in the farthest distance, there on the opposite shore (where the "castle" stood), it turned suddenly black. There was no place for the eye to stop, this was optical weightlessness, my eye established a connection so direct and unstrained that—where was I, where was the lake, and where, especially, was home? where was everything that didn't exist here and never had?

How could I look at the lake, and not be myself, and be the lake, at least for as long as the sunset allowed?

Imagine that—had I chased the idea so long and so hard that it finally caught up with me?

This, probably, is what I was thinking on the shore:

"I've never thought about death (never feared it?). But this incessant suffering, this desire and inability to merge with a reality that exists only in the present—isn't it an active (innate?) desire for non-existence? I could have been happy (unaware) even in my unreality, in my hammock between past and future, if I had accepted that unreality as my own. After all, I've always been like this, I've never consciously stayed within my 'programmed/desired/real' meaning, so why should I care about the world around me? But if love and happiness, in my experience, have been only those instants when I didn't exist (infancy is non-existence, 'I don't remember' is non-existence, the act is non-existence, death is non-existence), this means that I have been controlled, throughout my 'conscious life,' chiefly by the desire to disappear."

THIRTY-THREE

And the peasant? Where's the peasant?

All this time he has been walking toward me on the shore of the lake.

He has been walking toward me for a very long time now, and today he woke up, took a hair of the dog, and then got drunk, today being the holiday, Victory Day, and he fought and fought, went all the way to Berlin (to Berlin—that was a deviation from the route, of course, but closely calculated so that he would arrive this very day, at the moment when I would be sitting by the lake and thinking about . . .).

And now we can set an exact date: the week that I mentioned above is passing, has passed, and I will soon be, I am . . . thirty-three. The nails ache in my newly cobbled heels, and on this day memorable for Christ I am engaged in something of an ascension from lush and blooming Dilizhan, or is it Borzhomi, toward this lake, toward a peasant apostle in my gelid land . . . I carry my balking and deliberately heavy self to the other shore and sink my new heels into the dense wet sand. I see myself clearly from a distance, flustered and apprehensive, standing on the shore in a land of unexplored topics, and I grin maliciously. But it's too late. Over a smoking wick, in a blackened and dented pot (homologous, in this instance, with the morning shape of my head), a day-old mixture of stale beer, coffee grounds, dwindled cigarette butts, and she-loves-me-she-loves-me-not petals is beginning to heat up. The rising current casts up to the surface now a cigarette butt, now a blob of spittle—and back to the bottom, around the circle. Creativity aboil. Just you come here, little peasant, and I'll . . . write you.

He is approaching me from the right. Coming from the boiler room, or is it a pumping station, over by the railroad. Squinting against the light, swaying confidently in his conscientious total intoxication. He sees me . . . And I, apparently, am composing my autobiography, three years ago. But how can I catch the delicate, breaking thread of a poetic high that is already weighed down by interpretation and formula and coarsened by the drunkenness of a frantic existence?

Yes, it's him. He put in a stove for me last fall. A stove just as effortful, crooked, and honest. Never mind, it works . . . He suddenly took a liking to me, for no reason at all. Perhaps from (today's) disinclination to write, I was too willing to mix the mortar and hand him the bricks, when I needn't have done this at all; or perhaps we got talking about how it's okay to drink but you have to know how much, and *he* never had any problem, though of course it can happen, but everything in due time and in moderation; or about how they shouldn't have stopped at Berlin in '45, they should have gone all the way to America, and now we wouldn't have any of these conflicts we've got now; or about the Jews—a cautious, fumbling conversation . . . Whatever the reason, his cunning obtuseness, obtuse cunning—the peasant squint of a man many times deceived—vanished one day, and he handed me two rubles change from the five I had tipped him for vodka: "I'll accept for a half liter, no more." Ever since, he has needed me to talk to when he comes out of his yard, positions himself in the middle of our Lonely Street, stands there swaying confidently—as if on deck, but always keeping his balance, not stumbling at all—and stares into the darkening street, where the braid of paths is already being plaited into twilight . . . He stands patiently waiting, his eyes filled with a primeval yearning to communicate . . . but there are no passersby. "Tell me, Andrei . . . the patronymic's Yegorovich, I think, is that right? . . . So tell me, Andrei Grigorievich . . ." I smile; grieving at my own insincerity, I incline my head toward my shoulder, as if in affection, and hear him out. I answer laboriously, choosing my words, and then he says, "You went to school, now, you finished college. Now, I didn't happen to . . ." He listens to me, chews a moment, and suddenly —it looks as if—yes, his eyes fill with *hurt*. Grunting, he rocks each foot up from the ground separately and goes off without a backward glance—you hurt me, Andrei, why'd you turn me down, I've still got half a split—goes off to finish the bottle, and no doubt he'll grunt and wave a hand once or twice, in vexation . . .

So there he was, walking toward me and tearing me off again on the dotted line, like a page from a calendar . . . I was just on my way to get soap, I was busily absorbed in cataloguing non-existence, when a sudden illumination came to me, I merged for an instant with the world and the present, and was promptly snatched back from life to non-existence, but a seemingly inspired non-existence, a poetic one, and—not again! why the devil was this peasant walking toward me!

Today is May 9th, Victory Day, he was saying, and I went all the way to Berlin, I was three times wounded and shellshocked, it's been twenty years, why not have a drink, can't *not* have a drink, certainly nobody's going to say that *he* . . . or any problem like that . . . He had been walking toward me from the Reichstag, hup-two, for twenty-some years, apparently, and had planned it just right, so that I would be sitting here by the lake at this instant and thinking about . . .

I completely forgot it when he walked up. The neighbors had put on a record, and the noise of its rotation was winding the landscape into a gray, twilit ball.

"What are you doing here," he said to me affectionately. "Standing . . ."

"Thinking," I said rudely. From then on, not one single thought entered my head. A remarkable emotion spread through me in hot waves of shame. Then and there I started to apologize, to lie. "Understand, I was going . . . the sunset . . . I thought . . . the lake . . . too bad . . . the earth . . . sky . . . birds . . . You know."

And so, while I joined in the honesty of his intoxication, not meeting his eyes, which expressed wine's rainbow, reason's mother-of-pearl sunset in their smooth, darkening waters: vagueness and intentness, cunning and guilt, devotion and boorishness, smugness and a desire to please, deference and a strong doubt of my, your, their, his own words . . . privately I was selecting popular ideas, forever to doubt and discredit them.

"No, nothing exists anymore!" I exclaimed, all but weeping with insincerity, wallowing in apotheosis and pathos. "The bear at the zoo one day, that was the way he looked at me! . . . They might have spared a semblance, at least."

The peasant fixed me with his stare and leaned hard.

It was like this . . . A drunk was rolling a cartwheel down the road so that it wouldn't go to waste, such a useful thing, almost intact, and always sure to come in handy sooner or later (anything can happen) as a souvenir of the horse who cannot be. The wheel was an irregular circle, and it rolled the drunk irregularly behind it, jerking him forward and escaping from him. Tipping, it kept swinging him in exactly the opposite direction, he goes left, I go right. Meanly it paused to butt him, took another frisky hop forward, and—oof!—toppled sideways again. Now the emotion that had overwhelmed him began to intensify. What the hell was going on, when it was such a happy idea, beneficial and noble, so that there was even profit in it (he'd had his drink, but he was bringing the wheel), and suddenly it turned out like this? "I'll give you what-for!" he thought, overtaking the wheel and slowing it down with difficulty, only to have it snap awake and run over him this time, for no good reason. "But then you . . ." he said, and prudently he planted his feet wide apart, crouched down, and took a firm grip. "Heave!" But it proved suspiciously light, like a child's hoop, or maybe strong, like a spring. Maybe this wasn't him slinging it, but it slinging him, so adroitly across itself . . . "Oh no, you don't!" (Expressively sneaking up on it from the other side.) "Not a chance! I'll sober up, or leave you!"—this time meaning his wife, with whom the sincerity of his intentions would collide when the wheel finally rolled into the yard and bumped against the porch with a sigh. *She* wouldn't appreciate it, she who had let all his warmth and kindness suffocate, choke in his breast . . . He, she, it—the graphic image of the tipping wheel. Hesheit—a naïve tribe that has outlived civilization. Man's ritual dance with the wheel of effort, the belly of death, the word . . . And as the procession moved off down the road in their obscene jig, whirling and changing places, ashamed of nothing, driving ahead of them their shared mutual image . . .

. . . the peasant, gazing at me with his forehead bumps, stooped down inside himself to the bottom of his belly and caught hold of a certain word. He had laid it by for future use, and its time had come. He lifted it over the edge, glancing reproachfully at the dried-up wheel in the ditch . . .

"That's right," he said. "If man kills off all the animals, why, then, he won't be able to live, without animals. Why, he was created with the animals, from birth, so that there would be both beast and man . . . When the animals are gone, then he'll have to take them from himself. To make it even again."

"Yes, yes!" I confirmed ecstatically. The world was still beautiful, it still *existed*, if it had stored up another gift for me, ungrateful and unfaithful me! Someone had interrupted my thoughts? My thoughts, hell! The very air, water, and forest were thoughts—*they* were choosing *us*, at random . . .

We stood on the shore like calves with our heads grown together, the two-headed seed of radiation and trade union. His chemistry overflowed into my head, my thought overflowed into his. We were swaying on the shore, on the stem of a desiccated umbilical cord, when suddenly a faint terrestrial current ran along it.

"Thank the Lord!" I said prayerfully. "We're not alone on the earth yet, either of us!"

"So you even believe in God?" the peasant said to me, doubting and flattering.

"How can we not believe in Him, when look . . ." I said, gesturing roundly at the lavishness of the world that remained to us, as if I were stroking the subject of our shared thought, our little baby who had given birth to us . . .

"I don't think I do," he said. "I believe in nature. If He were above her, how could He let her die? No farmer could afford such a thing."

He was right—and I could not retract it.

I said, "Faith doesn't mean agreeing with God. Faith means never doubting Him, in any circumstance."

"So Doomsday is coming, is that what you think?"

"Why, yes!" I took him up, rejoicing in his logic. "We've lived to see it."

"But I feel bad for my little son," he said. "What do you make of that? If I love him and feel bad for him—then what? That's no good either, I tell you. You and me, now, maybe we deserve it. But a little boy, how's he to blame? It's uneven again . . ."

"You were right, what you said about animals," I said, extricating myself. "It's the same with children. We kill the *children* in them, and bring up ourselves in *them*."

"Aha," he said. "But when he's little, a wee little baby, what should we do?"

"As long as he's little, it can't be the end yet," I declared confidently.

"Then that's right," he confirmed.

"It's just as you said." I was speaking more and more loosely, content that he agreed with me. "When the animals are gone, man will extract them from himself, to make things even. So right away there'll be twice as few of him. Of man. And then, when the children grow up, there won't be much left of him at all. So, gradually, we'll be reduced to nothing."

"Then that's right." The peasant nodded his head in agreement. "If there's twice as few at first, then four times as few . . ."

So we stood on the last shore, embracing, capable of arithmetic and pleased to be capable of that much.

"Man is always a minority," he said profoundly, reaching the final word up from the very bottom. He stumbled. "There's twice of us, lesh go shtoke up . . ."

THAT IS THE QUESTION

We were sitting in the boiler room, which was more likely a pumping station. It stood on the shore of the lake, under the embankment; trains went by overhead. The place was cozy, so sealed off and isolated that you had to think to remember where it was: under the embankment, between the lake and a viscous green reservoir something like a bomb crater—you would hardly think they got their water from it . . . When a train went by, barely exceeding the steady mechanical drone and quiver of the chamber, you could imagine a sea beyond the wall, and yourself on the shore, perhaps because it was also very warm here. I kept forgetting where I was. Whenever I tried to remember, I passed through a phase of pre-memory: I was on a barge, or something of the sort, at night, in the middle of a large body of water; I was an isolated, weak-willed thing, like a small wave, or a balloon.

The technology housed around us was exactly the kind that can indeed, unlike liners, reactors, and lasers-masers, be designated by the word *technology*, as in childhood. Fat pipes loomed shaggy in the corners, lush valves grew as large as steering wheels, and two squat, green, froglike pumps made squelching sounds. In the center of the room, very large, merging massively with the darkness of the corners, sat a great-grandmother of the modern rocket. She wore two inoperative manometers, like eyeglasses tied on with threads, and snored softly through the gaping empty mouth of the firebox.

The peasant took good care of her: she brimmed with trustworthy old age and gleamed with rare burnished copper. This was a nice place for her, a nice place in general, warm, clean, and rather dark because of the economical light bulb. It smelled of . . . good Lord, how it smelled!—of rags, coal, oil, chalk, cooled heat, the darkness of the morning shift, and the deep blue of metal filings . . . A twig broom stood in an empty pail, a small mug on the little shelf over the basin, and a half-empty split of vodka on the shaggy knee of a pipe . . . A place for everything, everything in its place.

I complimented him on everything, and he listened patiently.

"Sure. The proletariat," he said opaquely, and we drank. "Now look, you're an educated man, you write books, tell me this. Why is it they publish the bad books and don't print the good ones?"

Impossible! I thought joyfully. How could he know this, too? Oh, ungrateful me!

"It's all for the same reason," I declared.

"Now look, who wrote *Hero of the Golden Star*, for example?"

"Babaevsky."

"Right," he said. "You know. So why won't they publish it?"

"But they did publish it!" I said in surprise. "They even gave it the Stalin Prize!"

"Oh sure, published it," he said doubtfully. "I read it by hand."

"By hand!"

"Well, a hand copy. A very correct book. It's about a *farmer*, you know. About land. Now, explain that! Why can't they print about land and a farmer?"

I really didn't know what to say. An apocryphal version of *The Golden Star*! Unbelievable.

"It's about a farmer, you know. And here's another thing, explain this. Why did they treat the farmer so unfairly? All he did wrong, you know, was keep his nose to the grindstone, he never saw the sky . . . The proletariat, they . . . I finished my shift, nothing to do, read the novel, my mind was like this!" He gestured wider than his shoulders. "And I left!"

This was expressive. We drank another half split.

"Well, how's the tile stove?" he said. "Does she heat up?"

So he was, indeed, the one who had put it in for me.

"Heats up just fine!" I nodded. "Only thing is, the bricks keep falling out."

"Does she smoke?"

"No."

"No problem, then. Few more fall out, give me a call."

"But don't worry!" I said. "It's fine."

"Beetle giving you any trouble?"

"Beetle?" I said blankly.

"I remember you folks were having trouble with a beetle—"

"Why, no, we're not. What kind of beetle?"

"Wood beetle. Eats wood. I'm having a lot of trouble with it."

"Sort of small? dark? hard?"

"But did you *see* a beetle?" he said in alarm.

"I saw one at my parents'. It was eating the chair legs—"

"But you saw the wrong beetle!" he said. "You saw a furniture beetle! You didn't see the real one! I'll show you!" Inspired, he jumped up and disappeared through a fortuitous small door.

He was back shortly.

"I still have several here." (Cautiously sliding open a box, so small in his machinist's hands.) "Two or three individuals." That was his word—"individuals." "Two," he said with disappointment. And I don't know how he did this, but, solicitous not to crush the "individual" in the pliers of his thumb and index finger (thus the *Science and Technology* film shorts used to startle us with the spectacle of a Wellsian jointed mechanical hand, holding a fragile little retort and adroitly pouring into test tubes a liquid symbolic of Radiation), he triumphantly held out to me—

Actually, I had pictured it all wrong. This was a soft, reddish, quite loathsome creature, halfway between a fly and a small cockroach. What most surprised me was that the creature was soft. In order for it to gnaw wood, you'd think the beetle would be as black as anthracite, something like a small coal-cutting machine created by nature herself.

"It's soft!" I said.

"*Soft!*" the peasant sang out venomously. "Don't make me laugh . . . Slimy!"

His eyes glittered with inspiration, his face flamed, and his speech flowed, as smooth and heady as a Pharisee's, easily crowding aside the labored speech of the apostle . . . This was rhythmic prose, about how the beetle had tiny little wings at first, and it flew out, landed, laid its eggs, and lost its wings (later I was struck that this was backward: it laid its eggs first and then flew out); the males had a special little chitinous key with a complicated groove, the female had a keyhole, just like a safe, no chance you'd get in with someone else's key . . . but, most important, when it was laying its eggs, I think, or perhaps when it was flying out, it was especially quick to devour houses, the female doing most of the devouring and the male being harmless, or maybe it was the other way around . . . but, above all, the beetle was devouring his (the peasant's) house . . . The peasant closed his eyes, and his speech acquired a new and fabulous epic strain, expanding into the saga of how he, a peasant, all by himself, had sallied forth against countless multitudes, he had flung down the challenge and charged into battle; he had chopped off their heads with dusting powder, Trichlorfon, kerosene, Disinsectal, but they kept growing back; he had sealed their burrow holes with wax, flooded them with pitch, smeared them with tar; he kept replacing the crossbeams of his log cabin and was losing the unequal struggle—the beetles fed on the insect dust, multiplied with singular rapidity in the Disinsectal, and acquired a peculiar lethal toughness and strength from the kerosene . . . He had written letters to the *Village Star*, *Red Life*, *Medical Pravda*, the *Yesterdaily*, and many other papers, he had subscribed to several specialized journals, he had tried forty suggestions—but he had not surrendered . . . He had started to burn them out with red-hot iron (literally—a nail), and his porch had burned down . . . Apocalyptic storm clouds, once more acquiring the frenzied force of the apocryphal, thickened over his tale. The locust twanged its steely wings, and inside of it lurked a live, plump, squishy little body.

If the misfortune he was recounting had not been so natural and great, I would have been lost in admiration of him, for his figure had suddenly grown tall and monumentally fiery, conveying the Passion and Death of the Fighter so well that Vuchetich would have envied it. But just then the sparkling and precious essence of his eyes narrowed again and filmed over.

"But now I know," he whispered voluptuously. "They can only be fought one by one!"

A faint shiver ran through my body.

"You don't believe me?"

Gently and insistently he took my hand. I stooped to pass under a shaggy pipe, which seemed to me alive and insectile, like the belly of a bumblebee. Shrinking down, taking tiny flylike steps, we passed through the fortuitous little door. It was a hole just like the beetle's, chewed through a solid, but by and for man . . .

I stood in a small laboratory, where—under medievally cramped conditions, dictated only (medieval times being spacious) by the nature of the work itself—a huge pulsating forehead, made zealous by the pure logic of duty fulfillment, was struggling and suffering in the heroic, exhausting labor of materializing an Idea; where, through the mere exertion of thought, even without the

Archimedean contrivance of the lever, he had made himself equal to the weight of the world and was ready to master the Idea, but each time, at the very gates, on the threshold, as his hand touched his goal, he was defeated by the sudden advent of a fainting spell, a treacherous coma; where, however, he came back to consciousness through the eternity of his faint, taking no note of his mad interlude, and turned to the happy, uncoordinated, superficial elegance of inventing as ends in themselves the objects that had once served the Idea . . . and thus, having discovered (through the sophistication of lenses, machined bronze bushings, and the curved delicacy of retorts) his skill at selling the very equipment of the Idea—that is, because he could not bear to strain his spirit further—he halted halfway and turned to technical progress, and then, with the faint skip, tick, and chime of micro- and macrocephalic little clocks made of straw, water, and crystal, he pushed time toward production, where the initiative of the man of talent (a Kulibin or a Polzunov), representing itself as the people's mental curiosity, coiled time into a spring that has stimulated productive energies, right down to our own day . . .

And where the naïve tribesman, in a voluptuous mood of genius, now invents the integral calculus to the amusement of professional creators of the infinitely small—there stood my peasant, who had recently invented a clock that was set in motion by the trains passing over the boiler room. There I, too, traversing an epoch, suddenly found myself. And never mind the clock, the peasant was holding in his hands a hypodermic syringe. Taking aim, like a surgeon, to create a narrow little jet, he was sticking the needle into the burrow hole of a grinder beetle. Several blocks sawn from the crossbeams he had replaced in the past year were neatly stacked together in the corner for experiments.

"Right now I'm injecting chloroform, but before long I'll have invented my own new compound . . ." And he gave me a sly wink, in place of the words "and then—!"

I looked at the clear row of test tubes on the workbench, the massive array of stout poison jars on the long shelf, the framed clipping from the *Moscow Evening News* on the wall ("Reader Ivanov, resident of Station T., asks . . ." with the "Ivanov" underlined in red pencil), the bronze harmonies of the sprayers, the motionless, gleaming tip of the vertically upraised syringe needle, whose tiny incandescent point signified the concentration (isolation) of the instant and expressed the entire surrounding space . . . The pause lengthened, the silence hung over us, and a long, delicate ringing stretched from ear to ear.

I looked at the injected block. The myriads of little holes, distinct and focused, were black daytime constellations, twisting galactic spirals, worlds and passionate antiworlds, where the density and matter of the remaining wood was merely a constellation of cosmic emptiness, where the wood was suspended in some fashion among the holes . . . worlds, holes, hole worlds . . .

"You inject every hole?" I asked timidly, in a bare whisper.

"Of course." Suddenly his voice sounded very normal and natural.

A train passed overhead, the test tubes tinkled gently in a harmoniously quaked row, the silence snapped, my giddiness left me. Shedding a frightful world, discovering an unfrightening situation, discovering normality in obtuseness and habitualness, I said, like the anecdotal villager who asked the visiting lecturer how the jam is put into bonbons . . . "But listen, how do you pull the logs out from under the house? Doesn't it rest on them?"

At first he looked at me dumbfounded. Visibly returning, on foot, from fathomless distances of consciousness, he caught sight of me far away . . .

"Good grief!" he said, with affectionate superiority. "I jack up the house, numskull. Highbrows!" he lamented ironically. "And not the whole house at once! First one corner, then another . . . What a screwball!" He burst out laughing, truly merry. "Let's go have a drink instead. I've still got half a split there."

"But we drank it!"

"You don't know anything. I've always got half a split there."

. . . I went out into the starless night. It was big and dark, like a bear. The moon shone through like a crazed eye, white and blind. The world had shut its bright eye. The blind eye stood directly above the chimney of the house in which lived the mistress of the cow who gave us milk. This house was even darker, in its benighted determination to be a farm and thus live by its own labors, feeding itself and its land by establishing a semblance of a cycle on its ten-hectare plot, where the cow's peaceful juice was now filtering down via the earth's vapors to the unsleeping potato tubers, and the skimmed milk was cooling in the cellar, and the cream was being digested in the people sleeping above. But the cow *existed* in this even greater darkness, and just now her sleep and breathing were doing more to make the world real than were the immortal patterns of physical spaces and bodies. She breathed around me, I plunged into a warm puddle of air stagnating between two haystacks, and I would have liked this night to have more of the cow in it than the bear. That would be an inequality, but no loss of the equation . . .

I can't say that I was thinking of the specific bear I have mentioned above. But they were all one and the same thing, the peasant, the beetle, and the moon. "Don't forget to tell them at home how a peasant is no different from an aristocrat"—I carried the phrase very alertly, along with the milk jug I had picked up from the porch. The jug was full, my foot did not recognize the microrelief of former puddles, the sole of my shoe had lost its sensitivity, and the milk ran down my fingers and into my sleeve, signifying, by way of consolation, that the cows of today were at least a little bigger . . .

Don't forget to tell them how much I liked the kulak bloodsucker. The beetle-eaten peasant—he is endlessly *not* exterminated. And behold, the cow still breathes, though no one hears her. Press your ear to the wickedness of the day and you will be deafened, cursing your life. Thanks to everything under the sun, you will someday understand these connections. Thank the Lord . . .

There was another old woman in my childhood, Pelageya Pavlovna. A little old kulak, kind as a cutlet—she's gone now, long buried, I didn't notice she had died, I don't remember it . . . I remember she used to tell the story of how her horse bolted while plowing. Young Pelageya did not let go of the reins. She couldn't let go, she feared for the horse, she feared her husband. Stronger than pain, stronger than blood, was the earth—the earth, too, was blood. "Stones grow," she used to say. And who can doubt it? This story, so literary that it seemed to issue from the black disk of the loudspeaker under which she sat slicing onions, was, it turns out, the truth, warmed by the cow's breath in this night . . .

The milk flowed down my fingers in the night of the crazed bear. Don't forget to tell . . . Whom? What? Don't forget . . .

What?

This, it turns out, is what not to forget. This, it turns out, is what I was thinking on the shore when the peasant came toward me and broke the thread . . .

To forget, or to remember—that is the question.

That's it, that's it! I don't live because I'm remembering yesterday and not living now; I'm intending to live in the future, through memory . . . Which means I must forget, in order to be alive and real now. But the world has perished because people forgot. Then must I remember? Remember, lest it all perish utterly! As the cow's mistress, disagreeable old woman, remembers her cow! As old Pelageya dragged her horse—remember!

And yet, remembering, I don't live, I perish in everything, with everything: forgetting, the last one who remembers departs from the world. Forgetting, I perish utterly, so that I'm afraid I'll die without having lived at all. To depart from the world by forgetting it, so that I myself can live; or to remain in it so that I can never be in it, can't be in it *now*?

Thus I rolled the drunken wheel home from my journey. Melting in my pocket was a piece of rock candy—a token gift out of my paycheck.

To forget, or to remember? Hamlet . . .

LONELY STREET

To the memory of Nikolai Rubtsov

Every spring, when I moved down to the dacha, I would catch up on the events of our street over the winter . . .

Ours is an odd street. It has no beginning, no end; it suddenly broadens out from a footpath in the swamp, then stretches on, in a legitimate and respectable display of houses, gardens, and neighbors—and suddenly stops short, a bright, swiftly narrowed cul-de-sac. A void yawns there, a blue gap among the trees. Anyone who doesn't live here, anyone visiting for the first time, won't guess right away what comes next: where has the street disappeared to? What comes next is a small bluff, a slope down—and a tiny river, a meadow, a floodplain. But to see it you must walk right up close, peering into the widening emptiness of the street's end, and only with your last step will you understand . . . Maybe this is why it's Lonely, because it's without end or beginning. And there, in that greening gap, dreamed in a light sleep after irreparable sorrow, I see the word *fate* written, washed away again, and rewritten. That is, at the word *fate*, this little nook is what flashes like a fish before my mind's eye . . . And I don't even notice . . .

A small house stands there, of a sort now plainly impossible in this life. In it live people who have never managed to become bad . . . They created their little cul-de-sac and strait by annexing half the street, because they had no land allotment as such but needed to live around the house. And the house—if you can call it that!—was someone's ownerless bathhouse in which, at some long-forgotten time, a certain newcomer settled, a stranger to everyone, and he has outlived them all, remaining forever a stranger and newcomer. And although there are people living all around him who arrived later than he, even later than I, even just yesterday, these latecomers are so stubbornly building their houses and growing in, putting down roots as thick and blunt as carrots or fingers, that of course *they* are the ones who live here (that man with such-and-such a woman, that woman with such-and-such a man)—not he. His little house has been crowded out to the end of the street, as if shoved aside. Its whole misshapen lot has slipped off it like a patchwork quilt, one edge trailing in the river . . . Somehow, as needed, the little bathhouse has surrounded itself with tiny rooms and sheds—because time passes, the family grows, and no one leaves—taking up the street and a corner of the steep bank. They have enclosed their homestead, their bit of meadow, with an undulating, flimsily transparent stake fence, and their life shows through for all to see, shady and unrecognizable: a hammock has been hung, a dishpan has been thrown out, and there is a single garden row, small as a grave, just for form's sake, in order to be "recorded" in this world as having populated it, a tiny garden row with everything under the sun (two carrots, three dills, and one sunflower), exercising the rights of a flower bed (it has to be watered, as a kitten has to be given milk or a puppy leftovers), there's nothing to eat from it and really no point to it—it doesn't produce at all.

We don't hear anything over there: they don't argue, don't quarrel, don't shout, don't explain . . . Someone swings for a while in the hammock, forgets his book; someone comes out barefoot on the little meadow, glances at the dishpan . . . and that's all. No chance you'll find out who it was. And all the rest of the tense, full-blooded reality that is gaining a foothold in the neighborhood has had to exclude this little nook from its consciousness, from the sphere of its infringements, as if the nook were an invisible part of the spectrum, an inaudible part of the diapason—non-existent. An accidental, fragmentary revelation of the simultaneity of another life, going on (such happiness is hard to believe) within frozen, uncomfortable, self-propagated, established forms . . . They look through us, we through them. And that is the only place on earth where things happen.

He is the man who got run over by a train one night when drunk, as I will learn that spring, or this spring, and I will live out the summer as if he did not exist. But nothing has changed, something has even been strengthened, in the little house at the edge. In the autumn I encounter him alive, missing a leg, and am surprised that I hadn't noticed that he had just one leg . . . But these are two different stories, and who knows which came first, whether he was missing a leg to begin with, and then he got run over, and just yesterday I encountered him alive and all in one piece, or whether, on the contrary, time passes in reverse at their house, coming to meet us or backing away. Time does not pass at our house; their time passes through us, and soon the grandson will finally have a grandfather. Over there, someone is occasionally added to the household, as if he had made up his mind and defected to them—I'm on your side! He looks over the fence, happy that he has gotten away from us, gotten away at last. Over there they all love spilled milk—who cares!

But they are also steadfast—not to our way of thinking, but to theirs. And what lives within their steadfastness, as they live among us? Isn't that where the cloud is, from which, in our dreams, the beloved dead come to us to arrange that we will meet occasionally, "but don't tell a soul," and you haven't even time to say what you wanted to, though you are bursting with the muteness of your love—"until tomorrow," and a finger on the lips, "not a word! it's a secret, yours and ours . . ." So that in the morning, as you splash water on your face, you notice the morning and—but what happened? what was it? Suddenly you remember that you mustn't remember—and you smile: a secret, yours and theirs. Isn't that where all this lives, clinging to the edge? Maybe over there . . . where those loving and living people are, the ones who are "not us" . . . over there, for them, she's alive even now, the only girl who didn't hang herself, didn't shoot herself, but whom I murdered, whom he murdered in me, and under whose name someone continues to live with me, outside her own soul (because her soul is stationed on the other side of the door), clumsily imitating her own former words and gestures, and made up to look like the murdered girl: oh, you can tell she's the wrong one, sticks out like a sore thumb, that's why I made myself up so badly, you know, so that everyone could tell, this is how we live, you know, this is how we do it . . .

It's all so terrifying if you exist among them, within love, over there behind the transparent symbolic fence, and you look out from there—from your own authenticity—at your own street, your own dwelling, your own self, as you would look at a vampire who donned the clothes of the little boy he had sucked dry, and then pinned the boy's name on the pocket lest he forget . . . We're all over there, Lord bless us. The reason the little house is so crowded is that we're terrified to leave it and can't and it's the only house for us all, and besides, the grandfather who once found this nook is still alive from under the train, having cut two wheels off the locomotive . . . Today he asked me for money for a split of vodka, but yesterday he gave it back, he's a good man, although why should he hurt me this way, even though I'm disguised as the little boy I murdered I'd be glad to forget the ruble, but he wants nothing in common with me, he takes the ruble from the next split and hands it back to me. Sad. Is there something nice I could do for them? Nothing, ever. Set a fire, perhaps? . . .

They have fire, they have murder, they have prison, they have one child after another, they do not have a cow or a vegetable patch, they do have these things that we don't have. They have everything, even a lack of what everyone has; we have nothing. May we come in? They don't hear. The wicket gate is always unlatched—we can never go over there. Conscience forbids. Which means that what prevents you from asking to visit them is also conscience . . .

Now it's another new spring—and the boy, the son, so very handsome, who last spring married such a nice girl (she was added, then, to the household on the other side of the fence, in the little lake of their void that slides down to the river) . . . the boy, the dear son, yesterday tonight they cut his throat with a bullet with a knife through the temple; he got involved with a gang, and then broke off with them, went straight when he got married; it may have been that, or something else . . . day after tomorrow they found him, their darling, murdered in the bushes, by Finland Station.

That's it, that's it! None of this happens to me! Ever, for any reason, by nature—it doesn't happen to me. Suicide is in the reserves. Fate in retirement. Soul pensioned off. Conscience laid up. Body under repair. Mind in storage. I am looking for a door in a field.

The married couple, accomplices, secretly ate the baby; his grandmother later found him in the vegetable patch, and now she sings him lullabies; the couple go down to the river, and the husband carries a basket full of clothes stripped from people they have killed, people whose size and quality they deemed suitable for murder. As the fence stakes are reflected in your pupils upside down, so, too, am I . . . and the little meadow is deserted now, it stares after me through the eye of the discarded dishpan. When they all rushed into their bathhouse in fear, they forgot the dishpan.

In that house is fate. It happens to those who were unable to become us, even if they wanted to, but who simply stayed, crouching at the very edge of our ironclay forms, unintentionally lodging themselves in this life as a mother to someone, as someone's grandma, or simply as a distant aunt.

This—and not songs, not birch trees—is the concept of *the people*. The people are the divine fate that happens to someone else in the world. Among them are all those who were, who are no more, and who have not been. Everything I loved and everything I still love because it remains, everything I had and everything I have left—it's very little, but by now it is all I love. Fate is the people, the people are fate; I, an excommunicate, am off to one side. Until all envy is gone, until I have placed on a greedy palm the generous crumb that is left of me, until then, I can never go to the place where everything lies in full view, through the wicket gate that stands always open.

Autumn at Zaodi

———

To R.G.

. . . We were coming down into the Alazani Valley. Autumn hung in the air, an autumn the equal of spring. With the beautiful difference that it made no demand on you, and you could exist in that crystal space as easily and idly, as unpretentiously, as a falling leaf suspended from a spiderweb. We drove through a little town nesting precariously on the mountain spur. A flock of ravens burst out from the crossless bell tower poised above the precipice—and a view of extraordinary depth was revealed to us. As we dropped unresistingly down the hairpin turns, back and forth, like that smoothly falling leaf, our eyes were opened, life relaxed, and we did not need to overcome. The world's clarity was ordered differently, in reverse: it began with unclearness, rather than ending with it. Haze did not gather in the distance—it was somewhere at close range, before our eyes. Then came a spurt of absolute emptiness above the valley, and beyond it, in the mountain view, lay cold, still, thickened air of astounding clarity, a property perceived not by the eye but by the tongue, like the clarity we taste when we drink from a longed-for spring. Over there stood clean, white mountains, and we were dropping like a leaf to the bottom of a huge bowl, where people had settled down to live, where they were being born and dying, while above them, soft and blue as a puff of cigarette smoke, hung their life's breath: from hearths, campfires, and braziers, from decayed leaves and spent vines.

The cry of autumn, when the smoke has cleared
And shadows of echo have settled on the lowland—
The ravines are narrower, darker, with the flapping
Of wings long since flown, the wings of cranes . . .
And the cry is gone. The campfire is dead.
Among the stars the air of night grows empty . . .
As hollow to the ear as the rooster's voice—
Beyond the stillness and the bird ellipsis points
At the valley's end,
*   where the mountain stands*
That stood there yesterday,—

so said a remarkable Georgian poet, brother of another great Georgian poet.

And we found ourselves in a verse of his autumn. Life is so cozy in a country where you can sense that a poet you know from your primer stood right here, at this same point and this same time of year, and looked out with the same feelings; your homeland is burned onto you in the tight, aching scar where you see the view from the window, the line from the primer, and your mother's face—and, without lifting your eyes, an escape from intolerability, and the first swallow of the wine at the *dukhan* . . . And autumn's clear wine carries with it the concept of that same air, that same hazy clarity, that same smell of destruction and love, which allows us to go on living—the smell of longevity and death: the leaves have been burned, the wish has been conceived . . . and has not been wished. It was as if the air held something that was *after* the smoke, *after* the flight of the flock, *after* the fall of the leaf, *after* the just-interrupted cockcrow, all of which we had missed, all of which had ceased to sound just before we came—it wasn't even an echo but *after* the echo, *just* after, when it had departed into a diapason inaudible to our ear. But we heard it! It was autumn. And the shadow—could anyone have said it better—that shadow, black and then azure, fading away in ravines and ridges so distant out there, beyond the valley, that they were as small as the fingerprints in modeled clay—that shadow was the print of the faded sound.

We were looking for "the mill." I had no idea what it was. My friends kept asking the way, and no one understood them. This was getting to be something of a mystery. From this authentic autumn, which I had been pursuing in my flight from winter and had finally overtaken . . . from such an autumn . . . to go looking for this out-of-place Russian word, *zavod*—and not find it. My friends kept asking the way, and people stared at us. Their gaze slid over our city clothes, smiled secretly, and led away deep into the landscape. There. There was the *zavod*. The landscape seemed to originate from their gaze, it *was* their gaze, and they couldn't see it . . . There was no one in the village. Old men. They were in no hurry to live, just as the autumn itself was in no hurry to die. They did not hurry to understand and did not hurry to answer. I had no idea how they managed, every time, to get my friends talking, but, every time, it turned out that my friends were no longer inquiring of the old men, the old men were questioning my friends. I had no idea why they started to smile, but those two poses were eloquent without translation, even to me, looking on as an outsider . . . The clear-eyed old man and the two flourishing old ladies, as well as the intimidated young woman who heaved her belly across the threshold, were enjoying us—we weren't much entertainment, but better than nothing on this back road, which we could never have taken if we hadn't been overinterpreting all the directions we'd received . . . Our driver was trying to understand these people, but how? By half opening the door of his "made-in-U.S.S.A." Fiat, planting one foot on the road, keeping the other on the gas, clutching the door with one hand, and freeing his other hand for a gesture that belongs in the Georgian alphabet as a letter. The pose of a man who has not a second to lose and wants to get back in and drive, if he only knew where . . . I looked again at these clear faces, washed by time and smoothed by its abundance. They were not so distracted and restless as to lose anything that had come into their keeping—time and dignity included. "*Zavod? Zavod* . . ." Musingly they inserted the mysterious word in their conversation. "*Zavod?*" They discussed it. "*Zaodi?* . . . Ah, *zaodi!*" And they pointed out the road, which we inquired three times more.

"The word had to be said in Georgian"—my friends laughed. "They don't understand it in Russian." But I, too, liked *zaodi* better.

Now we came to a place which on first glance was the least prepossessing of our entire quest. A black, dead ravine crossed the highway (or rather, vice versa). It appeared to have been additionally torn up, dug up, *autopsied*. There was not a blade of grass in its landscape (not a drop of color in its face). It was worse than dead —cadaverous, somehow. Its rims would become a hell at the first rain. There had been no rain for a long while.

"Look," my friend said. "This is *the present!*"

And from the way he livened, quickened, and brightened, it was suddenly obvious that all this time—while we had been riding and chatting and he had been listening, agreeing, and nodding contentedly—all this had been alien, not his cup of tea. He may have been sipping from it, but only as a kind and gentle person. Now he scented the approach of his own world, as a true hunter scents his prey . . . We dismissed the car. My friend was already walking ahead, not concealing his excitement and joy; he was leading me confidently to a place where he knew for certain, without ever having been there, that what we needed was awaiting us. Up ahead, perched precariously on the edge of the ravine, was a shed, or shelter, and in front of it stood several dump trucks, further underscoring the impression that the ravine was not a ravine but an excavation run riot.

The cabin faced away from us, and until the very last moment—until we came right up to it and entered by the back door—I still couldn't guess the point of it.

This is where we found ourselves.

Two hefty suckling pigs came out to meet us, with an oddly unsteady gait. They paid us no attention but wobbled over to a gnarled brush pile to scratch against the wood. We descended two steps, my friend's back obscured the entrance for a moment, and it took another moment, or even less, for my eyes to adapt to the diminished light so that I could make out what was in the shadow . . .

We were in *the present*. I am hard put to prove this sensation: like any sensation, it is unprovable. I can only swear that suggestion and autosuggestion had nothing to do with it. My sensation on finding myself in this semi-room (*semi-room* is the right word, because it had a roof and two walls, but two walls were missing. The architecture was bare necessity, just four posts, a roof against the rain, and the two wretched walls, boarded up with assorted trash lest anyone see in from the road. The view of the valley and the snowy mountains was unobstructed, as was the view of the ravine, the pit) . . . well, my sensation on finding myself here is hard to describe, I had never felt anything comparable, I can only offer a simile . . . The little ball whisks around the Coliseum of the roulette wheel, tapping and pouncing, describing large circles, trying to fly out of bounds . . . that's how we live! . . . but it weakens, its circles grow narrow, it bobbles among the pockets more and more indecisively, as though it still possessed the independence to choose itself a number, and perhaps it even has the momentum to pop out of a seemingly unsuitable pocket—but this will use up the last of its strength . . . and then—plop!—it falls at last into its *own* pocket, which now could be no other. One more faint twitch, from side to side, as if settling in more comfortably, and it stops dead, subsides: Good! That is exactly how I felt, as though I had been rushed and bobbled all my life and at last I had arrived, here I was, and I didn't even quite know where I'd landed (in which of the pockets), but I had landed, that was certain. Perhaps the aroma was what told me, the smoke. But I was *here*, and it was true, and at last there was nothing summoning me to doubt or strive onward. And since I was here, I could also look and see where I was—in what surroundings I was destined, this time definitively, to *be*.

It is very hard to give a sequential description of my cozy roulette pocket; I really wish I could render it visible all at once. But that is beyond the capacity of language. And besides, the way it happened, I was seeing first one thing and then another, as I tried to analyze the sensation that had come over me at the threshold (this is what they mean by "at first sight"!). The heart of this mausoleum (since this was the end of my hard life, as I have already said) was a stove. And a hot, blazing heart it was! It seethed and gurgled, choking on the future blood and joy (though I didn't know it yet) of my life. This heart (this stove), in turn, recalled one of the mausoleums I had recently seen in Khiva. The clay-daubed vat was crowned with a polished copper lid, like the golden dome, which had also had a little knob on top. The only thing missing was the crescent moon. The copper lid was the *richest* thing here —and that was why it shone, that was why it had been polished (which is why we're also seeing it first) like the sun. It was, however, slightly creased from long service, though all its dents shone just as blindingly, sending tiny individual rays of refracted light in the most varied directions. But despite being dented the dome had not lost the general impression of sphericality. It shone just as round and coppery as the man who must have polished it—Gogi, the "mill owner," who was busy doing things at the hearth.

"Bend down," my friend told me. "Look! See how the grate has burned through!"

Indeed, the thick bars over the fire had sagged, and they hung like a bubble. The firebox gave off such blinding heat, the logs were so blistered with round knots of coals, the open stove door revealed such a life-affirming, never-dull drama playing in this theater, that had you shown me an atomic reactor I would have curled my lip at its negligible, mediocre, imitative form.

"Would you believe," said Gogi, ceaselessly doing things but finding the time to smile serenely, so that his coppery cheeks rounded and sent off dancing reflections of the hearth light. "Would you believe," he said, with the pride of a pacifist, "for three months now, the fire on this hearth hasn't gone out."

I believed.

And besides, what could I disbelieve here? This fire? This half of a suckling pig, suspended from a hook on the only post that the walls did not touch—the pillar of this temple? This drunken sow, mother of my shish kebabs, who was rooting in the narrow strip between the mill and the ravine, but not falling into the ravine? These peaceable laymen, who had arranged their well-deserved feast at a narrow table that fitted into the corner like the narthex of a church? These hardworking peasants, drinking and conversing with a steadiness and dignity that no lord could muster if he had this much to drink? This shish kebab, sliced as I watched, from the leg of the suckling pig who had just been running around right here? This wine, the color of an autumn leaf? Especially since it wasn't even wine yet, but the material of wine, that is, innocent nature, not warped by instruction and long practice. Disbelieve the "material" of wine? These four posts? This copper lid? This roof against the rain, or this sky through the hole in this roof? That view, through the absent door, of the High Georgian Mountains, which reproached us with nothing, however, because we were infringing on nothing? Those mountains? My friend? Gogi, finally? No, I could not disbelieve Gogi!

Because the one thing I might have disbelieved, the one thing sought out by my envious eye, was a pink light switch fitted to a post. Gogi had gone over to electricity; whatever else may be said, electricity makes it more comfortable to stand the night watch. And that single object, of distinct and final form, was crude and strangely irregular in this hastily, crookedly, carelessly knocked together ship of the world, this frail bark of happiness, this dirigible after the seventh drink! I shall turn my gaze to that object no more: life is so beautiful. Let the man of petty soul dislike us! just as we pity him, for he is not with us.

Exactly here, at this point, the cycle of yearly life was completed, if one can find the beginning or end of a circle . . . But the life cycle is vertical, unlike a senseless rotation on the surface. And here was the beginning of that end . . . when, gathering speed down the mountain of the summer noonday, we arrive at tangency and convergence with the earth, with the special inertial force that pins us to the earth. The sultry heat had finished its work; the earth had finished hers and was now resting, mellow and empty, like a mother whose children have scattered to their families and the cities; the grapes had finished their work, having become wine and entrusted even their pressings to Gogi, so that he could distill from them a lethal *chacha*—for what was boiling and muttering so mysteriously under the shining lid was the caldron of a still . . . Even the pressings had finished their work, but, although they had become a thin, ugly, reddish gruel, it too had been put to use, because that was what the suckling pigs were ecstatically eating, in the narrow strip between the mill and the precipice. They were made happy by it, and very drunk, so that their transition to shish kebab apparently occurred without pain or fear; their innocent souls flew lightly away and entered freely into the soul's cycle in nature, where, depending on their talents and sins, they were awaited by a promotion or a demotion on the career ladder of evolution: to become the soul of a hen or of a horse . . . The men now drinking the "material" of wine had also finished their work, and they were every bit as honest as that "material." They were the honest material of men: neither overfermented nor vinegary, and free of added alcohol or sugar. Everyone had finished. Autumn. Gogi alone was working.

Now, *this* was "labor unceasing"! He was beautiful in work: swift and steady, but so free of wasted motion that he appeared to move lazily. He stoked the fire, split wood, seasoned the caldron, sliced kebabs, broiled kebabs, set the table, poured wine, was courteous and radiant—all this simultaneously, all in good time, everything in its turn. How solicitously and instantaneously—a conjurer!—he created a space for us to feast in, the single table being already occupied; how deftly he spread out a newspaper, the tablecloth; dished some pickled peppers onto it; sprinkled a handful of salt; spread a tattered blanket on a bench and smoothed it tenderly—sit down! And no servility as he waited on us, only dignity. No boorishness, only courtesy. He served wine in a pickle jar (and the jar, as if bewitched, was never empty, and I could not see when he had time to refill or replace it); he flipped the shish kebab into an aluminum dog bowl with style and snap, extracting the skewer as if swishing a sword from its sheath (and the bowl was never empty, but in this case I saw how he did it, because my shoulder was the one over which Gogi's hairy hand was thrust, and the skewer kept zinging past my ear). Such a table and such "service" I had never seen, nor will I ever again . . . No, absolutely, men do everything better—too bad they can't have babies . . . Things were so clear and good here, among men. There is so much tenderness and purity among friends—where else but in Georgia to understand this!

Never had we tasted anything so good . . . We weren't even devouring the meat—we were breathing it. To swallow such a quantity of scalding, fatty, half-raw pork, well rubbed with coarse crystalline salt and broiled on the open fire, and to wash it down with liter jars of the "material" of dry wine—I might as well have thrown my liver straight to the drunken pigs. But it was easier to die than to deny myself this delight.

"Understand, now, liver," I was saying. "You have to understand me."

My friend was riding high, my friend was king, his eyes shone. He sat increasingly erect; his hand holding the glass was increasingly steady and triumphant; the national line of his shoulder, the right angle between shoulder and neck, became increasingly square; and lo, he had stepped out of Pirosmani's painting *The Feast of the Princes*. Our tables had long since grown together; the man who looked so much like my father's young pictures gave me a ceremonious hug to cement this blood photorelationship; someone untied our little boat, and we drifted down the ravine toward the Main Caucasian Range; the pigs, perhaps to sober up, scratched themselves passionately against the tires of the dump trucks, which, quite obviously, would be staying here tonight . . . My friend proposed a toast, which I no longer had to translate from Russian to Georgian, for I now understood even Russian as well as I did Georgian . . . So happy was my friend that I realized that even he, although he possessed the gift of the world we were now in, found it much easier and pleasanter to get into this world from the outside than to insist on carrying it with him.

Alas, only another man's life can be life-affirming!

And just then, taking my friend's word that I was worthy of it, they gave me a little book, the only book that my adopted brother (who looked more and more like my father) happened to have. And this—who could have dreamed!—was a biography of Pushkin, in Georgian. I burst into tears at the symbolism.

It's wrong, it's bad for you, to drink from sorrow. But not to get drunk when you're happy is impossible. We can't walk away from happiness by ourselves, we haven't the strength (spare me those iron-willed people who, just at that rare moment, find the inner strength and heroism to turn their backs on happiness, only to weaken later and dissolve in protracted grief because they let it slip!). A man cannot turn his back on happiness, and yet time flows and corrodes, hastening the treachery of this very instant, which does not last, and will pass, and is gone—where? . . . Can it be that something for which we have lived all our life will come to an end? No! Never! Never will we betray this happiness ourselves! Simply —morning will wake us, to find that happiness is over.

Soon Gogi will have remade all the grape pressings into fire and burned the fire down to pressings. The grate in the hearth will break, cave in, burn through. Then Gogi will furl his mill, roll it up: he will remove the caldron and carry it home, dig up the posts and carry those home, too, prop them in his yard; the rest he will just leave, as trash. That's what they told me would happen after we drove away . . .

Such a sad ending . . . Gogi walks away down the ravine like a roving actor, his carnival booth furled: stooping under the weight of the logs on his shoulders, he carries the copper pot under his arm, and his side reflects the sun . . . Thus he departs into an infinite vista, taking with him my happiness, as though my coming here had not been chance, but his arrow had struck my heart.

If another great poet (granted, a Russian, but also of the brother-hood) had not said, "Cadet Schmidt! Upon my honor, summer will return!"—I would not have known how to console myself.

Everyone here had earned himself an autumn. We alone had received, for free, a happiness deserved by someone else. Kind and deeply touched, we would stop at the bazaar and purchase a jug and a shirt, scorning our paper money and envying them their riches.

The Palm of Victory

When asked whether the Scythians had flutes, he re-plied, "We don't even have grapes."

ANACHARSIS THE SCYTHIAN,
sixth century B.C.

Man cannot get used to the cold.

ROALD AMUNDSEN

MY FRONTIER IMPRESSIONS

This journey begins from afar . . . From Peter the Great—half benefactor, half Antichrist. My mother still omits prepositions in telegrams, "dislikes" taxis, and rides the train only fourth class (with a reserved seat). She does not hire a porter. If she counted up what she saves by all this, the difference would make her laugh. Yet I remember that after the war, for another three or four years, she invariably had a second bowl of soup, brimful, with a thick slice of bread. Only after that could she consider herself full—this delicate, intellectual beauty . . . In Europe, both soup and bread have become relics: you have to hunt for the soup, and they will bring you the bread separately when you express surprise that there isn't any. They're not economizing—they're keeping their figures, eating scientifically, people who are long since full. They buy a hundred grams of this, fifty grams of that (without standing in line)—to eat immediately, fresh. Yesterday's is thrown out. What a barrier we must cross, to be able to throw things into the garbage pail! Hunger and cold pierced us to the bone. Cold and hunger . . . We haven't yet outlived the extra bowl of soup, the second helping. SECONDS!

The "supplemental portion," the "fortified diet" . . . In English these terms convey nothing of our experience. When my mother has her routine liver attack, I can state with confidence that she "hated to waste" some stale bit of food. And she never needed to "keep" her figure: she was always like this. Starving people do not have good eating habits. They also cease to read books in a time of book famine—they just *get* them.

Bone-piercing cold and hunger . . . I was visiting a socialist country and had acquired the local semi-hard currency. I decided to buy a fur coat. This led to anxieties and problems, and what did they remind me of? Why, the purchase of a cow! My companion, a specialist in Russian literature (naturally, he was trailing after me through the stores, broadening his professional horizons), said: "Russian writers still have a Gogol's Overcoat complex." I took offense. (Especially since I did have the complex, chiefly vis-à-vis him. He was so obliging and well bred that I, as a Russian, a man of the empire, could easily suspect him of irony, mockery, and even of scorn.) I told him peevishly that as a specialist he might be better informed. It wasn't Dostoevsky who had said this, but Turgenev. And for another thing, it wasn't all of us (not all of us had come out of Gogol's "Overcoat"). After cooling down a bit, however, and after moderating my tourist complex (especially since I had not aborted my expedition or refused his services), I realized that I had said this myself more than once; I just didn't want to hear it from foreign lips. And, indeed, the gentleman's fur coat . . . the kingly fur coat . . . the royal gift . . . that is, from the tsar's own back . . . Pushkin's Grinyov gives Pugachev a hareskin coat . . . finally, "The Overcoat"—Gogol will never be understood, never be explained—a genius! . . . Mandelstam "in a fur coat too lordly for his station" . . . But certainly the fur coat has outgrown itself; it has become a symbol of prosperity, success. What, if not the fur coat, do people later sell and squander on drink? And steal, of course. "The forces that stripped Akaky Akakievich of his overcoat . . ." Or again, I had a friend, a Moscow prose writer, who rode the crest of his success to my city ("familiar to the point of tears") to wrap up a contract with Leningrad Film. He installed himself in the Hotel Europe and naturally started to drink. I had made his acquaintance not long before this fame: he had been splendid, shiveringly naked, and black with soot from the wood stove in his Moscow hovel. Now I visited him in his new status, in a deluxe room. Near the entrance hung a Mandelstamian fur coat (beaver, if my hazy impression is correct), from among Lensky's stage props. Perhaps I even unconsciously hummed his aria, "Whether I perish," or perhaps my friend, with the intoxicated sharp eye of an artist and parvenu, had immediately caught my glance; perhaps I was needlessly sober early in the morning; but our conversation, as compared with our last meeting, was aimless and stumbling. He looked darkly at the buzzer and pushed it with disdain—the waitress flew in so promptly that she must have been lurking behind the door. Her obsequiously greedy little eyes made me wonder how much he had already overpaid her. Caviar and a poached egg in bouillon arrived immediately, and not without a bottle, of course. He downed a drink, tossed the bothersome egg into the corner, and swallowed his chaser of bouillon. Sitting up a little straighter, he cast a glance at the fur coat (now I knew that my own glance had not escaped his notice). "We tinkerers!" he suddenly shrilled theatrically. (His complicated history also included a period as a dramatic actor.) "We all want to write *War and Peace*. But we can't pull it off. Can't pull it off!" he concluded, on an extremely piercing note. And went to bed. He was undoubtedly a decent person: I never saw him with the fur coat again. He had let it go cheap, he said, just as he had bought it. "I've accumulated a lot of vests," he complained to me once. What he meant was this: Each time he emerged from a drinking bout, he had an expensive three-piece suit made. When he sold it for drink, they would take the jacket and trousers, but nowadays who needed the vest? He had accumulated a lot of vests . . . I love him for that phrase. I'm not digressing: the vest, too, is apropos. Gogol also talked about vests. He had a liking for vests—there are various anecdotes about this, one of them recounted by Bunin, somewhere in his reminiscences. Galoshes, too, have gone the way of vests and fur coats; Bulgakov testifies to this. But the ladies' fur coat will never die out in our country. The fur coat may indeed be a complex . . . It may indeed, in our range of goods, be a luxury and a symbol of luxury . . . But people are cold! This must not be forgotten. When I am afraid of nothing, sure of myself and my lucky star, when all misfortunes happen only to others, never to me—even then, there's one thing that always makes me rein in my arrogance and confidence: the memory of working with metal at forty degrees below zero . . . Dark blue hoarfrost. That indigenous episode in my biography eats wormholes through my courage.

And I myself don't like to settle accounts in a taxi. On the train, although admittedly I don't travel fourth class like my mother, I take third. Anything above third gives me an involuntary spasm. And I understand my social position when I'm settling accounts: when I'm embarrassed to pay less, when I don't want to pay more . . . Luxury, you see, does not attract me. A yacht and a villa ("the Turkish coast and Africa . . .") are not what I need. I need a room of my own, and jeans, and I can't do without coffee. I don't need what is possible—I need what comes next. I have long had the means to travel first class, but I just can't skip third.

It happened once that my friend A. was going to Leningrad the same day I was. We decided to travel together, and I agreed to get the tickets. I was worried that there wouldn't be any, but for some reason he was not. He "always went to the station and got right on the train" and took "international" (first class). I could not consent to such a risk and went to buy the tickets in advance. I waited out the line—there were no tickets. Not for the trains that "proper" people ride (the Arrow, the Helsinki), not for a compartment, not even for international. At that point I got lucky: I bought two tickets from a scalper, for a compartment on a supplementary train. My friend was dissatisfied with what I had done: we would get there half an hour early and buy a ticket, he claimed. I arrived forty minutes early. He was late: twenty minutes early. He went to the ticket window and got two tickets, as usual: somehow there were some. We boarded our car and the train started. I had not had time to turn in my tickets. They were sweating in my fist. So off we went, on four tickets. I stood in the car's buffet, between two Arabs and a shabby rear admiral, sipping cognac and accustoming myself to my accidental luxury, persuading myself that I liked it. This cost me some effort . . . Despite all, I didn't quite like it. "It's not an admiral's duty to be admired," I said. My friend led me to our compartment. As we undressed, I realized that although *he* was traveling international, I was not. Different shoes, different socks, different underwear. Neither of us, I thought, wrote any worse than the other, had drunk any less, had loved . . . But he was ahead! Unbelievable. He had slipped into first class ahead of me. He had been to Paris, to Japan (admittedly, he hadn't been to America yet, but now he would go). He had been to countries I couldn't hope to get to. He knew people I had heard of, but who most likely hadn't heard of me . . . Here, of course, I have overdone my confessions. In my secret heart I hold an extremely high opinion of myself, apparently, and I envy no one . . . though I'm not sure that a flare-up of the complex isn't envy's little sister. Of course I'm a provincial, a Leningrader; of course I understand and cherish the idea that poverty is a characteristic, not a lack of money; even when broke, a rich man wastes incomparable means . . . But a man who has gone broke is not a broken man—he can go broke several times. To be broken by someone, by something, is irreversible. No, I will never be rich!

And why malign myself? After all, I like poverty. I dislike excess, though admittedly I want my necessities to be of the highest quality. I like having a poor little house, but in a place that I like; I like having one suit, but to my taste . . . Yet this is wealth indeed, to have my time free and no one bothering me! This is most precious of all. It turns out I dislike sufficiency, but wealth will do. Either feast or famine. It's more than pride.

After all, that sleeping car had appealed to me since childhood. I had loved to peer from the station platform at those glassed doors with their polished brass sprigs in the Russian *style moderne*. The idea that the car dated from before the Revolution pleased me. And there I was, riding in it for the first time. What was the matter with me? I didn't like the people who rode in it now. I subtracted myself. And A. From the compartment I couldn't see *them*. Which meant that what I really didn't like was myself in my new social aspect as a "Soviet bourgeois."

Curiously, cars of this class went out of production after the Revolution. This had its own justice: after all, there was no one to ride them anymore. When there began to be someone, enough of the old cars still existed. Which meant they had been well made.

I was confirmed in my reflexive vow not to ride first class. But then another occasion arose . . . My wife and I were returning from the south. There were no tickets, of course, and we needed to leave. At this point, taught by my first experience with A., I made bold to ask for "international." These they had. Enjoying the comfort in advance, I walked down the platform with an unliftable suitcase, overstraining myself in my effort to show the empty-handed porters that I was carrying it like a feather. Of course, our car was at the end of the platform. Five, four, three . . . I was counting off the cars I still had to pass. One . . . There was no car beyond it—and then there were cars again. In place of ours there was a gap, a hole. This seemed so strange to me that I failed to construct any bold hypotheses as to how such a thing could happen, and I understood only when I came up close. Our car was there after all, between the others. It was merely somewhat lower; when shielded, it disappeared from view. This was a new car, spanking new, of a kind I had never seen.

Sucked as smooth as a piece of hard candy, it shone like a dental crown in a ruined mouth; the neighboring cars, which had still seemed serviceable, were instantly rendered obsolete. It was brightly flecked with the nickel of foreign inscriptions in all three languages, in addition to Russian, in such classy, brand-new letters that you immediately wanted to steal them—unscrew them and affix them to something else. The lettering was perceived as a toy and did not serve its function in the mind.

I approached the door timidly, a sweaty passenger with his arms weighed down, who would now begin to rummage through his pockets, having forgotten which safe place he had hidden his ticket in this time . . . How was I any different from the old woman who reaches into her stocking for the little bundle in which her entire property is tied—a few banknotes, a railroad ticket, and a reference from the village Soviet? I regretted not hiring a porter. I should have arrived at these doors wearing another social aspect. Matters were partly righted by the conductor's unfriendly face—I dwelt on it with gratitude. Once again, the situation seemed understandable. This nice, tidy woman, who must have gained a reputation for her cleaner car and stronger tea, had been appointed to this unique sleeper as a promotion. When I finally found my ticket and handed it over, I tried to flatter her by admiring her new equipment—and wounded her to the quick. (Why is the painful spot the one that is called the quick?)

More boldly now, and not in the least offended, because I realized at once that her remarks had more to do with the car than with me, I walked inside to civilization. My foot stepped first on a row of little brushes, and then on a thick carpet runner. This was "Ah!"—and as yet I was in no shape to comprehend it. We found our compartment. The door had its own complexity, for you couldn't open it and get by, you could only get by and open it.

Similarly, the only way you could pass a neighbor in the corridor was to draw yourself back into the compartment, like an oyster sucked into its shell. But we mastered this and found ourselves inside the compartment, feeling slightly constrained by shame at being there, but also constrained by its size. The whole place gleamed with a peculiar home-away-from-home coziness, guaranteed to us by the high standard of design. Everything appeared to have been well thought out, down to the smallest detail. And so it had. Our first interest, however, was not the details but the large items: our two weighted suitcases and ourselves. We couldn't immediately find room for them.

Everything here folded back, opened up, collapsed. Everything converted to itself, apparently bypassing its very function. The little dining table converted to a washstand, the washstand concealed within it a bidet. That foreign word *bidet* happens to sound like the Russian for "offend"—and it does offend me. Almost as much as *konditsioner!* When they work, we don't yet know how to use them; by the time we learn, they no longer work. The bidet, possibly, wasn't working *yet*; but the air conditioner, certainly, was working *no longer*. The plywood apotheosis was sweltering. "Never mind," I told my wife, defending civilization. "They'll turn it on when we get under way."

I was no longer confident of this: I had managed to pick up a few slight hints in the brand-new perfection of this rationalized space. It had been overperfected! Too well mastered, assimilated, and digested—it had vanished. Yes, everything here had been conceptualized, systematized, and calculated to the utmost, to the words *rationality, economy,* and *efficiency.* The intended rider, apparently, was an equally rational creature, average in size, economical in his gestures and intentions. If our well-traveled conjugality should suddenly awaken in this romantic railroad intimacy . . . The mere fantasy cheered me thoroughly. That celebrated spy in the story read under the school desk—I wonder how she would have gone about it here? But there were lots of places to hide things: the wall was honeycombed with an extravagant assortment of little shelves and drawers, each conceived with its own purpose. I could not refrain from laying my toothbrush on one of the shelves and setting a bottle of beer in the bar. Beyond that, my imagination ran dry. Although, had I wished, I could have put away, as in a chest of drawers, the entire contents of the suitcases that I had jammed tight with such difficulty . . . a shirt there, a towel here . . .

Now it dawned on me. I was Gulliver, crossing the border from the land of giants into Lilliput. A shiver of self-congruence ran down my spine: when I was stuffing the suitcases so that we would have fewer pieces to carry, and secretly priding myself on my "packing skill" in front of my wife, wasn't I preoccupied with the same thought that the car's designer had had about *me*? German met German here. I recognized him. Very likely that brilliant designer had managed to cram into his sleeper one more compartment than in the previous design, while fulfilling all sanitary standards so that it "had everything"; he had inserted the very compartment that made everyone identically uncomfortable. Oh, no! I exclaimed to myself. Only a German is capable of elevating poverty to wealth and reducing wealth to poverty! This was third class elevated to first. And so skillfully! You couldn't tell the difference . . . But then where had first class itself disappeared to? This was a dialectical question. Suddenly I understood the brushes at the beginning of the carpet runner. No one's restricting your freedom. No one's forcing you to wipe your feet. You yourself, "by reflex," as you walk over the little brushes, will wipe your own feet. Willy-nilly, you will step onto the runner with your feet already clean. Which means an immediate saving on the carpet runner, or rather on the vacuum cleaner and the conductor's labor: one meter of carpet runner per ten thousand kilometers of travel, half a kilo of dust per hundred passengers . . . That is no joke, incidentally, when multiplied by all the kilometers and all the cars and divided by all the passengers! Oh, it makes me want to fold my arms, lie down with my face to the wall, and as usual do nothing useful, just wonder, idly, who rides? and whither? and why? . . .

The air-conditioning in the car must have been carefully thought out and trouble-free, since the windows were not equipped to open . . . The compartment and its meticulousness still hypnotized us, however. We sat on edge like poor relatives. There was no way we could get comfortable: the trash generated by unpacking was still in our hands, because we didn't know where to stick it, although there were so many empty pigeonholes, suitable for trash if nothing else. I went out to the corridor in search of a trash can. In the normal place for it, a passenger was loitering about, like me, also with trash in his hands. Perhaps the can converted to a chess table . . . by now, neither of us knew. Just then the conductor looked out, her face severe. "The pail is on the rear platform!" she said. So they did have this understandable thing! Pleased and relieved, we undertook to inquire about the air-conditioning. "I don't know. I know nothing about it!" the conductor snarled. "The engineer is on his way." "The engineer?" we both said, in amazement. "The engineer of the train?" "The engineer of the car," the conductor snapped. "The car has an engineer??"

But—life settled down. The engineer assigned to the new car did not turn on the air conditioner, since it had been turned off on general principle by a more senior engineer, lest it get broken. But our engineer did manage to turn on the hot-water heater for tea. The conductor had been slavishly guarding the only valve she had mastered, letting no one near the water heater, just in case. She rolled up the runner and took it into her compartment. One of the passengers, a foreman and skilled craftsman by the look of him ("Eyes afraid, hands busy"), managed to open, or break, a window in the corridor. At any rate, the engineer failed to close it back up. A cross-draft formed in the car. We sighed. Finally, at one of the stations, I spied on a scene that thoroughly mollified me. The conductor opened the door to the other side and emptied the pail of trash onto the tracks. So we had adapted, we were on our way!

We discovered the possibility of looking out the window . . . There was only what we saw. What we had seen whirled away. And again there was only what we saw. The crossing keeper's cabin, the peasant woman with the flag, children with knees, a horse resting its muzzle on the barrier—the traveler's honor guard. Crossing, clicking, coppice . . . we clickety-clacked along. What eternal, melancholy happiness! Scarcely heard, kindred, not yours . . . A delay en route, a stop in a field. Back in my post-war childhood, how many of these stops there were! The passengers would slide down the embankment, while even the locomotive, taking advantage of the stop, appeared to nibble grass. Back in a hurry: some with a bouquet, some with berries, some with mushrooms. Such a stop is a rarity now, and besides, you can't hop out. But we were standing still. And here is what Chance elected to halt before my worn gaze . . . an embankment plowed for potatoes. Not yet fully plowed, however. It was being plowed right now. Two peasants were harnessed to the plow, a third was driving. The plow was wooden, by the way. A wooden one is lighter. They didn't have a horse, then. Could this really be easier than a spade? It must be. The peasants still know what they're doing. They leaned into their work like Repin's *Barge Haulers*. But their expression was not unhappy; the peasants did not have an unhappy expression, I tell you. Did Repin exaggerate? These three peasants had a calm, shared, family face. They must have been plowing for themselves. Without coercion. The field they were carving out of the embankment was narrow, but long. Two motorcycles lay on their sides at the edge of the plowed strip. One a Yava, the other an Izh. Good machines. Something like fifty horses between them. Finally a peasant noticed me watching him. And I may not have been the only one gawking from the cars . . . Whoa! They paused, glanced at us without apparent irritation, but unharnessed themselves. Rightly so—smoke break, by law. They sat down sedately near the motorcycles and took out a bottle of Camus. With milk. Handed it around the circle, to our envy. Lit their cigarettes. Threw us an occasional indifferent glance, as they reclined comfortably on the embankment in the unconstrained poses conferred only by physical labor. Should I add that in the meantime a TU-144 flew directly over all of us? Too much? But the little white arrow of the fighter plane was creeping across the firmament like a bug—it's true. At last we started moving. The peasants got to their feet: That's enough lazing around, time to finish up. Now the one who had been driving went to the strap. His turn, apparently. Turn by turn, apparently, they would finish the day's plowing, then mount their steel horses and dash for home. They would probably camouflage the plow under a bush, so that they could come back tomorrow. But no, it would fit perfectly in the sidecar . . . They would dash away, with a tail of dust curling behind them like the old behind the new.

The compartment had even become spacious. I laid my Era electric razor next to my toothbrush and made a trip to the buffet. What if they have Camus in the buffet, I thought. Sometimes they do. Less often nowadays, but still, it happens . . . They didn't. I drank just beer, with fellow passengers on the rear platform, and followed it up with port. How cozy we were on the platform! The floor clanking underfoot. Gobs of spit, cigarette butts. The suppressed desire to pull, at long last, the emergency brake. The door kept slamming; the people passing through glanced at us with tact and understanding. The sun shone through the car window as if this were Russia, and outside the window the world flashed by as if this were Russia, and two menacing peasants were nice to me as if this were Russia, and I worshipped them as if this were Russia. But indeed it was Russia.

Germany was something else. The Germans really knew how to make things! The compartment had become quite spacious, and even the landscape had begun to fit in the window. Rocking cozily on my shelf in this little cupboard, this tiny house, I was becoming efficient, neatly packed, and cognizant of my place, like the toothbrush parallel to me. The thoughts I was having—rhythmic, well ordered, and portable—were about suitcases. A suitcase would seem to be a familiar thing . . . But if we tell even the tiniest little story about it, as about an experience, as about something "given us in sensation," the whole narrative gets hopelessly sidetracked. It sits there on the spur, waiting for the oncoming train, and all of a sudden it starts letting them go by, the oncoming trains, one after the other . . . We'll be late! But here is a grand consolation and solution—we are *already* late.

And so, a suitcase. In Russian it is *chemodan*—a word of Persian origin, as unexpected as *hippopotamus*. Or *crocodile*. Or crocodile leather. And maybe it *was* crocodile! I thought, happy at the memory, for I did have such a suitcase in my inventory. From my legendary Aunt Frieda, Elfrieda Ivanovna (Johannovna), my great-aunt. After the war she lay in our kitchen like a thing, but she was known to have been the picture of beauty, and to have had a *romance* in Paris, or a romance in *Paris*, I really don't know how to convey the enchanting, awesome ring of these words in the inflamed, blockade-weakened middle ear of 1949. We love ourselves. Nowadays, I am less astonished by the fact that Aunt Frieda had been there with her romance than by what I was able to make of that fact as a child. A romance in Paris is nothing unusual. Nothing unusual *now*. No big deal. Now it's a romance *in* Paris. The *in*, not Paris, is capitalized now. Well, in those years it was Aunt Frieda's enormous trunk, not a suitcase, that took up half the front hall in our apartment, just as Aunt Frieda took up half the window shelf in the kitchen. An enormous leather trunk with two handles at the ends. The leather was *real*. In those years, leather was understood to be like the sole of your shoe, not the skin of your face. Real leather—people clucked their tongues and sighed and rolled their eyes. Because mostly there was imitation leather, and even that was rationed. A limit on LeatherImit. And a chain of gold on the *chemodan*! A small bronze padlock on the chain locked the trunk, and the key was on Aunt Frieda's neck. I would creep over to the kitchen window and touch Aunt Frieda on the little key. Then she would open her eyes.

I did not know what was in the trunk. At our house it was considered so improper to show an interest in someone else's belongings that I simply didn't dare, out loud. The leather trunk was reinforced with thick leather at the corners, it was bound with two mighty straps, it had brass nailheads . . . I strolled up and down past the trunk, touching and jingling first the lock, then the chain: "Whoa! Giddyap!" I thought of a horse because they still existed in Leningrad then. A horse's harness, too, had brass nailheads. And besides, how could such an enormous trunk be transported, except on a sleigh . . . The trunk lid was embossed, so it may well have been "crocodile." The horse was harnessed to the trunk straps, the trunk flew over the snow, the snow dusted the crocodile's back . . . Whoa! The trunk turned out to have nothing in it. A broken umbrella with moldy ruching, and a bundle of letters not written in Russian, and a small bouquet from a hat—these were all at the bottom. It seemed to have been sprinkled with powdered butterfly wings. Aunt Frieda was carried out and laid on her trunk. Both leaves of the door were opened, so that it could pass through, drive through. I was sure they would be carried out together, united at last. But only Aunt Frieda was carried out. The trunk stayed. With its Parisian dust. When the grownups called this a suitcase, it was clearly a joke, to my mind; the older people grew, the fewer jokes they had left and the more often they repeated themselves, so this joke embarrassed me as "unfunny." How could they call it a suitcase! It wasn't even a trunk, it was already so much a part of the furniture.

Many years later I was enlightened by a certain philosopher, a mover from a furniture store. He was a fabulous personality, a man of great natural talent and little education, a mighty provincial intellect. He absolutely flattened me. That, indeed, was his intent. The minute he looked at me, he lost all interest in my set of furniture, his fee, and me personally—he saw in me a victim, he quivered with impatience. That glance of his, rather too swift and crafty, betrayed him. Of course he intrigued me, and I was hooked. I ended up with an inferiority complex, and a dependency on this original "man of the people." We were chatting at the very table, and in the very chairs, that he had just delivered. He found in me an enthusiastic listener; I think he was even disappointed that I surrendered so easily, without a struggle. I immediately acknowledged him to be the winner. As I now begin to see, there was a modicum of social arrogance in this, and it wounded him. So, within his apparent victory, he became suspicious of me, and now he wanted to win a victory that was not condescending, not merely formal, but real and complete. He needed me to acknowledge not merely that he had won, but that he was better than I. Otherwise, what was the victory worth? By all means; I acknowledged him to be better. He became even more suspicious of me and redoubled his pressure. And, also, we were drinking. His intellect kept growing and spreading. There was no end to him. At last his fathomlessness embarrassed even him, and he finished me off, as if taking pity on a vanquished foe. "Tell me," he said, "what's the primal furniture?" "You mean . . . ?" "I mean, what's the object that everything originated from and can be reduced back to, even today?" I looked around in perplexity—at the set of furniture, which seemed to have been arranged as a visual aid for the lesson. Obtusely, like a D student, I rested my persecuted gaze on first one object, then another, while he condescendingly shook his head. No, no, and no. "A trunk!" he proclaimed at last. Enjoying my bewilderment, he explained, "Sit on it, and you have a bench. Set it, and you have a table. Attach legs, a chair. Stand it on end, a cupboard."

Thus, my predilection for the suitcase acquired a belated theoretical basis. And I did have a predilection, if I scan my whole life with an eye to suitcases. In the beginning, my dream was a kind of small valise—who remembers it, ladies after the war even carried it as a handbag—of buckram, with a little round mirror on the inside of the lid, and a small pocket snugged with a piece of elastic. All such things, of course, come to us irreversibly late: after we have dreamed of being the first to have them, after they have come into style, or even after they have gone out. I will never have the first sheepskin coat or the first jeans! And yet they do come within reach. The gap between imagination and acquisition still spans the birth and death of the style, but the gap does decrease. True, it decreases only with the weakening of desire, which was once described so accurately by the epithet "passionate." Thus, my next valise, a so-called athletics bag, came into my possession more promptly—not before anyone else was carrying them, though not after everyone had stopped carrying them, either, but exactly when everyone *was* carrying them. Progress! Dear God, what a sea of emotions a man is plunged into by an increase in his status! That reddish bag with the metal corners, that brick with a handle—how it reeked of my sweat, which was shed in the name of a future when I would be trim, strong, and handsome! . . . when I would be one of the first to go for a stroll with my attaché case.

How quickly I have skipped ahead! How many other suitcases I have omitted, large ones and small ones, recording my life's journey like a fleeting dream. From out of them all, my warped mind generated the image of a kind of super-suitcase, the suitcase of suitcases, very much my own, very convenient, very personal—a suitcase that would take the place of everything for me. Among my papers I recently came across my numerous rough sketches, which had developed into a diagram, a plan. It combined the concepts of the easel, the drafting table, and the carpenter's bench—the office and the printing house. It could be packed up in a single minute, to go in any direction decreed by Chance; there, in a secret corner, whose sole requirement would be a roof, the suitcase would open up—again, in a minute—into a small desk with a typewriter, a hinged lamp of my own design, an ashtray, a coffee maker, and even (a debatable detail of the plan) a sort of small, modest icon case, which would fit my need for family and even God into one small page. (But why did I wax so indignant a moment ago about German design?) And so, in a minute, in any attic, I would weave my creative web, and when I captured a fragment of an idea I would suck out the *text*, digest it, and immediately pack up again and move, carrying in my hand the convenient little suitcase that contained all the things I supposedly couldn't live without. Whether all those moves from place to place signal an implacable striving toward an end called "destiny," or a routine defeat in the routine space of my life, I do not know. But the very idea of a suitcase so hastily packed with essentials is highly suggestive of escape. This objectionable idea, owing to the author's fortunate laziness, remained in the design stage. Besides, could so perfect an idea be final? The thought of locating the materials, and someone to execute the design, kept stopping me. My idea struck me as too modern to be executed on our backward level.

And *I* supposed myself progressive! I could not yet see that the level of execution was modern, but the idea was backward. It was obsolete. Like the concept of "skilled craftsman," "a trade," or "made to order." Nowadays, "not created by human hands" means something different—machine-made, rather than divine. A thing can be yours only as property, only as the cost of the item. It's not really yours. Only the money was yours. The possibility of giving substantive expression to your individual taste has been undermined, chiefly by the fact that the thing has ceased to bear the stamp of the individuality of the pastry chef and the cobbler, the master suitcase-maker. He is gone for good, having floundered but a moment in the surf of the new era, under the alias "solo handicrafts-man." How could I miss seeing this in my own instance!

Not the worst things, certainly, but the ones marked by the imprint of unique craftsmanship failed to survive competition. Similarly, the mammoth did not die out because he had become weak and sickly (and the very last mammoth, especially, was the greatest of animals, since he had outlived them all). The mammoth died out because he never met the last she-mammoth. Two beautiful and mighty beasts failed to find each other in the brand-new geological epoch that had come to replace them. The myth of the defectiveness and degeneracy of the departed is merely the self-flattery of the survivors.

But let me interrupt this wordsmith's lament with a real-life impression . . . In a city whose name, to us, means Peter the Great—Amsterdam—I visited a luggage shop. It was packed to the rafters with *my* suitcases, and even my starved imagination had not sketched for me such a diversity of individual functions, such a quantity of stocked items. I can't say that this delighted me—it disillusioned me. My personal, my individual idea turned out not to be new at all, but fully mass-produced and even modish. Well, all right, so they've outdistanced us, especially in the sphere of consumer goods; who cares that if a thing has just occurred to you as a theoretical possibility they already have it, and it's about to depart into the past; who cares if every idea finds a form of merchandise for itself, is exploited, and disappears like a one-day butterfly, leaving behind the dead form, as the butterfly leaves its chitinous integument; who cares if every idea promptly gives way to a succeeding form and another busy idea, which promptly becomes a business . . . But what's the rush?

For the remarkable thing about the Russian fascination with imports is this: they have taken the place of handcrafts for us.

Possessing jeans or a tape recorder distinguishes us from the crowd as a person of taste and social privilege, as an individual. What melancholy disillusionment, what a soulless sepulchral chill, wafts from the obvious notion that there are *millions* of these jeans or these tape recorders, identical down to the last button and screw, identical down to the last molecule! The charm of possessing Western things in Russia is that they individuate us. We inspirit them with soul. This inspiriting of the product guarantees the monstrous speculative price of jeans: they cost as much here as authentic handwork does in the West. How patriarchal is our idea of jeans in Russia! Jeans are an archaism, if progress means the degeneration of handcrafts and cottage industries as backward forms of production.

No, the comparison with barbarians swapping gold for false beads (although that, too, takes place) is not what I'm thinking of here, but rather nostalgia, the Russian's paradoxical dual nostalgia: for progress and archaism simultaneously. The two have been fully diffused into each other, perhaps more than once. Never separately, always simultaneously, in lockstep—these two ideas, archaism and progress, have exhausted Russia by their invincible coexistence, blocking our transition from a state of time to a state of history, and from a state of space to a state of culture. Here, even jeans are an icon (literally so, in terms of cost), and a rocket is a magic carpet.

A great country! Our people will break or use any toy of civilization with no special delight or surprise. The conjunction of "old and new," so characteristic of revolution, is not a moment of transition from the old to the new. Both old and new exist, each on its own. Dismounting from a late-model motorcycle, we plow the embankment with a wooden plow. Settling back for a routine smoke break, we inhale a Marlboro, which cannot be had in Moscow but which, once in a lifetime, we find piled high in our village store, with a dust-covered Napoleon on the top shelf, and the usual lack of household soap and Russian cigarettes on the bottom shelf. Inhaling the Marlboro, we look at the sky, at our much laundered heavens, where a supersonic fighter, our magic plow flying to the stratosphere, weaves its fatal thread. And our spaceship is not so very distant from the wagon, in our consciousness; it was conceived, in due time, by peasants so clever and skillful that they had once been able to bind up a wheel with a rope because they needed to drive on. That is why we are still capable, although more rarely with every try, of approaching the unprecedented with extreme simplicity, undertaking it unexpectedly, and getting it done in short order, as a matter of course—or else suddenly doing something so fantastically complicated that even we can't figure it out for three centuries.

And when I shift my gaze from our "backward" to their "advanced," from the barge haulers on the railway embankment to the impeccable interior of the compartment, I am not so very upset or embarrassed. God forbid we should learn this. What a nightmare it would be on our scale, what a loss of soul, if we were forever unable to inspirit our space, as I have been unable for days to inspirit this exemplary compartment. What scares me is not that we can't make this kind of thing yet, but that we already want to.

Apropos of Amsterdam (of my having been there) . . . that is, of Peter . . . that is, of both of them (or the three of us) . . . that is, I was reminded of him by something in myself (naturally, I draw no comparison)—I recognized myself in him. I should note that Amsterdam remembers Peter well, even today. Not just for the benefit of us Russian tourists. They remember. He made a strong impression. By his size, which was proportionately representative of the empire itself, though they had little conception of that. Even now they'll tell you about the ceiling he spat on, and show you the tree under which he fell after the *assemblée*. He made an impression. But he also received one. It was a powerful impression, in a brilliant mind, but perhaps sometimes a bit vague. The maelstrom he stirred up in Russia when he returned has some similarity to my own recollections—the shock of comparison—against the background of foreign ways. The difference is that I will have neither the resources nor the desire to translate the impression into practice and make my recollection a reality.

Having begun with Peter, let us end with Peter. And by the way, about the palm of victory: one of the best Russian poets now living, my friend V.S., when we found ourselves shaking with the early-morning chill in some new locality on New Year's Day and visited the station restaurant, which, however, turned out to have neither beer nor anything else—he looked at last year's empty tablecloths, and at the potted palm triumphing over the twenty-five-below cold outside the window, and said, "Those palms, old friend . . . they're Russia!"

WHY I KNOW NOTHING ABOUT BALLET

A change of geological epochs, although it defies understanding in its irreversibility, is actually somewhat less drastic than a change of historical epochs. The difference is that history takes place before our eyes. Our facile regret over the mammoth and the saber-toothed tiger is basically no more than the triumph of the survivor: with them gone, we're viable. Any sort of graveyard or burned-out building serves mainly to exhibit the fact that *we* are unharmed. This is the reason why man feels so victorious on earth.

My grandfather was born in the days of serfdom, and my daughter was conceived toward the centennial of its abolition (1961), which was not commemorated here in any way. The psychological reason was deeper than the ideological: it was too recent—your own grandfather could well have been a slave. To us, born under the new regime, the concept "before the Revolution" was just as remote as "before the birth of Christ." And yet the Soviet regime was not quite twenty years old when I was born. There were still many things, and even more people, left over from that other epoch, but already I was unable to perceive them: both the things and the people were finishing out their lives but not living, for life is reproduction, not self-contained life processes. By the time I became capable of reflecting on this, the only things from the past that were still being reproduced were Herzegovina Flor cigarettes (pre-Revolutionary man had smoked them, as it turned out); Maria crackers, for some reason (albeit in a new spelling); and also the ballet (in my time the familiar name Mariinsky was being supplanted by the new Kirov, and the change is now complete) . . . Most significant in that series, although I did not immediately realize it, was the very city in which I lived, a city called by a new name and inhabited by new people, but ever the same—Petersburg. In this city, everything was correlated with something that had been before it. The Northern Venice, the Northern Palmyra, the second Paris, though not the second Moscow . . . Here I learned to walk in the second square in Europe (Palace Square), to see the largest cathedral after St. Peter's (St. Isaac's), to note one of the largest mosques (this time, not the second in the world, for some reason, but the third). If not the first, the largest. Why, right across the street from my home, according to our information, grew the largest palm in Europe (of those growing in hothouses). Like the only elephant (probably also the largest, at least of those living on the sixtieth parallel), it was hit by a bomb during the blockade . . . The palm and the elephant perished on the periphery of childhood consciousness, but Petersburg again escaped destruction—the Peter and Paul Fortress, the Winter Palace, the Bronze Horseman, the Rostral Columns, and the Sphinxes (positively the most northern, even though ancient Egyptian) . . . in sum, the *Petersburg* in which "I, too, was born, perhaps," in which Pushkin, too, was living and which Peter was founding, the Petersburg in which classicism and the baroque were going to be slightly more correct (slightly more classical and slightly less baroque), in which the striving to catch up signified a suppressed "Excel!" And this invented city, imposed on Russia, has a palpable eternity that belies its youthful age (some two or three hundred years). (Incidentally, black humor from an architect: "What would be left if they dropped an H-bomb on Leningrad?" "Petersburg.") It is not eternal in its life and antiquity, like Rome—it was conceived as "eternal," it was already eternal in Peter's mind, before the first ax. It is fixed in consciousness. That is why its every visitor finds himself not in the city of his imaginings, not in the city of Peter, of Pushkin, of Lenin; he finds himself in the very same eternal Petersburg in which those men too, though they made its fame, merely came and went—and in which "you, too, were wont to shine." From the human point of view, Petersburg is not the city of Peter and Pushkin, but the city of Yevgeny and Akaky Akakievich. Its grand stage sets will fill you with the same emotions that troubled the souls of these heroes, and troubled the minds of their creators, we must suppose, even though we are not their equal. And Petersburg, in this respect, although second and third in its squares and architectural ensembles, is finally and forever the first and only city. Its riddle, posed by Peter, has gone unanswered from Pushkin's day to ours, because there is no answer. A phantom, an optical effect, a camera obscura, a window on Europe, with an imaginary European landscape installed in it instead of glass . . . And here my disjointed allusions—the mammoth, serfdom, the palm and the elephant, the baroque and the ballet—all come together in one: "Can an ideal be materialized?" It cannot. Yet here it is! Petersburg, in itself a work of art—can it symbolize a symbol, abstract an abstraction, idealize ideals, fantasize a fantasy, allow convention within convention? Come to Petersburg in winter, in autumn, on a White Night (preferably in clear and uncrowded weather)—and

you will enter a Chirico painting, you will find yourself in the
situation of a literary hero from a work that you haven't even read,
that no one has even written, and before you know it you will feel
you are wearing a pelerine over your shoulders or a top hat on your
head, or your legs are sheathed in tights and you are gliding from
the wings to the proscenium at the angle of Chagall's heroes, kicking
your feet in flight, aware, like Pasternak's Hamlet, that you are "the
focus of a thousand binoculars." A man born in Petersburg was
born in a ballet. How was he to interpret that dusty, clumsy convention when he was taken to the famous Kirov Theater (formerly
the Mariinsky) for the first time? I can still feel the first nauseating
dizziness brought on by convention within convention, convention
imitating convention . . . In those days, convention was imper-
missible in stage sets. They were "like real"; the spectators were
peculiarly eager to applaud a change of scenery (now I think I hear
in that applause the sincerity of relief, a discharge of tension, on
encountering an intelligible and accessible mind): we saw a real
Peter and Paul Fortress, which we had already seen today in real
life, there was real snow falling . . . To our applause, a naked
ballerina came fluttering out in the snow, wearing a snow-white
tutu. By her leaps across the stage she was "expressing" the bitterness
of an encounter with the man she loved. We had all had time to
read about it in the program note during intermission, so we sat
holding our breath, matching the just-read with the just-seen, and
in the right place we guessed that we were to clap, from the expression on the prima donna's face . . . I have never gotten over the
burning and unconquerable shame and discomfiture that I felt as
a child—and still can't admit to anyone—at the element of assignment and compulsion in our ecstasy, the universal duty to a glory
born long before us . . . Time and time again, as if my chair had
collapsed under me, I sat invisibly red and sweaty, itching with
shame, inferior to the entire auditorium in my aesthetic development, and never confessing this to anyone, until now. Even today
I perceive these things in nearly the same way, though I have
somewhat squandered my capacity for shame, somewhat trained
myself to appear cultured: "It's regrettable that the 'second
position'—so unaesthetic—is the one most often encountered in
ballet. Sideways leg movement is very vulgar. What can be more
unsightly than splayed legs? What movement can be natural in this
position? Yet a majority of the *pas* are built on it: the *glissade*, the

assemblé, the *échappé*, all the *entrechats*, et cetera. Why has ballet technique been largely reduced to this very ugly, banal body position?" Or: "The celebrated *fouetté* is considered to be the most typical, most balletic, and most loved by all worshippers of 'classicism.' To me, it is ballet's most abhorrent, most untruthful contrivance. The ballerina twirling in the *fouetté* is expressing a sort of ecstasy, her swift movement is supposed to express gaiety and élan . . . but what, meanwhile, is expressed by the ballerina's pose? Quite the opposite. The ballerina is seeking balance in her pose, and that is what its whole meaning boils down to: the body is held erect, so is the head, the arms are symmetrical, the eyes fixed on one spot. And what is expressed by the face? The pursuit of balance, and the fear of losing it." In some things, it is true, we may have held second or even third place—but in ballet, indisputably, first. Just as the Petersburg baroque was more perfect in some respects, so, too, our ballet—extorted from serf actresses, later than in Europe—was probably more perfect in some respects. But why, in a world that had replaced and banished all other values and symbols of the old world, did ballet alone survive at its previous, ineradicable level? The phenomenon of the serf actress, who was now a free and unapproachable goddess of the new life, gave way to the phenomenon of the new spectator, whose status had been elevated to the point that the dancer "belonged to the people" and was dancing "for us." No, none of us knew about the backstage intrigues that enabled this particular art to stay alive and survive—all those vinegary considerations could belong only to a future epoch. But how this most conventional, most seigneurial, most elitist of the arts became also the most "popular," subject to neither ostracism nor doubt, was a mystery to me even then. I was born a lover of the ballet, and I can't love it anymore. With the same primitive coarseness, I can't stand the universal pair-skating on television now—although that really is primitive. Today, in the era of distribution, ballet has finally assumed its proper place, more or less: tickets to the Bolshoi (and the Kirov, too) are impossible to get, and you should really wear diamonds . . . while figure skating on television is what ballet was supposed to be for us, but at long last it's for everyone . . . "That's not nice, I'm an angry man . . ." But even now I am angered by the same thing, and we will never understand each other. The West is quick to name a phenomenon, finding painfully concise and exact words. *"Poor eating habits," "poor-boy fashions"*—in English, these are well said and beautifully expressed, but to this day they sound outrageous in Russian. There I sit, still seven years old, dressed in the style of the future, with a half-eaten dry bread crust in my pocket. Far easier for me to grasp, even now, are concepts never translatable into English: "supplemental portion" and "fortified diet" . . . There I sit, and Mama, after standing in line for two freezing nights, has gotten tickets for Ulanova's tour, for *Giselle*, which makes no sense to either mind or heart or stomach, and I'm not letting Mama watch, I keep poking her in the side and tugging at her sleeve when anyone makes an entrance: "Is that her?" Mama is annoyed, she keeps snubbing and shushing me. I exasperate her. And suddenly I've forgotten what I'm waiting for . . . I did not ask again whether it was Ulanova. Never since have I seen anything more beautiful. But, dear God, how much still lay ahead of me, to be seen, recognized, and understood! And in all of what lay ahead of me, there was no longer Ulanova.

Georgian Album

———

Is it because Georgians have trouble remembering their addresses?
. . . All ethnic generalizations are feeble. For the umpteenth time
I am mounting the same steep little street, which really ought to
have stairs. When they dictate the address, do they scramble the
numbers of the house and the apartment for spite? I have been
trying to contain my suspiciousness. It would be most insulting.
Although, to be sure, as the famed Georgian hospitality migrates
into our communications era, the tradition can be ominous for the
host. Apropos, I am reminded of an episode from *The Thrush*. When
the hero is at an apogee of flurry and tardiness, a pair of tourists
arrive at his house to stay for a while, and he can't seem to remember
the name of the person who sent them. What a telling episode, I
reflect. Especially since we have just one Georgia, just one Tbilisi,
and just one of your house. And you yourself, *you*! Unquestionably,
we have just one such director—Otar Ioseliani. But I am inclined
to think that this number-scrambling, which is more often encountered here than at home, has a different explanation: Georgians
still find it more natural to say "So-and-so's house" than "house
number such-and-such." Rather than search for the wrong house
number, I should ask for "Ioseliani's house." The fat, mustachioed,
T-shirted man who is lazily draped over the balcony, side by side
with a striped mattress, and who perhaps for this reason looks com-
ically like a tiger, would examine me, consider me, and at length
accomplish the feat of changing position to point at the house across

the street. I would tug the surviving brass pull, and somewhere in the dusty unknown distance awaiting me I would hear, to my surprise, the tinkle of a bell . . . For a long time no one would answer, for a long time I would study the blank door with the sensation of studying the inside of my eyelids, for a long time footsteps would shuffle. The door would open—and I would think I had the wrong house again, I would apologize to the tall, thin old man, apologize for being like this, always coming to the wrong house. He would look at me with the curiosity that is especially lively in the faces of people who always maintain their dignity.

"Does Otar Ioseliani live here?"

"That's my son," the father remarks with some satisfaction, and he lets me in. We proceed to the second floor by a small staircase. He invites me to go right, and he himself goes left, and I will not see him again. Otar (for some reason, this is characteristic of him) kisses me warmly while looking past me, as though kissing someone else. Thus, he veils his eyes first to the left, then to the right, and then moves on. It turns out that I have caught him at home only by a miracle—he is just leaving. In a way, this is a piece of luck. I am present at the filmmaker's preparations for a trip. "Our Russian comrade paid a visit to the Georgian director on the eve of his departure at the invitation of Estonian cinematographers."

He is enjoying getting ready. His house surrounds him. As someone who has seen his films, I find it interesting to look about me. Here is the faded tapestry, woven of twilight and dust; here is the familiar bamboo étagère that crumbled away in my childhood; here is the porcelain borzoi, or perhaps the little shepherd with the reed pipe, I don't even remember now. Here is his daughter, who sculpts, draws, plays the upright piano—here is what she has sculpted, here is what she has drawn, here is a song without words . . . In this house, everything that survived the epochs and the haggling because it had no value (no one would even buy it) still stands, serves, and is recognized as priceless. Here on the wall are photographs, and I seem to have seen them before . . . People used to love having their pictures taken. They trusted the gramophone. The ones at the back are standing on chairs, while the ones in the very front lie on the floor, resting their heads on each other. Carefree people, regimental comrades and district officials, graduates and jurors, they seem to be trying to halt time, which is passing. If only they knew that it would depart entirely, if only they knew what an opportune moment they have picked to be photographed . . . How many men there used to be . . . So this is the first episode of *Falling Leaves*! A great many men in photographs, and only women sitting around the table alive. I saw these photographs in the movie, I see them on the walls. The only man in the house is a personage of the time, the personage of Otar.

So I look about me, gaining a rough acquaintance with the artist's world, and feeling gratified by the resemblance in its first layer. With a face like that, I muse, looking at Otar's (which is really extraordinarily long), it's no wonder he knows faces and is able to judge them . . . The ability to understand a face means everything to a film. Only two or three directors, perhaps, understand . . . "And socks," Otar says, interrupting and unwinding my thoughts, "the ones I brought from Moscow last time, remember?" The director is giving orders to his wife. "Red with a green stripe. Thick wool. And some long white shoelaces . . ." The director has a corn. Well, that's all, he's taking along a black turtleneck, hiking boots, shirts—one's enough, he'll put this one on—he's not taking anything more. The details of his scenes are as laconic and selective as the things going with him; the contents of the valise are as laconic as a scene. And again, the same surprise: Have I always seen Tbilisi the way Otar photographs it? Or do I see it that way only after Otar has shown it to me? Does Otar live like his heroes, or do his heroes live like Otar? Is Tbilisi like Otar, or is Otar like Tbilisi? Is his world a reflection, or an expression? What do we recognize, and in what? The world in the reflection, or the familiar reflection in the world? The world with which the artist will astonish us is just an arm's length away. As I compare the world he has expressed with the world surrounding him, I discover that Otar has not gone looking for anything. And this means that everything has turned up of its own accord, thrust itself into his hand, always existed . . . A simple matter, one might think . . . He needed only to be born in this house, on this street, in this city, in your time and mine—there were no further prerequisites for the birth of this specific individual talent. "And my notebook, the long one—put that in the valise," Otar remembers, threading the long laces into the heavy boots. "How I wish," Otar says with a grunt as he laces the boot, his long face peering up at me from below, "how I wish you'd come and visit me . . ."

———

You arrive—and you weren't expected . . .

But another time it will turn out that when you were introduced in the street the day before yesterday and didn't learn the name, their "Do drop in" was said in earnest, and your "Yes, yes, of course" became a promise. In your utter idleness, carving out the time for this unexpected evening will prove very difficult—a whole project. The commotion raises the incident to the level of an event. You are going "to a house, to listen to music."

(The invisible spirit of Otar stages this episode for me . . .)

Except for trust in your companion, you possess nothing—neither time nor concept. This trust-and-ignorance system wakens the imagination. You can't recall a certain atmosphere, a certain astringent taste: something reminds you of the sensation, with a high degree of vagueness, an uncorroborated concreteness . . . You are immersed in childhood. You are led by the hand. You are going "to a house." Before your eyes there rises a "house-in-general," for some reason with little columns, a balcony, a tree—goodness knows why, it's not the kind of house that is built, in your experience, but all your life you have pictured to yourself exactly this kind; it has survived only in your mind's eye, at the verge of sleep . . . This infantile vagueness is romantic, even novelistic, that is, learned (or withheld) from some book. Inside, you are flowing with positive feelings. But you approach your destination at last—and it is indeed that kind of house, there is even a semblance of columns . . . not exactly columns, but still . . . Across the way, behind a fence, construction goes on even at night: the roar of bulldozers, the blind beam of a floodlight, as in a prison compound. Dissolving in celestial blackness, an unfinished skyscraper: the Georgian Council for Economic Aid. So, next door to your huge, unfinished modern experience, this little house has survived after all, like a babyhood memory: perhaps you remember it yourself, or perhaps Mama told you. You are going "to a house," "to visit a nice family," and in your bare, book-learned imagination you see a living room, a painting, a tablecloth, cherry jam, and around the table the hosts' blurred faces, expressing cordiality and dignity, attesting that they love you in particular, for some reason—why should this be? And in all this pleasant approximateness, the question "But where are we going?" brings an answer that lingers especially sweetly: "Nona is a remarkable young lady." This opinion is corroborated by another friend whom we encounter along the way: he joins us. And although she can only *become* "remarkable," and she *should* be a lady, this bride has grown weary with waiting, just for you.

What are you expecting?

It all turns out to be so. Even more so than you had unconsciously imagined. You are let in. Surely this isn't a housemaid?

She escorts you up a small staircase and leaves you in a small transitional room, which has a large mirror, armchairs, and half-closed doors leading inside. A room whose function is not quite clear to me: too furnished for a vestibule, too unlived-in for a room. A few superfluous items have been moved out here from the unknown rooms beyond: the piano they will play for us, cabinets with random books, a wobbly-legged antique escritoire, on which one could write no more than three lines on a quarter sheet of paper— the little desk will withstand one more postal kiss, and the photo album, which lies there as if by chance.

Holding back the heavy portières, my friends stand and smoke by the dark tall window, as though there has been a difficult conversation but they have settled everything: what does it matter. I sit in all the chairs, am reflected many times in the mirror. With burning interest and small shame I leaf through the photo album . . . Here is Grandmother, who was Grandmother even before the Revolution. She wears a kind of bridal veil, held on by a little round black hat that suggests the tambourine in a dance ensemble; but there is something elusively different in the fact that this attire is natural for her, these are her clothes, not a national costume. She looks at you with uncensorious non-recognition, and you might be faintly uncomfortable under the gaze of these young eyes in a face as old and wise as the earth. This gaze surprises—as if only purity that has lasted a century knows all. Here is a highland warrior, thrusting out his chest, not tangling his sword knot with his aiguillette; he looks at you, concealing behind his luxurious mustache more intelligence than a man is obliged to have. Grandfather? Papa? Perhaps he was the one she glanced at so gaily and directly, as though someone had suddenly called to her but there was nothing to fear, nothing was hiding in the sunlit, yellowed bushes and trees of the garden, what could frighten her, this young woman in the long dress, with her high, untidy hairdo and the huge broach on her high bosom? Why would she be afraid in her own garden, as she bent over the wicker basket on the grass, where lay, not yet hurt by the future, her full and contented baby—son of the photographer,

none other. Whom else could she have looked at with such frank-
ness? He unfastened his aiguillette, shifted his saber, and struggled
a moment with the tripod, smiling in his uncomfortable position
. . . The birdie fluttered, and the woman, with a shy curiosity and
the consciousness that things were forever all right, glanced directly,
shameless creature, into the eyes of the man, the photographer, and
this is how she has stayed, this is how she gazes even today, through
the page that has separated them, at the man with the mustache
. . . So that, several blank pages later, a little girl, standing on a
tree stump and clasping to her outthrust tummy a long, awkwardly
dangling kitten, stares at you with the same round eyes, and so does
the kitten . . . The mistress of the house has Grandmother's nose,
but Grandfather's eyes . . . No, she definitely looks more like
Grandmother than the little girl, although this little girl, a few pages
later, is most probably she.

Where have these faces disappeared to? Never again will anyone gaze so fully into the camera, so directly, glad of everything,
bashful about nothing. Who would have thought that the clumsy,
three-legged messenger of progress could make the young mother
laugh so! She wasn't frightened at all, didn't shy away, only her
curiosity was shy . . .

By now, however, we have settled down in this drawing room;
an hour has passed, another half hour. The hostess should have
made her entrance long ago, in a floor-length gown, no less, and
played this whole yellow stack of sonatinas and waltzes, revealing
an astonishing ability to read music . . . My fantasy has already
gone so far that any conversation with me can turn only to Pushkin.
My friends roll their eyes heavenward and say, "Ah, Pushkin!"—I
must read "The Poor Knight" aloud to them, forthwith. I take down
the slim volume, and the page has been torn out. But even this
enchants me.

Because, with no small surprise and suddenness, I realize that
just like this—well, perhaps not quite like this, but in just this
role—people lounged about in drawing rooms in those unforgettable
times and certainly did not count their time lost, while I am ex-
asperated at the mere thought that time is passing *in vain* and I'm
not doing anything. Although, in point of fact, I had done nothing
for a long time prior to this hour . . . But they leisurely passed their
best years in drawing rooms, these very men who filled volumes
and became part of the school curriculum! They wrote the collected

works that now serve as models of labor, they wrote numberless
letters to their friends, while I, like Private Ivanov, cannot write a
line to my mother . . . They sat like this for a lifetime, not counting
it wasted, and their lives contained so few superfluous events that
everything could be remembered and told. That is why, in our
century, their biographies read like fairy tales.

Even to me, it will seem that I'm exaggerating when I populate
the nineteenth century with myself. But, as confirmation that my
emotions have a kind of accuracy, the hostess will enter at last, after
about two hours, smiling most charmingly but offering no apology
whatever for having made us wait. Her gaze will caress me, when
I am presented and click my heels; it will be reflected in the mirror,
from which, with absolutely the same eyes, round and clear, her
grandmother will peer out, or she herself; her gaze will slide over
the sheet music I have jumbled, it will light on the album. Suppressing a faint sigh, Nona will exchange kisses with my friends,
and we will go through to the dining room . . . But—the round
table! the tablecloth! the framed painting! the frame itself! It will
all be exactly like an uncorrupted dream, and just what you pictured
to yourself in childhood at the word *table, tea, jam,* as if the Larins
had made it behind the scenes—it will all converge to corroborate
your picture, and you will remember how it was supposed to be in
the very beginning, before you forgot, before it ceased to be so.

With surprising irreversibility, as in childhood, the instants
have rolled into the past. Just now you were waiting, imagining,
and then it began, came true, and now it is over, like the New
Year.

After such expectation, you are seated at the round table, that
very one. And again, not everything comes clear to you right away:
what comes after what, what follows what. Nona herself has baked
the pie (that is what has kept her these two whole hours), her pie
is very charmingly burnt, and this, the fact that it's slightly burnt,
is especially becoming to her today, like her blouse, like her hairdo
. . . Because the pie burned especially for you. Otherwise, the
housemaid would have baked it, and it wouldn't have burned; and
if Nona, for some reason, undertook to bake it today, it implies
such readiness, such promise! For some reason, this crumb of charcoal in your teeth is a guarantee of buoyant happiness, of an infinite
morning as rosy as a peignoir, as a shameless bashful smile. You
are plunged into a sea of fathomless coquetry, the secret of which

is that everything suits its lovely possessor, everything becomes her—even if the pie, for example, had been a splendid success. And such a long courtship lies ahead . . .

Just at the right time, late, my friends' wives appear. A twittering, kisses . . . School friends, they equalize the age of the beautiful Nona, who, growing suddenly older than her years, is so wonderfully well preserved. This, like the pie, begins to flatter her with accentuated force. It's as if expectation has subtracted from her age the period by which you were late—for she had been mired in a single protracted day, many years long, waiting for you to arrive here on the morrow. She promises her girlfriends she will dictate the recipe for the pie . . .

This is Woman! Whatever I believe of her she will give me. Singular grace—no gesture is determinate, each torments and promises, harboring within it the ultimate deceit of good breeding, when you don't know what you'll come up against until the very end, until you have gone to all lengths to slake your inflamed curiosity. But such curiosity can be slaked just once, and then with poignant clarity you will see the consummation, the determinacy of all these indeterminacies, of this smooth grace over which you have come sailing in, for when it has been exhausted its flowing line will be echoed in the faint breath that stirs the bridal veil—you're already at the altar. If the bonfire catches, you will be the one who has lighted it; if it doesn't begin to die down, it means that for your sake she has gone to all lengths, even to something she could forgo just as easily as she breathes. Ah, how touching you will find this cold readiness and submissiveness, taking it for purity or shyness . . . And suddenly you'll remember the crunch of charcoal in your teeth.

No, no, and no! I've already been through this twice. I haven't done anything that would obligate me, as a decent man, to— But just at this moment I dribble jam on the tablecloth. This is such a trifle, and I should so certainly pay no attention to it, that—my God, I'll never settle the debt, to my dying day! "Oh, no, I didn't get married," a Georgian friend once told me. "I just discovered one day that I was sitting in the kitchen having soup."

But after living out my life so swiftly, after measuring the ever-ageless Nona for widow's weeds, which are just as uncommonly becoming to her as the bridal veil, and after watching a small funeral procession made up of my two friends and their wives, so sincere

in their lament as they follow the coffin of this Georgified Russian
. . . I am born again to a new life, realizing that I have it all wrong,
this is not Nona but Nina, and Nona—here she is! she enters in
the middle of our tea party, with ink-stained fingers, having failed
to solve a problem about two trains. And while the trains race full
speed toward their inevitable collision (through the fault of the
charming mathematician), I tenderly examine my error . . .

Something had once made an extremely strong impression on
me, and I'd never even noticed . . . More and more often, as the
years go by, you search for a cause in the past and do not find it.
Then, in the thinned-out expanse of childhood, it will seem that
everything is in plain view. My first visit to Tbilisi was during the
era when boys and girls went to separate schools. I was fifteen; that
is, this segregation already had basic significance. I stood before the
tomb of Griboedov with great excitement. In an effort to be honest,
I will confess that this had little to do with *Woe from Wit*—my
emotion was for the tomb, and was akin to envy. "Thy wit and
works are immortal in Russian memory, but to what purpose has
my love outlived thee!" The elegantly genuflecting mourner pressed
her cast-iron forehead to the cross. Our guide said that the widow
herself had served as the sculptor's model. I trusted his accent immediately. There was no way I could see her face, behind the cross,
because the grotto was closed off by a railing. "Lucky man!" I mused,
undoubtedly, dreaming of the beautiful young wife who would be
a widow all her life when I was gone. Youth does "have its head
in the clouds," if I could think it happiness to be buried and mourned
in a foreign land! . . . I was in love with the more modest neighboring
tomb, that of Nina herself. Without ever having loved, I was day-
dreaming beside her tomb about my young widow's fidelity . . . As
a certain great Russian writer has said, only a Russian boy can fall
asleep in a soft bed and dream of suffering, imprisonment, and
penal servitude. I'm not sure he's right about all the terms in this
statement—but I did dream. On that grave, I wanted to die of love.
I recall this here, as another great writer has said, exclusively "for
the Viennese delegation" (meaning the friends of Freud).

I do not recall it as I sit at the table with the sisters. Possibly,
however, Nina, or rather Nona, is supposed to play me a Griboedov
waltz—brilliantly, with her inky fingers . . . In any case, for some
reason this particular adolescent loveliness, untidy and clumsy, does
not preclude absolute pitch. Or so it seems to me, as I watch her

wriggling at the table, spilling pie crumbs and tea all over herself, perhaps scorning our senile conversation, perhaps depressed by it as usual. I catch the older sister's glance of vexation, as though apologizing for the younger: No, she has no idea how to behave at the table, but you should see the transformation when she sits down at the piano—it's as if she were a changeling . . . the bearing of a queen . . . where does she get it? . . . The older sister might well speak such lines, but she does not. I am privately in accord with her implied statement, I nod, I already believe in the girl's stunning talents. From the depth of Nona's indifference (which I already see as feigned) shoots a single sudden glance, which seems to me un-usually clever; it suggests nothing less than a keen sense of humor, a distinctive feature of the next crop of young people, unknown to me. The vulgar fear of being left behind by the rising generation pushes me to make an effort. Though still addressing myself to everyone—particularly her older sister, who meanwhile adds to her own virtues the very rare ability to listen, which may or may not mean to understand—I find myself waiting for this flash of attention in Nona's babyish disdain. I am trying to ingratiate myself with her generation, hoping for encouragement, like an old dog . . . Their dignified grandmother catches me at this undignified pastime. Ma-jestically and modestly she sails into the dining room, with her large, slightly tremulous gray head held high, and examines me with a long, prominent stare, at the limit of propriety. Ah, much expectation is concealed at the bottom of this stare! A quantity of disappointed hopes, a hope of not being disappointed. All of these are so secret that her majestic, proud eyes, filled mainly with a sense of self-worth, express nothing but concealment. Alarmed by me, Grandmother sits down and allows a cup of tea to be poured for her with all granddaughterly respect, though she does not drink it, merely consecrates it by a faint quavering of her head toward her lifted cup. For a little while longer, she stares straight ahead, past me, her prominent clear eyes magnificently uncensorious of any-one. Reassured, whether about the dangers or the hopes, she pre-pares to withdraw—and just in time, because the younger sister finally crowns my efforts by spattering everyone with tea and pie. (She leaves me somewhat bewildered, because, although I have been honing and modernizing my humor, I have achieved this ultimate success without making any joke—just by using the word *parrot,* or maybe *fool.*)

And so, the venerable woman's face will be barely illumined by a sincere chagrin, an embarrassment that her favorite has behaved so improperly, and she will hasten to retire. "I hope she wasn't offended?" I will ask Nina, drawing closer, to the distance of a relative. "Mama? Why would you think so? No, not at all. She liked you very much." "Mama?" I exclaim in bewilderment, looking at Nona. "She has such a young daughter—" "Ugh, Nona," Nina will say, "you spat all over me!" "I didn't mean to, Mama," Nona will say. Mama? Nina already has such a grownup daughter? . . . And in the time it takes for the sisters to be detached in my mind, and for the grandmothers and granddaughters to be reversed and assume their places, exchanging themselves for mothers and daughters, I will reflect with bewilderment that this solution, even from the very beginning, was the one most clearly implied. "Is Nona going to play for us?" I will ask, emboldened, because Nona's giggling confirms me in the belief that I have gained her friendship. "Me?" Nona will say in surprise. "Nona!" Nina (now her mother) will exclaim. "Why, she can't even play 'Chopsticks'! Her sense of pitch is so bad it's brilliant." I will burst out laughing—and this will become my most successful joke. Because it starts everyone laughing. We are so suddenly gay, so causelessly and infinitely gay, that I quite forget what century it will be when I walk out the door. Because life was this gay only in those faded, yellowed photographs, and mine is not among them . . .

Nina will banish her cheered-up daughter to finish her homework, and this will summon to the girl's face an unfeigned sorrow, which I will construe as reluctance to part with us. The cups will be cleared from the table. My friends and I will return to the living room to smoke. The three girlfriends, Nina and my friends' wives, will sit closer, shoulders touching; they will put their heads together and start chirping in their native language, like birds. I will see them from the living room . . . The sense of closeness will so permeate me that I begin asking for a light from my friend's cigarette, concealing the fact that I have matches in my pocket. "That's funny," I will say. "A foreign language. Just now we were all sitting together talking. And suddenly—bang! I don't understand a word. What are they talking about?" "What about?" my friend will say, not bothering to listen. "What else. About us."

About me . . .

> *And, perhaps, on my sad decline*
> *Love with farewell smile will shine.*

(At this point, Otar halts the scene. He winds the film backward and rehearses me in a different variant: at the same tea party, I undertake to lead a chorus of "Moscow Nights." I can't pull it off, and Otar is forced to find himself another performer for the role . . .)

The Doctor's Funeral

A sunny day recalls a funeral. Not every sunny day, of course, but
the one we speak of as sunny—the first one, sudden, at long last.
It is also clear. Perhaps the clear sky is what matters, and not the
sun. At funerals, first and foremost, there is weather.

. . . My aunt by marriage, my uncle's wife, was dying.

She was "such an *alive* person" (Mama's words) that we found
this hard to believe. Indeed she was alive, and indeed it was hard
to believe, but the fact was that she had long been making preparations, even though secretly from herself.

First she tried her foot. Her foot suddenly became painful and
swollen and wouldn't fit into her shoe. But Auntie did not give up.
She would tie a pre-war slipper to the "elephant" (her word) and
come out to the kitchen to wash dishes with us; then Alexander
Nikolaevich, her chauffeur, would arrive, and she would drive to
her Institute (disability evaluation), then to a board meeting of her
Society (therapeutics), then to some sort of alumnae committee (she
was a Bestuzhev graduate), then make a house call on some titled
bandit, then swing by to see her Jewish relatives (who, by a tacit
agreement of forty years' standing, did not visit our house), then
return home for a moment, feed her husband, and have trouble
deciding whether to go to the banquet celebrating the dissertation
defense of Nektor Beritashvili, an assistant professor at the Institute's
Tbilisi branch: she was very tired (and this was more than true) and
didn't want to go (but this wasn't quite true). Secretly from herself,

she wanted to go. (Having repeated this "secretly from herself," I begin to realize that the emotional capacity for such a thing can be maintained into old age only by people who are very . . . alive? pure? kind? . . . good? . . . I mutter this incomprehensible, now defunct word, secretly from my own self . . .) And she went, because she took all human gatherings at face value, she loved them, she had a passion for tokens of kindness, the whole brocade of honor and respect. To forestall possible mockery she had even taught our self-important family the Jewish word *koved*, which means a respect that doesn't necessarily come from the soul and heart—respect pro forma, according to status, as a display, respect as such. (Russians have no such concept, no such word, and here one might say, with the affectionate smile of a person who secretly from himself is an anti-Semite, that the Jews are a different nation. But although this insincere word does not exist in our language, it has become a fact of our life—and besides, why is everyone so convinced that rudeness is sincerity?) "You understand, Dima," she would say to her husband, "he's Vakhtang's son, do you remember Vakhtang?" She would sigh with distress, and go. Her desires still outweighed her fatigue. Nowadays we can't understand this—people used to be different.

At last she returned. She never stayed long, only for the ceremonial part, which she loved poignantly, imbuing its every ostentation and hypocrisy with her own generous good sense and faith. (It is curious that they sincerely believed themselves to be materialists, these people. We will never be like them; to achieve such a paradox, one must possess exceptional . . . again, that incomprehensible word.) So she came home promptly, because in addition to her foot she suffered from diabetes and could allow herself nothing at the banquet, yet she came home high: the speeches of the ceremonial part affected her like champagne. Younger, pink-cheeked, she would buoyantly and happily tell her husband how nice everything had been, how warm . . . Gradually it would become clear that she herself had said it best of all. If you looked into her face then, you could hardly believe that she was about to turn eighty, that she had the foot. But she did: it was tied to the slipper, you had only to look down. And after she finished chattering, after she gave her husband his tea, after he went to bed, she would fill a basin with hot water, lower her foot into it, and sit for a long time, suddenly lifeless and shapeless, "all in a heap" (as she put it). She would sit there for a long time, all in a heap, staring at her already dead foot.

She was a great doctor.

Doctors like her *don't exist* nowadays. Easily I catch myself using this ready-made formula, which has struck me as absurd ever since I was a child. I tell myself (with a "sober" grin) that things have always been the same. Identical. No better. Easily I catch myself, and easily let myself off: from the altitude of today's experience, the formula "they don't exist nowadays" strikes me as both legitimate and accurate. Expressive. So they don't exist . . . It wasn't that Auntie cured everyone. Medicine was the subject on which she had the fewest delusions. She didn't feel that everyone *could* be helped, so much as that everyone *must* be. She well knew (not in words, not from science, but from . . . again, that nameless quality) that she had *no* way to help, but then if she had even a *small* way to help, you could be sure she would do her *all*. This inability to do even the slightest bit less than her all, this need to do absolutely all she could—this imperative was the very essence of "the old-time doctors that don't exist nowadays," doctors like her, the last of them. And it was provocatively simple. If you had a cold, for example, she would inquire whether you were sleeping well. You would ask in surprise, "What does sleep have to do with it?" She would say, "He who sleeps poorly will feel the chill, and he who feels the chill will catch cold." She would give you a sleeping pill for your cold (allergy was still a fiction of the capitalist world), and suddenly this forgotten tempo of Russian speech and Russian words . . . "feel the chill" . . . made you so happy and affectionate that all was right, all in good order, all ahead of you . . . you glimpsed an unreal morning with gray sky and white snow, fever happiness, someone riding by under the window on a horse, smoke curling from the chimney . . . If you said, "My nerves are playing tricks, Auntie, could I have something for my nerves," she would give you an icy look and say, "Get hold of yourself, there's nothing for nerves." But another time you wouldn't even ask for anything, and she'd thrust a medical-leave certificate into your hands: "I saw you smoking in the kitchen last night. You need rest."

If an observant intellectual had articulated it for her—even this way, in her own words—she would never have understood. She would have shrugged: What are you talking about? For she

knew no mechanisms of experience. The way she entered the patient's room! No amount of self-control could have wrought such
a change. She was simply transformed. Nothing but ease and
steadiness—no eighty years, no handsome young husband, no thousands of snotty, sweaty, blue, pathetic patients breathing in her
face—no experience, either professional or personal, no vestige of
the residue of her own self and her own life, her eager life. How
she let the patient complain! How affirmatively she asked, "It hurts
a lot?" Precisely—*a lot.* There could be no "It's nothing" or "You'll
get over it" from her. At this moment only two people in the whole
world knew how it hurt: the patient and she. They were the elite
of pain. After she left, the patient was all but proud of his initiation.
Never in my life will I see again such a capacity for *sympathy.* One
doesn't take an exam in sympathy in medical school. Auntie showed
sympathy instantly, and at the same moment renounced forever her
old age and pain. If you were truly sick she had only to turn and
see your face, and with the speed of light you were bathed in her
sympathy, that is, in a total absence of the sympathizer and a total
awareness of how you felt, what it was like. This astounding capacity,
devoid of everything except its own self, empathy in pure form,
became, for me, the Essence of the Doctor. The Name of the
Physician. And nothing false, nothing forced, no "old chaps" or
"my dear fellows" in the Moscow Art Theater style (although she
believed religiously in the Moscow Art Theater, and when it was
on television she would settle down in her chair with a ready expression of satisfaction, "which nothing modern can bring, isn't that
so, Dima dear . . . Ah, Kachalov! And Tarasova is the ideal of
beauty . . ." At the word *Anna* she shapes her fluffy hairdo with
trembling hand . . .).

From her hairdo, I begin to see her. To the end of her days
she wore the same hairdo, which had once suited her best of all.
As someone's compliment had stuck in the young woman's mind
—"She has beautiful hair," he had said—so her certainty of this
had lasted for half a century and a whole lifetime, and so the graying,
medicinally tinted wave was fluffed up every morning and a tor-
toiseshell comb was jabbed—her hands trembled violently—was
jabbed into it in three tries, back and forth, higher and lower, and
at last exactly in the middle, always in the same place. Her unsteady
hands were very skillful, and in my mind's eye I can also see her
adjusting their tremor, like artillery fire: undershooting, overshoot-

ing (a narrow bracket)—bull's-eye. That is, I can still see her hands, shaking but always hitting the mark, always doing something. (That's not my typewriter tapping, it's Auntie washing dishes, the characteristic clink of her cups against the faucet. If she broke a cup, which did happen, and her cups were expensive, then of course she felt very bad about it. But—with an indescribable femininity, also arrested in the era of her first hairdo—she immediately announced the event to all the kitchen witnesses, as one of her eternal charming blunders. "Again," she would say. Even her figure changed as she tossed the fragments into the garbage pail; even the curve of her waist—what waist? . . . —and the tilt of her head were once more maidenly . . . because the behavior most forbidden to the witnesses in such an incident could only be pity. We must not notice her age.) Even now I long to kiss Auntie (which I never did, even though I loved her more than many I have kissed) . . . as the cups clink against the faucet.

She tossed fifty or a hundred rubles into the pail with the gesture of a very wealthy person, forestalling our false chorus of sympathy . . . but what came next was the most difficult for her, though she was resolute by nature and didn't dawdle or procrastinate: for just an instant, with an assortment of cups in her hands, she stood frozen before her door . . . became still more willowy (even her round back straightened, it was hard not to believe the optical illusion) . . . and promptly threw open the door and fluttered in, almost with the summery chirp of a Serov morning early in the century —again, in her youth. Washed sunlight through washed leaves dappled the polished parquet, a bouquet of dawn lilacs stood motionless in droplets, there was all but a peignoir and a Scriabin étude . . . as though the reproduction on the wall were not a reproduction but a mirror. "Dima, such a pity! I've broken my favorite Chinese cup!"

Ah, yes! All our lives we remember how we were loved . . .

Dima, my dearly beloved uncle, remains beyond the door in these memories. I see him in shadow, his legs crossed, next to the bouquet, a kind of bouquet. He drums on the tablecloth with a surgeon's musical fingers, waits for his tea, smiles attentively and gently, a good man who has nothing to say.

So first I see her hairdo (or rather the comb), and then her hands. Right now she is stirring jam: an antique (pre-catastrophe) copper kettle, burnished like the sun; in it, a scarlet layer of very expensive select strawberries from the market; and on top, the coarse sharp slivers of old-time (loaf) sugar, shining faintly blue. All this is precious, a crown, scepter, and orb all together (in our family we like to say that Auntie is as majestic as Catherine) . . . and over this empire rules the hand with the golden spoon—it catches itself trembling and pretends that it had planned to make exactly the motions that occurred (this is very picturesque: governance by chance as an artistic method).

I see the comb, the hairdo, the hands . . . and suddenly, vividly, all at once, my whole aunt: as though I have been laboriously rubbing a transfer picture, and finally I peel it back, holding my breath, tormenting my own hand with my smoothness and slowness—and it works! no rips in the film! here come the brilliant big flowers on her crimson Chinese jacket (silk, buttoned) . . . her round back, with a bouquet between the shoulder blades . . . and the foot with the bandaged-on slipper. The flowers on her back are splendid, lush, a Chinese variety of chrysanthemum, the kind she loves to receive for her eternal anniversary (every day a basket is brought to us from grateful people, and my aunt's room always looks like an actress's after a benefit performance; every day, in exchange, the next faded basket is set out on the stairway). The flowers on her back were the same as in her coffin.

In our extensive family, all living together, we had a number of standardized formulas for admiring Auntie. What I don't know is how the questionnaire data—age, sex, marital status, and ethnic origin—were factored into them. Naturally, our family was too well bred to stoop to the level of a personnel department. Such things were never spoken of. Yet a hundred-percent silence always speaks for itself: the silence said that one did not speak of these things, one knew them. She was fifteen years older than Uncle, they had no children, and she was Jewish. For me—as a child, a teenager, a youth—she had neither sex, age, nor ethnic origin. Whereas all the other relatives did have these things. Somehow I saw no contradiction here.

We all played this game—of unconditionally accepting all the conditions she set—for our indulgence was too lavishly encouraged, and our clumsy performance had a grateful spectator. God knows who outplayed whom in nobility, but everyone overplayed. She could nevertheless see it from a higher perspective, I think; we could not. Weren't her pre-established conditions a lofty response to our own unconditionality? Wasn't this why the only person she feared, and cultivated beyond all measure, was Pavlovna, our cook? Pavlovna didn't need to play our game. She *knew*—that Auntie was a Jew, that she was an old woman, that her husband . . . that they had no . . . and death was near. She had a knack for revealing her awareness of these simple but mercilessly precise facts with exaggerated servility, stopping just short of verbal expression. In return for her silence, with bustling gratitude, she helped herself to anything she wanted, even those cups.

We really did love Auntie, but our love was also proclaimed. Auntie was a "Fine Human Being"! This has a bitter ring to it. How often we speak with a capital letter, specifically to hide the questionnaire facts; our automatic membership in the human race is racist. Inordinate delight in someone's virtues always smells. Of either toadyism or apartheid. She was a *fine human being* . . . great, broad, passionate, *very* alive, generous, and very *meritorious* ("Meritorious Scientist"—that was another title she held). In sum, I now believe that throughout the forty years of her marriage she *worked* as an aunt in our household, with all her remarkable qualities, and came to be *like one of the family*. (That was another reason why she and Pavlovna were able to develop a special understanding; Pavlovna, too, was a "Fine Human Being.")

We had every cause to extol and deify her: none of us did as much, even for ourselves, as she did for everyone else. She saved me from death, she saved my brother, and three times she saved my uncle (her husband). The number of times she helped just for the sake of helping (when there was no threat to life) cannot be counted. With the years the list grew and was canonized, item by receding item. Our custom, however, was to remind about these things but not remember them, so that the phrase I let slip a moment ago is correct: like one of the family . . . She was also—as I learned considerably later, after her death—*like a wife*. In all those forty years, it turned out, they had not been registered as married. This old news immediately acquired legendary chic: the independence of truly decent people from formal and meaningless formalities. The rest of the family, however, were registered.

Time drains away. A silted river bottom. The rustily protruding framework of a drama. This, it turns out, is not her life but its plot. It is lifeless from retelling: years later, in our family, information germinates in the form of a tombstone.

And now I'm constructing a pedestal from it . . .

She was a great doctor, and I've never been able to resolve my uncertainty: what did she herself know about her own illness? Sometimes I think that she *must* have known; sometimes, that she knew nothing.

She tried her foot, and then she tried a heart attack.

The heart attack nearly cured her foot. One way or another, she pulled herself through the heart attack. Knowing that she had squeaked by (as a physician, she could tell herself so with confidence, in this case), she felt so much happier and younger, and even fitted her foot back into her shoe, that we couldn't stop rejoicing. Again came the meetings, governing boards, dissertation defenses, house calls on officials (cure the murderer! unquestionably, a sacred principle of the Physician . . . but isn't it wrong to treat them more vigorously and responsibly than their potential victims? . . . no, it's all right: the law is alive where its paradoxes are alive, as in England) . . . and I see her again in the kitchen, ruling over her gleaming sun-kettle.

But her sun had not risen for long.

Auntie was dying. This was no longer a secret from anyone except herself. Even she had lost so much strength that every day she wearied, forgot, and took a small, involuntary step toward death. But then she would catch herself, and again fail to die. Her foot turned quite black, and she resolutely insisted that she wanted it amputated, although everyone, except her, knew that the operation was already beyond her endurance. The foot, the heart attack, the foot . . . a stroke. And now she clutched at life with fresh strength, of which she alone, among us all, had so much.

A bed! She demanded a *different* bed. For some reason she was especially counting on my physical assistance. She summoned me to give instructions. I couldn't understand her thickened speech very well but agreed to everything, seeing no great difficulty in the task. "Repeat," she said, suddenly articulating clearly. And oh!! with what annoyance she turned away from my unparalyzed stammer.

We brought in the bed. This was a special bed, from a hospital. It was complicated, in the clumsy way in which a thing can be made complicated only by people remote from technology. Naturally, none of the contrivances for changing the position of the body was operative. Many times recoated with a prison shade of enamel, the bed was both non-adjustable and ugly. We carried this monster into Auntie's mirrored-crystalled-carpeted-polished coziness, and I did not recognize the room. All her things seemed to stampede away from the bed, hide in the corners, huddle up in presentiment of social change. Actually, it was just that a space had been hastily made for the bed. I remember an absurdly youthful sensation of muscles and strength, an exaggerated awareness, inappropriate to my task as a mover. My biceps were emphatically alive, on display for the paralyzed, dying old person. Because of this a peculiar awkwardness pursued me: I kept bumping into corners, tripping, and banging my knuckles. The bed seemed to be forcing me to resemble it.

Auntie sat in the middle of the room and directed the move. That is how I remembered it—but she couldn't have sat in the middle, for she couldn't sit up, and the middle had been cleared for the bed. Her gaze burned with an ember light; she had never had such deep eyes. She passionately desired to move from her bed of forty years, she was already in the bed that we were just carrying in, and thus I remembered her in the middle. We mustn't damage the "apparatus," since we knew nothing about it; we must flatten it a little here and bend it a bit more there and set its permanently fixed planes higher-lower-higher, we were doing everything wrong, we couldn't possibly be this thickheaded, she herself would obviously have to . . . The impression also stayed with me that she herself finally rose, arranged everything right—see, nothing to it, just use your head—and after adjusting it lay back down into her paralysis, leaving to us the transfer of pillows, feather beds, and mattresses, a task more nearly accessible to our stage of maturity, although here, too, we made scandalous blunders. Good heavens, she hadn't changed in thirty years! When we sawed firewood together in that same kitchen, during the winter of the blockade, she (a woman of fifty) used to get just as cross with me (a child of five) as she was now. With our saw flexing and groaning as we rescued each other's fingers, she would be aggrieved to the point of tears in an argument over who should pull in which direction. "Olga!" she would cry to my mother at last. "Make your hooligan stop! He's tormenting me deliberately. He's sawing the wrong direction on purpose." I, too, was greatly aggrieved, not so much by her outcry as by the fact that they suspected me of "on purpose," when I had no ulterior motives at all, I would never have done anything for spite or on purpose

. . . at the time I was a tolerably good little boy; quite good, it seems to me now. Sobbing, we would abandon the saw in the half-sawn log. Ten minutes later she would cheerfully come and make peace with me, bringing her "last," something mouse-sized: perhaps a little crust, or a crumb. Well, I alone had changed, it turned out. And she still couldn't accept the only change that lay ahead for her in life: she did not believe, of course, in the Next World. (No, I will never comprehend their generation! Confident that God did not exist, they carried Christian commandments higher than I do . . .)

After we moved her, she spent a long time arranging herself, with obvious satisfaction and not another glance at her deserted conjugal bed. Now I imagine I heard a great sigh of relief when we tore her from it. Of all the things that she still, despite her medical experience, did not understand, this she understood irreversibly: never again would she return to that bed . . . We did not understand. Like idiots, we understood nothing of what she knew perfectly well, better than anyone: what it meant to be sick, how the sick person felt, and what he really needed. Now she herself was in need, but no one could repay this debt to her. And then, when she had arranged herself, she told us "Thank you," with profound first meaning, as though we truly had done something for her, as though we understood . . . "Was it very heavy?" she asked me sympathetically. "Oh, no, not at all, Aunt! It was light." That was not how I should have answered.

Yet this bed didn't suit her either: it was objectively uncomfortable. And then we brought in the last one, Grandmother's, in which all of us died . . . Once she was in it, Auntie put the pillow right for the last time, smoothed with her trembling hand the nice, even fold-back of the sheet on the blanket, half closed her eyes, and sighed with relief: "At last I'm comfortable." The bed stood like a coffin in the center of the room, and her face was at peace.

She passed away suddenly, that very day . . . the woman who had been the subject of the drama.

Auntie survived her. "At last I'm comfortable . . ."

The bed stood in the middle of the strangely deserted room, where her things had abandoned their owner a little more hastily —an instant sooner—than their owner abandoned them. They wore cheap expressions: these sides and surfaces, precious since childhood, turned out to be merely old things. They shunned the metal

bed in the middle, they were mahogany, they were Karelian birch
. . . Auntie was comfortable.

She would not be able to take them with her . . .

But she did.

In the middle of the burial mound stands a bed with nickel-
plated knobs, some of them worn down to the brass. Reclining
comfortably in it, with her eyelids half shut and her jaw bound up,
Auntie wears her favorite Chinese jacket; on her lap is the sunny
kettle filled with strawberry jam; in one hand she holds her stetho-
scope, in the other an American thermometer that looks like a timer
for a bomb; a Riva-Rocci blood-pressure machine lies at her feet.
Not forgotten are the surviving cups, the dissertation submitted for
review, the yellow Venus de Milo with which (as the story goes)
she arrived at our house . . . Uncle, with the chauffeur behind
him, stands discreetly at her side, already half covered by the earth
falling from above . . . Driving soundlessly down upon them is a
car with a gleaming deer on the hood (she regularly transferred the
deer from one model to the next, ignoring the fact that it had gone
out of style). So the deer is here, too . . . And our whole apartment
is already here, under the loose, friable time that is showering down
from above, bringing with it my entire past and slivers of blockade
ice, everything for which I am indebted to anyone is sinking into
the burial mound, time showers down with its living humaneness
and Darwinian humanity, with principles and decency, with everything that the principled and decent could not endure, with everything that made of me the pathetic creature who is called by analogy
a man, that is, with me . . . but I myself manage, shaggily, after
throwing the last shovelful, to be transformed into the blackly glimmering warmth of honest bestiality . . .

Because, since they passed away—first my grandmother, who
was still better, still purer than Auntie, and then Auntie, who took
my grandmother's place as in a relay race, and now her place stands
empty for . . . I will not forgive them this. Because, since these
last people passed away, the world has grown no better, and I have
grown worse.

Lord, after death there will be no memory of Thee! I have
already looked into Thy face . . . If a man is sitting in a deep well,
why shouldn't he think he's looking *out* from the world, rather than
into the world? And supposing I extricate myself from the well,

what if there's nothing there? all level, all empty, in all four directions? except for the hole of the well I've climbed out of? I hope the terrain in Thy country is slightly varied . . .

Why has Thy inept but diligent pupil been incarcerated at the bottom of this bottomless cell and forgotten? In order for me to spend my whole life observing one star? Granted, the star is farther than the eye can see without the aid of the well . . . But I have already learned it!

Lord! Uncle! Aunt! Mama! I weep . . .

Sun. The very sun I began with.

In your native city there are apt to be spots you have never visited. Especially in the neighborhood of tourist attractions that overwhelm their surroundings. The Smolny Institute, and on its left the bell tower of the Smolny Convent—I had always known that they were here, that this was the place to bring a stranger, and I no longer felt anything more for them than for a postcard. But now one day I had to locate an address (there were also houses and streets here, people living here, it turned out), and off to the left of the bell tower, to the left of the Regional Komsomol Committee, to the left of the honeycomb of convent cells, I found a crooked street (a rarity in Leningrad), century-old trees, Auntie's Institute (the former Invalid Home, which is why it was so handsome; not very many medical facilities are constructed—sooner or later you will come across an old building), and suddenly I was in such a good mood that even the blank fence looked beautiful to me. Everything seemed to have survived here, in the shadow of the tourist attraction . . . Well, there was a checkpoint instead of the watchman's booth, a board fence instead of the eliminated grillwork . . . but the main gate was still intact, and a handicapped old doorkeeper was at his post by the entrance to the Invalid Home (one of their own, probably). Both halves of the flowery baroque gate stood open in expectation. On the plaque I finally read what Auntie's Institute was properly called (Ministry of Public Health, Regional Executive Committee . . . a great many words had replaced the two, Invalid Home). I had to step aside for a black Volga with an epaulet flashing in its interior. The invalid, on his stump of a leg, jumped up and saluted. Low to the ground, with a surfeited swish, the general moved away down the brick lane in his fur coat of "black Volga."

I followed along, onto the premises. "You're going to the funeral?" the invalid asked, not from severity, but from a sense of dedication. "Yes."

The red brick of the lane matched the maple leaves that were being raked aside by a diligent Mongoloid. He looked like a home-made stuffed toy, of a poverty-stricken wartime pattern. Another man, a little brighter, proud of the tool entrusted to him, was spearing papers and cigarette butts. A cripple with a brick-red face, who stood confidently on a wooden leg with a black rubber suction disk on its tip, was crushing brick for the lane with a heavy instrument that resembled his own inverted wooden leg. Drab, laundered old ladies hovered here and there about the park like the autumn cobwebs—senile Ophelias with nosegays of sumptuous leaves . . . Outdoor work therapy, a nice sunny day. The air had grown empty, and the sunlight spread evenly, unobstructed, as if it were the air; the shade was gone, illumined from within by rays from the flaming leaves; a premature puff of smoke (don't let children play with matches!) had collected an intent, retarded group around it . . . The ancient smell of decaying leaves, the revivifying smell of burning ones. The fall cleanup. Things were all strewn about, but a forthcoming order was beginning to show through the chaos: space had been tidied up, the air had been changed, even the lane was freshly reddened. The morning's half-asleep retarded people, early-to-rise cripples, and autumnal old ladies were in great harmony with autumn. "Over that way," an extreme oligophrenic told me respectfully. Where was I going? . . . I was standing at the end of the lane, which had brought me to the hospital courtyard. I had to step back off the shoulder into a pile of leaves, which sank agreeably under my feet, and the oligophrenic wisely got off on the other side: more Volga sedans drove between us, two at once. Aha, over that way. That was where I was going. Auntie was already there.

At the morgue there had been a hitch. We hadn't recognized her: she was lacking her hairdo. None of us could lift a hand to fluff up the usual locks. Nor could she . . . It was Nektor Beritashvili who proved to be her true friend. He arrived leading a hairdresser, practically in handcuffs. "No one needs the money!" he said indignantly. "How much?" we wondered. "Oh—" He brushed us aside. "A hundred." The answer was as crisp as a new banknote. Auntie had not stinted.

Now Auntie looked nice. Her face was properly calm, beautiful, and significant, but slightly on guard. She was plainly listening to what was being said, and not finding it fully satisfactory. They were listlessly cataloguing her merits, piling up the corpses of epithets—not a single living word. "Her radiant aspect . . . Never . . . Eternally in our hearts . . ." The general who had been first to speak (three Hero stars, a good general, stout, preoccupied, and lifeless) drove away: through the conference-hall doors, open to the autumn, we could hear the disrespectfully hasty departing roar of his Volga. "Sleep in peace," he had said, bowing his head over the coffin, and already he was slamming the car door: "To the Smolny!" He would make it to his meeting. He had found time to dwell chiefly on her wartime services: "We will never forget!" They had forgotten already—the war, the blockade, the living, and the dead. They no longer had time to remember Auntie: I realized that she had been written off long before she died. The changed historical circumstances allowed them to appear at the funeral service—that was something, at least. Times were different now, how could old men be expected to keep up. And if the general, panting for breath, could still make it to his next Hero star, it would be on just one condition—that he not leave the carpeted racetrack for an instant . . . After the general, people were shy to speak, as though his white-haired ear and the golden gleam of his shoulder board had been left behind when he sped away. The next orator droned on exactly as he had, and so did the next . . . they simply couldn't catch fire. The deceased's family, parted by the coffin like streams parted by the prow of a boat, looked like poor relations of the orators. We were clustered on the left, the Jewish relatives on the right. I hadn't known there were so many of them. Not a single familiar face. One man, I thought, I had seen briefly in our foyer. He caught my glance and nodded. Gray eyes, attentively perplexed, as if near-sighted. But why had I never . . . none of them . . . I didn't realize it, but I had begun to feel awkward, ill at ease—in sum, ashamed. But I supposed I disliked the orators, not us, not myself. "Your merits were duly . . . with a medal . . ." Auntie was a fine human being . . . her merits could never be . . . Death is death: I was beginning to understand something after all, and the cultish flush left my cheeks . . . Stalin was dying a second death, fifteen years later. Because in all that time I no longer had anything to remember except Auntie, a pure and honest representative, it nevertheless turned out, of the Stalin era.

Auntie was more and more strongly dissatisfied with the droning of the orators. At first she had thought rather well of them—they had come, after all, the academicians, the professors, and the generals—but then she utterly died of boredom. At one point I distinctly felt that she was ready to stand up and make a speech herself. *She* would have found the words! She knew how to speak from the heart . . . Her temptation to give a person joy was always strong, and she contrived to find heartfelt praise for people who didn't deserve even one degree of her warmth. This is no exaggeration, no figure of speech: Auntie was more alive than anyone at her own funeral. But here, too—just as she hadn't been able to come to her own aid when dying, and no one else had come, though we were all clustered around her bed—so now, around the coffin . . . here, too, there was nothing left for her but to turn away in vexation. Auntie lay back down in the coffin, and we carried her out, along with her bed and her utter dissatisfaction, into the autumn sunshine of the hospital courtyard. Once more I lent my strong shoulder, of course, side by side with the attentive, gray-eyed man, who nodded to me again. "Not at all, Aunt! It was light . . ."

The courtyard was unrecognizable. It was thick with people. Nearest the door were the nurses and aides, sobbing with unusual respect for the deceased's merits, as evidenced by the guests who had come. Sullen, hung-over orderlies mingled with the cripples to form the next rank, their communal navy blue shoulder forcing back a crowd of retarded people, who in turn forced back the old ladies humbly standing behind an invisible boundary. The steady light of a timid ecstasy illumined their faces. That light fell on us as well. We assumed a dignified air. At a funeral the relatives, too, have rank. The coffin tassels, the galloons, the lid, the little cushion with the medal, the sobbing head nurses . . . the general!! (it was another one, who hadn't been in such a hurry) . . . the cars with chauffeurs opening their doors . . . the autumn gold of the brass band, the breathless sun of the tuba and cymbals . . . oh, my! They stood humbly and solemnly, patched but clean, never breaking discipline, leaning on rakes and shovels, this anti-rebellious mob. The general got into his car and gleamed inside it as if the tuba were being carted away . . . they watched with a united gaze, unblinking. The coffin sailed like a ship, its prow parting the human wave into two humanities: the defectives on the right, the above-normal, successful, and distinguished on the left. The two streams, separated by the breakwater of orderlies, did not close up behind the coffin. "We're just like them!"—that was the pride I read on the shared, unformed face of the retarded. They gazed ecstatically at what they would have become, had they risked going out in society, like us. They were what we had all started from, so that now, at the end of our careers, we could flash our noble white hair and rattle our medals. They were part of us, we were part of them. They hadn't risked it, for fear of the orderly; we had suborned and then subordinated him. Arduous and glorious our careers had been, as doctors and professors, academics and generals! Many of us possessed exceptional talent and vitality, and all this vitality and talent had gone for advancement—so that the door would obsequiously slam shut on the prestigious coffin-on-wheels . . .

If they were only half a man, so were we . . . They had not taken, and we had lost. But the half that we'd lost was the very half that they still kept intact. We ought to sort ourselves into pairs, as in kindergarten, hold hands, and pass ourselves off as a whole person . . . only thus can we come before Him without fear . . . Never, never should we forget what we would have been, had we not embarked on all this . . . Here we stand, in a respectful gray column, with large heads and tiny flowerlike heads, the micro- and macrocephalics, with the border-guard orderlies and the coffin of the last living person in between! . . . We trudge along, we who have given our all to become the objects of your merited ecstasy; we who are dead bury the living, we blind the living with our brilliance! . . . They're *alive*, the retarded! Like an autumn chill, the thought ran between my shoulder blades, my taut young muscles. Alive and sinless! For what sin do they have, other than in their fists, in their pockets . . . and their pockets are prudently sewn shut. But here we are, with the coffins of our achievements and experience on our shoulders . . . If you look first into the soul of an idiot, if you see in his eyes the near, blue, inmost depths of his soul, and then abruptly look into the soul of that general, or indeed of any of us —my God! better not look and see what we deserve. We deserve much, as much as we have paid for this. And we have paid our all. No, far be it from me to peer into the musty, treacherous blind alleys of our life, the inevitable peristalsis of a career. I fully believe that everyone in our procession is a hardworking, crystal-pure, talented, dedicated human being (even with a capital letter!). Only this soul do I propose to look into . . . our own, under no suspicion . . . and I turn away, frightened. That's why they don't cross over to us—they are rooted to the spot, not merely by ecstasy, but by horror! Not only the retarded, after all, but we, too, are hardly able to separate horror from ecstasy, ecstasy from horror. And we never will, never having understood. How could the retarded person . . . Wisely, he took fright at the very beginning. Even then, in the cradle, or even earlier, in the womb, he would not come here, to us . . . There he stands in the cradle, with his toy rake and shovel, and he does not weep for his doctor: the doctor is alive, you are dead. Not one of us could truly look Death in the face, not because we feared to, but because we already had. The souls of the unborn in Paradise, the souls of the dead in Hell; Auntie flowed between us like the Styx.

We filed lifelessly along the blood-red lane of the park. It had been thoroughly neatened up (when had they found time?). Kept back by the orderlies, the retarded had stayed at the end of the lane, still in formation, like a gray wall, and now they melted into the board fence, vanished. My last glance saw only an utterly empty world: beyond the cold, painted park rose the burial mound, whither the patients, one by one, were departing to their doctor.

Which of the two of us is alive? I myself, or my conception of myself?

She was a great doctor, yet even now, after all these pages, I still haven't resolved my banal uncertainty: what did she know, as a physician, about her own illness and death? That is, she knew all right, to judge by the pages I've written . . . but how did she deal with her feelings about her own knowledge? I never did answer my own question, and I still wonder what methods a professional employs to deal with his own knowledge, in an instance when he can apply it to himself. How does the writer write letters to his beloved? how does the gynecologist go to bed with his wife? how does the prosecutor take a bribe? how does the thief bar his door? how does the chef feast? how does the builder live in his own house? how does the voluptuary manage in solitude? . . . how does the Lord see the crowning achievement of His Creation? . . . When I reflect on all this, of course, I conclude that even great specialists are also human. For, in these critical instances, the narrow and secret maneuvers by which their consciousness bypasses their own skill, reason, and experience are such a triumph of the human over man—always and in every instance!—that we can only turn our long faces once again to Him, who for our sake consists of blue, stars, and clouds, and ask: Lord, how much faith hast Thou, if Thou foresaw even this!

Direct Inspiration

NO VIEW OF DZHVARI . . .

. . . I was walking on the grass, around the Cathedral of Sveti Tskhoveli. It was so quiet that even the ringing in the ears that comes when all is still, even this, died away in the quilted silence. My footsteps were muted in the grass. No sound, no breeze, no footsteps, no hum of blood. Not even a bird flew over.

All was astonishingly constant: the light, the air, the grass, the stillness. The world was without shadow. Such was the weather—in the sky there were neither white clouds nor storm clouds nor sun—only daylight. There was no sky.

From here, one usually has a good view of Dzhvari, on the mountain across the ravine . . . It, too, was invisible in this milk. No view of Dzhvari.

The softness of the lighting was extraordinary. I do not understand how I gained any impression of dimensionality, given the total absence of shadow, but the cathedral even seemed especially three-dimensional: I saw the whole of it all the time, my gaze curved and embraced it. It was quite alone in this world—there was no other object or body in my field of vision—only myself, a visitor. The cathedral remained silent.

But I had arrived in this dream on a train—that I remembered. Especially since the train had been pulled by a small steam engine, and the cars were old, with protruding running boards; it was quite some time since I had ridden cars like these. They brought back memories. I sat on the running board and smoked, as in days gone by. Tiled roofs, treetops, and small courtyards drifted past under my feet—very close, as on the Kuntsevo line of the Moscow Metro. Sometimes the villages disappeared, revealing below them a river "so very turbid," the Kura. Peering to one side, past the handrail, between the cars, I saw, above the jolting bumpers, the uniform shear of the cliff that the train was hugging as it made its way along . . . All this I remembered well. But now . . . when I was walking on the grass, around the cathedral, in this total gray-white stillness, as though I were in a very old silent movie . . . now, in this dream, the train and my arrival here seemed like a dream within a dream, languid and half forgotten.

And I no longer had any memory of the indifferent sights I had passed on the walk from the station to the cathedral. There had been something around me, obviously—there must have been . . . A wall enclosed the cathedral, and when I was walking alongside the wall in search of the entrance I still hadn't seen the church, or hadn't fully seen it, or it wasn't conspicuous, or I paid no . . . I took the worn steps and went through a small door in one side of the large double gate . . . It was a day off for the monument— there were no people, a lock hung on the cathedral doors—and I found I was there.

The cathedral was surrounded by a fortress wall. ("Surrounded" is not quite accurate, because the enclosure was square.) And although the function of a wall is always exterior—it is built primarily outward, so to speak, in order to protect, keep out—this wall had been built inward. That is the difference between a fortress and a prison: the wall always faces the enemy, and in a prison the walls look within. But here was something of a third kind, a monastery wall: it fenced the eye. Only a tree violated the wall, by peering in from the other side, drooping its curious crown over. But the courtyard between the wall and the church was a treeless meadow, covered only with grass, except for the path leading from the gate in the wall to the cathedral doors. The path was made of large flagstones—gray, like the sky of this day—and they, too, had grass pushing up between them. Meager bushes grew from the cracks between the stones of the wall. Beyond the wall there was nothing, the uniform absence of today's sky. In other weather there might have been a view of the distances, the mountains. Now there was only the flat, grassy little island with the church in the middle. A pontoon with stone sides, floating in a white absence of sky, sun, and shade. In silence.

White, whitish gray, and greenish . . . the three equally pale hues shaded into each other, and each contained the others. The cathedral walls, wrought of regular but unequal slabs—like the sky, more white than gray—were brightened here and there with symmetrically arranged slabs of a greenish cast, like the grass in the courtyard. You could blink away this faintly glimmering color difference, I thought, and then—where would the sky be, where the cathedral, where the land masses, in this suspended, incorporeal small world? . . . Let a cry ring out, and this hazy construction of air, stone, and grass would quiver and fly away, leaving you in an empty wasteland, I thought.

I did not see any visions, however—I had neither the predisposition nor the inclination, and certainly my mood hadn't been prayerful or even emotional when I walked in here. But I know nothing to compare with the sense of absence that overcame me at the threshold. The outside world and I myself were not so much unseen as non-existent.

I walked in silence all the way around the silent cathedral, on the mute grass. I was unready for insight—the cathedral brought nothing to mind. It differed from the Armenian churches, which are mighty in their faith, "bull-like," as Mandelstam said. It was not so classically finished and symmetrical; it did not assert itself as a uniquely correct thought which must inevitably occur to you as you approached, overwhelming you and dissolving you in its idea. This church did not force you to believe—the church itself believed, with a faith that was somehow gentler, more timid, even uncertain.

It was not final in its idea, or even insistent, like the Armenian churches; it was not predetermined. It was poignantly noble and seemed to make no demand on you. The mood it inspired was lofty but not exalted. A man wearied by false zeal might not have found the sudden strength to perceive true zeal. The church was not symmetrical, but neither was it deliberately asymmetrical in order to differentiate itself from the perfect harmony of its predecessors. The asymmetry quietly gathered force as I walked around, though it was manifest only in the fact that my psyche was not overwhelmed, there was sympathy for imperfect me—strictly speaking, I didn't even notice this cardinal violation of the tested proportions . . . the image, instead of establishing and impressing itself when I had walked all the way around, simply cast off and vanished into thin air, and I did not immediately notice that I had begun to walk

around the church again. It seemed unfinished, and even un-
crowned, for the dome is a necessarily symmetrical part, and therefore its dome had somehow been made inconspicuous, light,
unobtrusive, as if the walls were the central feature of the church.
Of course I don't mean to debate the subject of domes here—this
particular church was as I have tried to describe it (without destroying
it with impressive words). Or it was, when I was looking at it.

I was unready for insight, I wasn't expecting anything, and
indeed the cathedral brought nothing to mind. Yet all of this
together—this weather, these colors, this disengagement, this muteness and stillness—definitely reminded me of something I had once
seen or felt, although in completely dissimilar circumstances. But
of what, and when?

Somewhere I had listened to such muteness, somewhere I had
seen such silence, somewhere I had heard such stillness . . .

The recollection pursued me—which meant that I could not
recall it.

Very strangely, when I searched for this moment of recognition
in my own life I did not find it. I remembered that I'd already lived
through this once, the spark of the experience was smoldering within
me unrecognized, but I found no burn. I couldn't imagine, of
course, that the recollection might prove to be something that had
not happened in my life but had been perceived with special force
or communicated with special force (just as a book—not merely
the reading of it, not merely the experiences you associate with
reading it, but what happened in the book—may prove to be an
event in your life). I couldn't imagine that I had once heard a
stillness exactly the same, a stillness with exactly the same meaning
. . . not in my own soul.

IVANOV'S QUESTION

If you ask, you're making a mistake; if you don't ask,
it's an act of defiance.

People's shared agreement not to trespass on areas of disagreement
is much greater, on a percentage basis, than their desire to agree.
It is actually their main agreement. A compact. I have no interest
here in dropping hints about "what's all right and what's off-limits,"

or "what everyone knows but doesn't say." As soon as you permit people who think this way to say what they "know," they can't do it. The only thing people truly don't know is what they've forgotten.

I am talking about a different shared agreement: the methodology of shared life, so to speak. Husband and wife, pupil and teacher, child and adult, chief and subordinate, reader and writer —all of them, always, will remain silent about anything they both know perfectly well. Above all, they will remain silent about the fact that they are husband and wife, pupil and teacher, and so on. They will remain silent about *their situation.* They will say nothing about the fact that each knows what the other knows about him, and knows that this is precisely what the other is saying nothing about.

The writer says nothing about knowing what the reader knows about him. For example, that the reader knows that he (the writer) writes badly. The reader says nothing about knowing that the writer knows this. I believe this compact is called authorial self-esteem.

All right. I had meant to begin more gently, from a distance, in a roundabout way . . . But instead of a courtship it turned into brute force. Don't assume something, then, where it doesn't exist.

I had meant to begin as if speaking of life itself, and reveal that it had a natural story, a thread of plot, so that I could then make the transition to literature as an individual likeness of life, and accordingly discover the same plot here.

The plot goes like this: I, you, he, she, they. We. Every one of us is different. So. We live. As we live, we display a variety of characters, programs, ends, and means. We try a great many approaches to the problem of life, and as we mature in our diverse approaches we display a mutual dissimilarity that is more and more striking. One person is fussy, another person lucky, one energetic, another idle, one unsociable, another frivolous, one faithful, another compliant; greedy and selfless, wasteful and thrifty, generous and wicked, curious and reserved, irascible and perfidious, and so on to infinity—one and another. First, innate potential; then traits of character and environment; then the wife, colleague, and neighbor who have surrounded you; the result—different people. No one, as we say, wishes evil for himself. Everyone somehow begins to adapt to the possibilities, to his environment, even to himself. People grow accustomed to themselves, and their traits become a technique for living; each person's traits define for him a way of life. Even such traits as dullness, meanness, wretchedness, weakness, sluggishness, drunkenness, and dissoluteness—though we might think them burdensome, depressing, excess traits, from which one could only wish to be delivered—become, in due course, not merely ineradicable shortcomings but qualities to be exploited, i.e., a technique for living, convenient for its possessor, and even shrewd. All these people have arranged to live as they live and as they are; they accept themselves and live with themselves, often ably, cleverly, comfortably, and skillfully, while fulfilling life's demands and finding fulfillment in life, each in his own way. Even the clumsy man has his own grace, the maladroit his own dexterity. Adapt to yourself, then adapt yourself . . .

And here's the result for you.

A letter arrived at the editorial office. "Dear Editor: I am interested in a certain question. Or even two. Because the second question is why no one can give me an answer to the first. The question is: Why were there geniuses in the last century, but not now? and why have our good writers written so little? not just worse than the geniuses, but also less? why can't even the bad writers, who write any old way, get as much written as a genius did? All this appears to me to be one question. When I ask it, I get the same answer from everyone: 'Oh, everyone knows that.' 'But I've never heard anyone ask such a question, except me,' I say. 'People don't ask because they don't have to. Everyone knows,' they answer. Then I say, '*What* do they know??' Usually at that point they tell me where to get off. And then a third question arises: If everyone knows this, why doesn't anyone ever explain it to anyone the first time? Please forgive me. I'll be waiting. Ivan Ivanovich Ivanov, Goatville."

"By the garden gate," my colleague snorted. He read the letter aloud, and everyone laughed at the author's naïveté.

"Whatever next . . ."

"He's a bit simple . . ."

"A simple fool."

"But *why* is he a fool?!" I said resentfully. I spoke before realizing why I resented it.

I resented it for this reason: I myself had been just such a fool for many years, though I had never asked anyone the question; I may have known instinctively that people would say something hurtful. I used to be very quick to take offense.

I had asked myself that question almost before I began to

read—namely, why the word *great* and the word *genius* were used only of the dead, or even the long dead. *Genius*—that was a childish graveyard word for the time when I hadn't existed. Granted, this is a slightly different question from the one in Ivanov's letter, but I don't think I asked it even then, when they would merely have tousled my hair and smiled affectionately: "My little philosopher . . ." And from the very moment I failed to ask it, at that tender age, I already knew that there were no geniuses or greats in my time, just as there were no sorcerers, no dragons, no Baba-Yaga. Just as there was no God . . . (That's not quite true, about God: in a childish way, much as one fears the dark, I was privately unsure—but again, did not confess.) Later, after I began to read, as I progressed through school, I was still asking myself the same questions as Ivanov, except that I didn't put them to others. Only after taking up the pen myself, perhaps, had I ceased to draw the comparison; is it easy, in one's own case? . . . And now, when my colleague read Ivanov's letter aloud for everyone to laugh at, I was so transported through time, into the long forgotten, that I could smell the rag with which we had wiped the blackboard . . . inside, I was aching and squinting from the swiftness of the flight . . . and that's where I was when I suddenly heard above me the laughter of these big, unfamiliar grownups and discovered that I wasn't in class at all.

"But *why* is he a fool?" I said resentfully. And all of a sudden . . . the big jumbled storeroom of my head . . . amazing that I had never seen this little door, all these years I'd been living right here (in my head), how do you like that, right under my nose and I hadn't noticed . . . a sort of idea, the color of authenticity, crawled out like a snake and slithered away, but still I hoped that . . . They were staring at me in surprise.

"A fool he may be, but Ivan the Fool gets the princess," I said stupidly, risking a reputation as a Slavophile and watching with some regret as the idea slithered away.

Now I gave them a brief account of my instantly pale and dim associations, and everyone contrived to look thoughtful, out of respect for me.

"But who would allow the truth to be told about this?" a colleague said, in the sympathetic, "you-and-I-both-know-it" voice used of a general evil, which everyone here (in the room) knows about, and in which they aren't implicated only because they suffer from it.

"But who wouldn't allow it?" I said, turning disagreeable.

"No one would."

"You wouldn't?"

"Oh, I would, but as you know, it doesn't depend on me—"

"But it depends on you to understand???" I said angrily.

"Understand whom?"

"The truth! What we're talking about . . ." I said, throwing up my hands.

"But everyone knows it!"

"So there," I said. "Reread Ivanov's letter!"

In sum, I became indecently angry. Mostly at myself, no doubt, for having started this whole quite useless conversation. There was no need to wound these nice, perfectly innocent people— Stop! How abysmally disrespectful this is, to consider a man innocent!

Yes, I was angry at myself, in a way, but that was the anger of hurt feelings; in another way, genuinely, I was angry at the very thing I began with: the compact. Why had they laughed when they read Ivanov's letter? They had laughed to avoid violating the agreement about disagreement—the compact. Why had they become cool and watchful when I started to defend him? Because I had violated still another compact, the professional understanding as to "all right" and "off-limits." Why had I behaved rudely with them, especially when even I could see that my behavior was ill-mannered, tasteless, and provincial? Because *I was no better than they, that I should have this right*. What right? To violate the agreement.

So I walked out—rude, disgraced, loathsome even in my own eyes—and each step of the staircase was a word I had not said to them:

"The one thing we *can* do is tell the truth. Truth, after all, is not what's all right or off-limits. Truth is what is. You believe that the truth is the opposite of what's permitted. Maybe it's unfortunate that the opposite of what's permitted is forbidden. Because someday the forbidden will be permitted. And for you, it will disappear as truth. The forbidden and the permitted, in that opposing sense, are one and the same, an identity. You won't be able to separate them: the forbidden will immediately be permitted by the vacuum. Let's suppose that what's permitted is meager, small, and false; well, then, its opposite will be equally meager and small, and truthful only insofar as the permitted is false. This, comrades, is too facile a technique for orienting oneself in the world. The false and its opposite . . . You believe this out of laziness, so that you need never think, never exert yourselves . . . Someday, comrades, the world will be a little bigger than this!"

There were as many steps in the staircase as there are words here.

It's not the reader who should be asking himself this question—the writer should ask *himself*, at least once, at least raise the question, never mind answer it, I thought, emerging in the fresh air. He's not all that simple, Ivanov and his question. It works out to be a poem, a fable . . .

Somewhere, perhaps, people do write a lot. Although I'm not sure. I don't mean to speak ill of our time, but something seems to have happened to time itself in our time. Something has happened to physical time. More and more of it is required; there is an increased demand, so to speak, for time. It holds less and less, it has contracted convulsively, things don't fit in. The production of time has not been adjusted, and we are at a disadvantage when we observe our individual achievements against the background of huge world events. It seems that either the world moves within time, or the individual does. In idyllic times, from which we are separated by less than a hundred years, time was measured by the dimensions of individuals who broke through it and set it in motion. Now we just wish we could keep up . . . But not with someone (vanity protests). With something. Our age, though we think of it as highly productive, resists the productivity of the individual artist. The marvelous concept of the craft has vanished, yielding to the concept of the profession; it could not withstand "high" professional demands. If the soul has vanished from things, yielding to functional convenience at best, then the same fate threatens language: professional literature.

There is something dishonorable, of course, about blaming "the time." Something lazy, permissive, conniving. Too facile. Blame is too easy: "There's no time," or "Times have changed . . ." This should not be indulged in. But we can't all be reproached for doing it. We are never all at fault. Blaming the time, except when it serves as self-excuse, does indeed have some objective validity.

Every writer who is responsible in his use of words probably knows the shock of diminishment when he puts his writings together in a book: he writes and writes and writes—everything taken separately is resonant and large—and now he puts it all together, and it's not much. I peer into rows of bookshelves. Here is a row of one-volume editions, small books; these are my contemporaries, and they're all pretty good. A man writes for ten years—one volume. Twenty years—also one volume. A two-volume edition in his declining years, and at that, the second is half the size of the first. He hasn't included everything, of course. Understandably. He has been responsible.

The loose multivolume edition has vanished. We don't write letters to each other. Only the suspicious keep diaries. Practically speaking, there will be nothing to fill the final volumes. The sum of modern one-volume editions equals one collected works. Even taken together, then, they're not much.

I begin to consider them individually. This man, we know, is a drunkard—he's destroying his talent and does little work; this one is too painstaking, he works too hard over each word, and therefore he doesn't get much written; this one is delightful, he's just a shirker; but as for this one, we all know exactly how much he works, he doesn't drink, doesn't smoke, he runs every day and does calisthenics, every day he writes—and again, a one-volume edition. What's going on, I wonder. There is some hidden factor here.

Oh, we're all working together in a great common cause, we're a great production brigade making one common literature. But here's the curious thing: just when there are masses of people involved, the sense of a Common Cause vanishes. Why should we write letters to our friend? What about? Let's just tell him.

No one wrote so little, except perhaps the upstart intellectuals: Pomyalovsky takes up no more shelf space than we do. Naturally, the space that must be set aside for Tolstoy is intimidating as a modern example. But Goncharov was a notorious loafer, and so was Kuprin. Drunkards, too, were not uncommon.

To write as well as, write better than, set an example for someone. And pass by. That is the effect of the one-volume collection . . . Of course, everything depends on the quality. When I speak of the one-volume collection, I am thinking only of excellent quality. "Excellent quality" is the production principle. And how often, in that sense, those great men wrote badly. Quality wasn't the point. They tolerated carelessness. They frowned slightly—and let it pass. They didn't care about that book; there was still the next, which hadn't yet ripened.

It may be said, of course, that they were not only great talents

but also great toilers—that we are inferior to them in industrious-
ness, if not in talent. But if we simply ask a modern "best writer"
to turn out the same quantity of work as a "best writer" of the past,
he'll have to write like a machine from morning to night, renouncing
all else, and he won't be sure that he can cope.

It is unlikely, however, that they (let us jealously call them
"they") renounced life. The wonderful thing about their literature
is that it wasn't even labor. According to high-school legend, they
denied themselves nothing. They had more opportunities for this,
by the way. We are incapable of renouncing our own opportunities,
much less theirs. People have always been human. And even especially human. So one should say that they wrote in between other
things—in their life itself, within it—and not in between living.
Their lives had not been divided into life and work. This is why
they wrote a lot.

Herein lies the essential superiority of quantity over a reworking
of each word. If words like *quantity* and *quality* exist, then, even
reasoning dialectically, quality cannot exist independently against
a background of absent quantity—there is nothing for us to cultivate
and grow. If we don't have quantity, we will get some bouncing in
place, but no great leap forward. The everlasting jump-rope work-
out, the locker room, and the shower—and not a single battle.

The rebuke to my own time in this comparison does not interest
me very much; blame is foolish. Time and the time. It was theirs,
it has become ours. What interests me, rather than the vulgarity of
blame, is the lesson.

Since "they" certainly didn't renounce "life" in comparison
with us—on the contrary, they even displayed a characteristically
Russian breadth of soul (let's believe they did)—then the answer is
that they had more time than we do. They had time. We do not.
Something constantly and irritatingly hinders us, plunging us into
the subjunctive mood. The moral man has to tell himself that he
is his own main hindrance; this will be his technique. The immoral
man will blame someone. The stupid man will blame something.
But the real answer is that *everything* hinders us. We do not have
time to write. We do not write too little. This is a heroic feat, how
much we've written compared to those men who filled dozens of
volumes. This is a renunciation of life, a will to triumph, and a
fighting character—the full complement. No, we do not write too
little. We write even more than we can. We are *unable* to write.

That's the answer. They had time to write, and they could. We don't have it, and we can't.

Nor should we. Neither labor nor heroism is valued in art. That kind of thing is valued in a person. And it is never without consequence, even if he doesn't write a line. We are goading and forcing ourselves because we misunderstand our task. We have been overwhelmed by shining examples. But we will never be able to do as they did. Because they were they, and we are we. We want to learn, but we need to *be*. This is our whole task. To *be*. Have we allowed ourselves this to start with? Because if not, in all fairness, it's impossible—pointless, idle, and benighted—to take pen in hand. The values we want on paper we must try to attain in ourselves. If what we don't even have doesn't work for us on paper—small wonder. That it does not work is the lesson of the time. But we don't care to learn it.

And so, for those who have misunderstood me, I declare: In any and all circumstances, I exonerate our time of blame. It is folly to blame where we need to understand. There is no right path in wrong circumstances. The circumstances are always right—they are the given. There is a wrong path. It always inflicts suffering on the mind. We do not have time when we do not *live* in it.

Time exists independently, we exist independently. Time is not understood. But writing is entirely optional. No one is forcing you. If you can't write, don't. There is something more important, which in the meantime—inevitably, irreversibly—is passing you by, while you are preoccupied with the fact that you don't write. You don't write because the one who writes is absent.

I stopped and reread this. Such resolute words. Something was falling between them—undershooting, overshooting. There is meaning even in the fact that the target lies between them.

A word has a somewhat higher magnetic force than I do. It outpulls me, but, dear God, how wrong the word would be if I summoned the strength of a dozen men and pulled it to me! I really didn't know some of the things I see here in my own words. For example, that to be "unable" is to be "disabled." Obvious, one would think.

The best writers . . . foolish phrase! no "best" writers exist! Simply, out of the multitude, those who were writers wrote a little—let's say, one book apiece. They did all they could. A man cannot do what he's unable to do. They did as much as they were

able, as much as they had time for in their time, to the extent that
they and the time were one. I want to talk for a moment about the
quality of their silence in the rest of their time, for that is mainly
where they fitted their lives in. Their silence is not purposeless; it
is, in fact, the enormous labor of time working with us and on us
—the school of time. This silence contains far more meaning for
the future than anything you can hold and turn the pages of. Only
an idiot could consider it unproductive.

Ignorance is not, by any means, insufficient knowledge, but
rather an insufficient regard for Knowledge. So our own twentieth
century is ignorant. This is the ignorance that even creeps up on
the now rare people who know Greek and Latin and have read Kant
and Comte. Today they are "experts." The gambit of an ignoramus
is to say that knowledge can be used for something other than the
development of the soul. That it has a purpose and can be applied
. . . useful and useless knowledge . . . and so on. Recipes, advice,
recommendations . . . Even Tolstoy, in the twentieth century, from
time to time said something Hemingwayesque about how one ought
and ought not to write. Unwittingly, he had been infected by Chekhov. They had been forced to share living space. But we, from
lack of experience in their space, mistook him for an equal, mistook
this for life, and started to draw a lesson from someone else's experience . . . This was the beginning of instruction based on bad
example—a widespread form of modern education. Karamzin visiting Kant, whom he had never read, and writing out the names of
Kant's works on a special card, under Kant's dictation, so that he
would not forget them and could read them later, was much more
enlightened than any modern acolyte who has created a fetish and
obtained an introduction to his idol, even if he has mastered his
new little Kant by heart.
    We should not confuse understanding with thought, enlight-
enment with education, proficiency with experience, mastery with
skill, creation with work, cause with effect, nature with God, God
with morality, morality with principles, principles with rules, rules
with techniques, techniques with means, the means with the end
—for the end is morality. God help us to free ourselves only from
that from which we should be free! The ignoramus always frees
himself from the wrong thing . . . even if he suffers from the loftiest
of progressive motives. Music, after all, lies more in the written

notes than in the musical instrument, although the instrument, and not the page of the score, is able to make the sound. The man who is illiterate but enlightened may fail to explain some of these philological subtleties to you, but he will never confuse them in his practice of life. To be enlightened and to be moral are synonyms.

We must write in silence.

All this is truly difficult for me to say. I want to surround silence with a babbling stream, so that the silence will be delineated by a ripple over the underwater stone. I want to convey silence in words. The task is like the desire to fall in a faint. A linguistic fainting spell. You can't faint.

But it's equally impossible not to fall when you're already fainting. A man does not slump back from his desk when he has written what he wanted to, but when he has arrived at his goal at last, after all those words, and does not have the strength to endure it. At the limit of his potential—again impossibility. And so, until tomorrow.

POSTSCRIPT

No, silence cannot be conveyed in words! I wrote these pages in one night, and fell silent for six months. My capacity to string words together was suddenly gone, cut off. Mumbling cannot express, can only suggest, the inexpressible. The inexpressible is itself expressive, like silence. Those six months were more profound than the book. I had been writing it as if settling accounts with life. Well, the book had done its work: I never did finish it. But I'm free again.

I tried to reread it, the unfinished book, as though I didn't exist but it did . . . An odd experience! In the first place, the book really did seem to have been written by someone else, and this gave me satisfaction. The only parts I would have liked to delete were those that I myself had written. Wherever I encountered myself, I felt a sour boredom and shame. In its concept, and even in its construction, this book is the ruins of a temple that I spent quite a few years trying to build. Ruins, it seems, are my end result. But they are the ruins of a temple never finished. For the reader, deciphering them is a task akin to archaeology. He must search for non-existent pieces, find the stones that have been dragged off to the neighboring villages, before he can puzzle it out: Did it have a dome? Maybe not . . . And yet! After digging, after completing it in his imagination, someone will draw a reconstruction diagram—with the dome, the right dome, the only dome, growing up from the unfinished walls! But it never existed, it never stood in time . . . But it did, if they've reconstructed it! Yes, it did—and it didn't. Because it does exist. It existed *before* it was built. People before me saw it and did not attempt it, I saw it at last with my own eyes, and someone else will see it. The culture does not stand empty; only the time stands empty, outside it. The culture *exists*. But it will never be made visible by nostalgia alone. Nostalgia, at best, will erect ruins, as a memorial to the only image imprinted on its mind. No, culture is not reborn—it is created. Culture cannot be interrupted, just as life is not interrupted. Culture is eternal and uninterrupted, and we either know the culture or do not.

What has come of all my effort!—a woodcut bear holds in its paws a woodcut depicting a real bear. I applied my paint to each separate scene so evenly, so systematically and rhythmically, never losing touch with the realities . . . only to discover—after sketching a timid dozen arabesques, after dealing this game of solitaire—that all together, laid out side by side in an unintended overall picture, they are beyond the control of my imagination.

Over each day in this book the sun rises, and then, when all is in order at last, I hear the rooster crow. All my life I have winced at his cry. I've never understood what was wrong: why did it upset me that he crowed? Suddenly I understand. The rooster is real, he's always *now*. And his cry is now. But I, at that instant, am always not here and not now. I am unreal. Hence my fright, hence my fear . . .

The thrust (in desperation, by brute force) to reality—this is the face of revolt.

Homeland or Tomb

———

THE POET'S HOMELAND

The border guard raised the barrier, and we drove across from Georgia into Georgia. It became so quiet that we halted. The Kura still flowed on our left, but the river was not the same, nor were we. It was . . . higher. We would have to grow accustomed to ourselves. Somewhat deaf, stretching our legs . . . Across the border is where other people live, not we. No others were here, but it seemed as if we weren't either. There was nobody. Both sky and greenery were now of a different color, although they couldn't have been. They were of a different *world*. This halted world happens only in autumn, when the moments spin in place and you suddenly feel, although this is your first visit, that you have already been in this very time and space, where you've never been before. You haven't existed in it, but you've visited it. The feel of the next world.

Autumn was a long way off in mid-July. The next world was closer.

Both yesterday and this morning were far in the past, much further than they had been. So were the still-faceless campground, with its already faceless tourists; the courtesy of the Borzhomi authorities, who had glanced at us with remote kindness as if we were long-forgotten relatives; the incomprehensibly lengthy wait in the reception area for the frontier stamp, which arrived with implausible abruptness; and we ourselves—our same selves, but now with our document, now with our stamp—a bit alarmed by the misspellings in our names, but not risking an attempt to correct anything . . . and already very slightly *not* ourselves, jumping out of the car at the last minute to buy sneakers at the sporting-goods store (you can't get them "over there") . . . and the pimpled archangel with a submachine gun, who, after wearily fending off a timid but impudent small group of dark-faced, guttural "locals," had admitted us in accordance with our document, which fully satisfied him.

. . . From a river which had yesterday, in another world, been called the Kura—from a river which seemed merely to issue from the Kura, so that now it flowed without a name, between nameless banks under a nameless sky—our children emerged with perplexed, washed-off faces, blinking whitely, as if born anew and surprised by us and by themselves, as if baptized, no longer nameless but christened Levan and Anna . . . We don't seem to have said anything to each other. We held back, I think.

It was strange to see our own tracks on this shore. The imprint of the sneaker tread on the black sand was not ugly, by any means, but it looked absurd. The remote rumble of a lone truck, from the highway we had left, disturbed nothing. We were just as extraneous as the white trail of the fighter plane in the sky. A different planet. Strangers. Wanderers. In Russian, oddly enough, *wanderer* and *cloister* share the same root . . .

No new prototype can be invented. A few things were invented by primitive man: the flint and steel, the pocket, the wheel, the sheet, the trunk. Modern man has merely inflated these forms: the cigarette lighter, the attaché case, the Zhiguli sedan. He has cut up the sheet, he has diversified his steamer trunk with doors and windows, and he rides in the trunk, too, from house to house and floor to floor. In Tbilisi I was impressed by the pipes to which people fastened their Zhigulis to keep them from being stolen. How clever and resourceful . . . But these were simply hitching posts! A remembrance of horses—just one generation . . . Received opinion holds that, while external forms have changed, man's nature has not. I'm afraid it's the externals that are unchanged; not very much abstract thought is required to discern the same old primitive stick behind its various attachments. Nor is it very difficult, on the ancient plaque of the saints' lives and passions at the entrance to Purgatory, to pick out scenes of the contemporary customhouse. Rather, the change is in man, for he now believes fully that his existence is coextensive with his own lifetime. That is, the power of abstract thought is the very thing he has lost.

Fairy tale and myth are much less fantastic than reality. They

are common sense. It's easy not to believe that you will be greeted
by a God with a beard, but it's entirely possible that there will be
an apostle with keys . . . The symbols of a faith are easier to believe
in than its *realia*. Granting that this world exists, why can't the
other? Any schoolboy knows that you can't chop a magnet in two
so that one half has just a plus and the other just a minus. Only
for us do this world and the other occur at different times (the other
one next, after). They are simultaneous, the other world and this;
they have never existed separately, because only together do they
constitute life. Like the moon, like a medal, life cannot have just
the one side. Life is not one-sided.

But what is it like over there? Don't they have the same problems? Overpopulation, Malthus, ecology? If, according to Dante,
one still has to get into Purgatory; if even Hell is a kind of career
for the soul, and the crowd (all the people who have not fulfilled
their destinies) marks time beside the Styx, having been denied
admission to either place—then what kind of crowd is this, compared to our world's four billion? The elite won't be able to get
through to the ferry. A modern bard had a brilliant vision: "An
enormous convoy of prisoners, five thousand kneeling men . . ."

A certain hairdresser recently lost her mother. She wept cop-
iously, and her mother came to her in a dream. "Please don't cry,"
her mother said. "I'm having a very hard time as it is." "How do
you mean, a hard time?" her daughter naturally wanted to know.
"It's very harsh here." "How do you mean, harsh?" the daughter
wanted to know. "Could I send you something?"—meaning warm
clothes and food. "Oh, no, we have everything we need, everything's
fair. It's just very harsh."

The conversation is given word for word. What will modern
man understand by the word *harsh* here, and what will he understand by it over there? Perhaps the moral norm of mankind is what
modern man finds harsh?

But what *is* it like over there?

Like this. Something like this, right here, where across the
border from Georgia it was the same Georgia, where the same river
and the same mountains had lost their names, and with them the
property of belonging to us. Here, the only thing that belonged to
us was the watermelon we had brought. We had been cooling it in
the river and let it slip. Now it wasn't ours, it was floating away
from us, homeward bound—it had escaped us. The bite of the

gadfly belonged to us, blindly symbolizing the fact that something (we did not know what) or someone (we did not know who) in the next world (which for us had become this one) was irritated by us.

We drove on, but this no longer changed things very much. Beyond the border that we had crossed once upon a time, the world was constant and bright: all of a kind, all of a piece. The contours of the cliffs changed, the species of the groves, the flowers of the glades—and yet nothing changed. This seemed to be one and the same world, rotating back and forth before our eyes, rather than us in a car, winding into a new hairpin turn. Our freedom was conditional. Certainly we ourselves weren't changing the space around us. It was thrusting itself upon us, backing off, turning toward us and away from us—we were stationary. There was neither freedom nor tyranny. It was harsh here.

Not that harsh. But still harsh; this place, for some reason, raised a question that is removed by human society, where you're always viewed in relation to others: the question of who you are. Who are you, why are you here?

Where *were* we here? Here was like there. We entered and it drove up to us, we approached and it bore down on us . . . And now we discovered that we were standing still, apparently going no farther. What was this?

Rustaveli's homeland.

I won't claim to have recited lines that I had known since childhood. But the name of a poet, even a poet you haven't read, carries peculiar conviction. A hundred times the ear will hear a sound that corresponds to someone's name, and the sound will have no name in it. But just once let the name be uttered by a man who knows what it means, who knows at the peak of his own love—and you will hear and believe. The word *Rustaveli* falls from the lips of a Georgian in that same convincing manner. You no longer doubt. You do not need to verify it.

So this was where he had lived! Had he lived in Paradise, or we in Hell? Had the place been such that it could serve for so exalted a birth, or had the poet been such that he exalted it to the level of his own vision, whereupon Nature was forced to match the impression she had made—and became like this? There is no doubt, however, that owing to the border, or to other circumstances, Nature here has remained in the same state as in his lifetime. He is gone.

Long ago he departed to a world even more "other" than this. The world stood still to watch him go, and remained rooted to the spot. This spot.

"The world is a mere instant," my friend said, possibly quoting. The instant between Rustaveli and us slipped past—we were standing in the same world with him. The instant stretched on. "A mere flick of the eyelashes, instantaneous . . ." We stood there, afraid to blink.

The tourist center was a mote stuck in the eye. But the rest was as it had been, merely an eyelash flick later. Turning away from the tourist center, we saw.

We could not immediately have said what was special about this spot. Beautiful, of course—but that wasn't it.

The opposite bank of the river stretched skyward, several gigantic sheer cliffs rising in space very musically, overwhelming their surroundings. The bank was yellow. But now, in the sun's setting rays, it was gold and pink. There were small black holes in it, almost dots from here. The same is true of little rivers at home: the steep bank is speckled with nests, and the swallows dive swiftly into them, dart out with a cry, miraculously avoid collision, cut space into many triangles. That is life. There were no swallows here. If there had been, they would have been eagles; from here, the eagles would have looked smaller than swallows. The scale—that was what hypnotized you. You didn't know what this was, what you were seeing. That is, there was no scale.

And the place remained silent. We, too, remained silent— silent not from shock, rapture, or some other such literary emotion, which would later be discharged in words or exclamations; silent not because we were stunned and had temporarily lost the gift of speech. Silent because words did not exist here. Or had one day ceased to be . . .

There was once a monastery here. That is, those holes had been the entrances to caves, to cells. People would explain this to us the next morning, when, after calisthenics and porridge, we would be led across the river for a tour. The monastery was founded and rapidly grew to be a cave city of a size unprecedented in history. Churches and domestic outbuildings; spacious cells, some with conveniences, some ascetic; ever higher and higher, with inaccessible staircases and passages, some suspended, some hollowed out in the cliff; terraces, galleries, and bridges . . . Georgia's heart and spiritual stronghold, in that intoxicating era linked with the names of Shota Rustaveli and Queen Tamara.

But not even a century passed. "The world is a mere flick of the eyelashes, instantaneous." An earthquake of a force never recorded before or since, even to this day, tumbled the cliff into the ravine, and with it the city. Thus, what we now see is like a draftsman's vertical section—a tragically graphic illustration. "Next, look at this fresco," urged the romantic tour guide, who wore jeans specially accenting the narrowness of his hips, a loose white shirt specially accenting the breadth of his shoulders, and an open collar specially displaying his powerful neck and the cross next to his skin, and who never glanced at the specially attentive girl who edged forward but did not glance at him either. "In this fresco you see an animal's ears," said the tour guide, who was actually a hunter and warrior, and only temporarily, for the moment, a tour guide. "By its ears, this animal is a horse. But the artist wouldn't have painted just the ears of a horse; clearly he was painting the rider on the horse. This means that the rest of the fresco fell into the ravine . . ."

The question "Why?"—which every nation asks itself, at least once in its history—echoes in this ravine. This is the same "Why?" that echoes from the lips of Russians when they try to understand their "today" in continuous connection with their day of birth, when some recall the Novgorod Republic, others the Tatars, and still others Peter the Great. After first quarreling at the starting point, they all forget, during the argument, that they are proceeding from a shared perplexity. "The artist wouldn't have painted just the ears," I heard again, from a tour guide no less stern and romantic, leading the next group.

Was it a sign from above? How else could it have been interpreted back then, when a faith beyond the grasp of our reason was building these nests and creating the spiritual fortress of a nation? A catastrophe is a catastrophe. What was lost was lost, and those who survived departed. Very likely it had been a laconic era to begin with. Monks and caves in a taciturn land; a thrice-willed separateness from the world, separateness through self-reliance, through inaccessibility, and through prayer. This world was cut off with razor smoothness—by the sword of chastisement, none other. Silence fell, a silence far more profound than the mere absence of man—

the silence after catastrophe. It, and not the landscape, is what we see. Even within us it remains wordless. It cannot be described. One can never speak silence, just as one can never paint music or write paintings, no matter how the art critics busy themselves with encouraging such crossovers and mutual enrichments . . . And I won't try.

Only silence begets a poet. Although Shota Rustaveli's life story is so little known as to allow the most unfounded inferences, still, how easily this particular place and this tragedy convince us that the poet Rustaveli was born in one of the people born here. As for the border, it's hard to see which it protects against which: the inner world against the outer, or the outer against the inner. The question is, which side are we ourselves on . . . But—a schism. The fortress we defend is our homeland. The fortress we're confined in is a prison.

> "See, my brother, what has become of me.
>   How will I hide my pain?
> Life is a burden to me. Yet by fate
>   am I forced to prolong my hour.
> I have no life, but life still lingers.
>   Death fears to come to me."
> He stopped. The silent tears streamed down.
>   How sad that tale!

You gaze into the distance across the river, at the might of the cliff, at the human honeycomb . . . They dug like worms, these people, with inarguable industry and stubbornness, without machinery or explosives, by hand almost, but with extraordinary speed. Like worms—but also like birds! Not in vain is the cliff so high, and striving ever higher. Not in vain the association with swallows—your first thought here. Both worms and birds. People. You are silent. You look. You don't see, don't hear, can't tear yourself away. You don't know what to say here. Not only is there silence, but also—time. Time has stopped here. It is the same time as when the first ascetics climbed up here. The same time as when the last departed. The same time in which Rustaveli, from out of the stony inexpressibility of this muteness, began to speak.

World lamentable. Fate sleepless.
Why do you cast about, perturbed?
Why are you eternally grieved?
Who will believe in you as I do?

Everything in Rustaveli's biography is mere conjecture, and while the authors of these conjectures are always certain, the facts are not. Everything about Rustaveli is hypothetical except Rustaveli himself. Rustaveli's museum is under the open sky, and it has no exhibits except his lines. Nothing disturbs their resonance here.

Yet still God sees and loves us.

THE POET'S HOUSE

I have a memory that I don't believe. There's no doubt of it—but I don't believe it. The war was over, I was nine years old, and Mama took my tonsils to Yalta. It was the first time I had flown on an airplane. What must I believe here—that I flew on an airplane? That the war was over? (It had always existed; before it, there was nothing.) That I was once nine years old? That I can recall today events of thirty or forty years past? But even less believable is the following, which at my nine years of age was not a fact to be either interpreted or experienced.

The wicket gate opened and an old lady admitted us to the garden. She gave Mama her hand but, as I understood, was not an acquaintance of Mama's. Mama explained that we were from Leningrad and would very much like to see . . . After appraising me, with a shade of doubt, the severe old lady wordlessly admitted us and shut the gate. The inside of the house looked like our apartment—nothing impressed me. I felt neither love nor hostility, as yet, for the elderly author of "Kashtanka."

Then we had tea in the little kitchen in the annex. It was just like home; even the sideboard was exactly like ours. Mama told about her Petersburg high school and Leningrad conservatory; the old lady about her brother, but not Anton Pavlovich, another one . . . I remember nothing of what Maria Pavlovna told us. I do remember a little turtle that crawled out on the garden path as we said our grateful goodbyes.

(That happened in the year when the number of years that had elapsed since Chekhov's death equaled the years that he had lived, the years that Mama had lived then, and the years that I have lived now. To be solved: What is the date today, and what have we written in this time?)

Mama took me along on her vacations, and I visited many other houses besides Chekhov's. I also went to Georgia—to Kazbegi's house, and Pshavela's house, and also to Gori once . . . In each I remembered an iron bed and a narrow-necked, tarnished green jug in the corner.

As a man of thirty, I began to find myself in these houses a second time. People took me to them. I revisited Chekhov's house with a well-known filmmaker, to whom we are especially indebted for screen versions of Chekhov's works (he had already filmed *The Lady with the Little Dog*, but not his wonderful *Duel*). Naturally, all doors were opened to us. The velvet barrier protecting the exhibits from visitors was unhooked for us, and we were allowed up close. On the night table next to Chekhov's bed lay a French book on solitaire; the date on the tear-off calendar was forever May 27 . . . I recognized none of what I had already seen. Maria Pavlovna was gone . . . The director bemoaned his million visitors a year, the State Plan, and the lack of subsidies. We shared his views: the wooden staircases, adequate to the tread of a small family, were not meant for a public spiritual watering place.

I visited many houses with Mama—I try not to visit them anymore. There is some kind of heartbreak every time, whether pain for the poet or for yourself. There is something you absolutely cannot forgive the era, or, again, yourself. It's hard, visiting . . . Hating the tour guides, mentally disassociating them from yourself, and arriving at the conviction that you're no better than they are, if not worse.

Besides, the houses aren't so very easy to visit, for some reason. You don't make special plans, and when a natural opportunity comes along, seemingly of itself—which you immediately want to interpret as a sign, or fate—even then, either they're closed or something worse happens.

I was returning by car from the south and had already come to the central zone, which I was trying to cross as fast as possible, fatigued by the long high-speed drive and the monotony of the view ahead . . . when suddenly—what was this? Such joy to the eye! A landscape stunning in its cultivation and freedom. Then came the answer: the sign read "Spasskoe–Lutovinovo." Fate itself had ordered this—when else would I be lucky enough to find myself here? But fate had also locked me out: I did not have the wherewithal for even the modest admission fee. I discovered my wallet missing—no money, no documents! Evidently I had lost it at the last filling station, almost five hundred kilometers back . . . I paid no visit to Turgenev! But perhaps it was just as well. Why bother? The visit might have upset me even more than my wallet.

Of all the poet's functions for his people, of all his services, one is yet unremarked, though indisputable: the conservation of nature. How much history, how many cultural monuments poets have preserved for us, by their names alone. But also—how many landscapes! If not safeguarded by their sacred names, these, too, would have melted away. The grove would have been felled and the country house dismantled had they been nothing special, "no one's." The right to the property remains with the poet; it is sacred. What sanctifies it, however, is our right of property *to the poet.* That is why we are able, even now, not only to learn about them through their excellent works but also, in some measure, to see with our own eyes how the man lived and what his surroundings were when he still existed. The inkwell, the gazebo, the avenue . . . the walking stick in the corner, the oak tree on the shore, the only century-old oak in the entire region . . . "No, I shall not wholly die . . ." In our age, nature is a space just as chambered and cultivated as the poetry about it. And if, as you drive along a Russian highway, the road suddenly—in relief of the endless, deteriorated, non-commercial little groves and logged areas that blend into a collective clearing, in relief of the decrepit huts and fences tumbling right out onto the thoroughfare—suddenly makes a graceful curve and enters a broad-chested, pristine forest; if even the topography is ennobled, if picturesque hills and glades appear from somewhere, if clear water sparkles, if nature exudes cultivation (for even wild nature, without interference, arrives at its own culture) even before you catch sight of the truly cultivated, planted, and not subsequently felled park or orchard, before you glimpse the clean little church with its cross not broken or bent, before you see, in a modest and most felicitous spot, the cozy residence . . . you can be sure that you are approaching the home of a poet. Delve into your erudition: which one . . . The poet is the last peasant. His homestead is intact—both whole and undamaged.

Maybe you shouldn't go there by car? We were planning an expedition—my friend wanted to show me the city of his birth. Along the way we would be able to stop wherever we liked. Take a side trip. But where to? Gori, say. Or even before that—Saguramo. Gori or Saguramo? I didn't want to go to museums. At the moment, I was far more attracted to open space. And I had been to Gori . . . when? Thirty years ago? Impossible! I was horrified. But everyone wanted to. Everyone wanted what I wanted. That is, everyone wanted me to want to. Saguramo, then. At least I didn't know what was there. I was slightly less unwilling to go there. We left the highway with the mysterious relief engendered by a turn: going where you hadn't planned to go at all . . .

What might I have missed seeing there? The car scraped over the crushed stone, steeply up the mountain. The Mediterranean dryness of the rocks and bushes was gaily arresting to the eye. And here's a curious thing: when we're getting ready to see something for the first time, we always have some picture of it in mind! Our view is blocked by some vague monstrosity, made up of sights already seen and sights we shall never see: a kangaroo hops along in the tundra, and the Petersburg drizzle falls on Montmartre . . . As we went up that mountain, I was seeing Chekhov's trampled little house. The health-spa crowds ascended its rickety, complaining staircases, and the bright memory of Maria Pavlovna (whom I did not remember) hovered sadly over the cement sepulcher in which the house had been buried alive during her lifetime. But the house I was seeing was both Chekhov's and not his at all—the staircase I was climbing in memory led me to the quite different upper story of a small, wood-heated dacha in Sestroretsk, and it wasn't Maria Pavlovna but Vera Vladimirovna, still alive, who was ushering me up those steep stairs: "Careful! See the little placard on the lintel? Mikhail Mikhailovich wrote it himself. So that guests wouldn't bump themselves." *Watch your head* had been carefully lettered, on an equally careful bit of plywood, by the hand of the master. Submissive to his will, I bent involuntarily as I entered . . . They say that the entrance to Napoleon's sepulcher is so constructed that each visitor bows his head, willy-nilly. But what a difference there was in these two great figures and their greatness!

Of all the writers' museums I have visited, this was the most alive. Alive like a last breath, like an autumn cobweb, like a room where the people have left but their footsteps are still audible. Alive and airy like the old lady's light tread, like the silvery down haloing her face, like the constant girlish chatter explaining things to slow-witted me . . . I sat down at his desk. "He also made these two blocks himself, to keep the shutters from banging." She opened the window and inserted a small block between the jamb and the frame. "Very convenient." Outside the window was an unpretentious garden, where the board fence was supported by the woodpile, and a crooked outhouse rested its shoulder on the branches of the elderberry that had grown into it . . . At once timid and brazen, I picked up from the desk a tiny pair of spectacles that had folded their little paws like a grasshopper: two dusty wads of cotton had been fitted to the nosepiece. They, too, had been "made" by Mikhail Mikhailovich himself, as it was explained to me; the spectacles had chafed! But they had chafed the bridge of a living nose! The cotton had touched him! Touched his nose! . . . No, I could bear no more . . . Gogol's successor, Chekhov's heir! . . . I turned over in my hands a little document, some sort of form, on a half sheet of paper the size of a travel warrant, prescription, or summons, and signed by a personnel registration inspector. The document was a notice that by decision of . . . he (Mikhail Mikhailovich Zoshchenko) had been awarded? avouched? assigned (that was it!) a personal pension, the modern equivalent of a hundred and twenty rubles. "You can't imagine how happy he was!" Vera Vladimirovna explained. "At least I'm sure now," he had said, "that you won't starve to death. After I'm gone, you'll have half." She had tried to dissuade him from making the trip (he wasn't feeling well): You have plenty of time for the formalities, the matter is already decided. He suffered from a nervous disorder—couldn't eat . . . (like Gogol? really? you don't say! I didn't know . . .) He said, "You know me, I won't rest until all this is . . ."—and he went, no matter how I tried to dissuade him. He came home very bad . . . That is, he never had time to receive it, his first pension check. The shade of Akaky Akakievich spread the folds of his fur coat over the great satirist . . . The old lady, in the same chiming voice (her speech was striking for its absence of pause), told me how they had met, how handsome he was, how he was just back from the front, still in his greatcoat, and he wore a turban, and they were on their way home from school, and her girlfriend said to her, "Look at that turban!" So that's what we called him, "the Turban," and then one day he came up to us. A high-school girl—that was what the wonderful old lady had been

and still was, prouder of her personal acquaintance with the notorious Charskaya (she had written her a fan letter, and can you
imagine! she answered!) than of having become the wife of a great
writer . . .

But there, that was it! She had married, not the writer, but
the handsome twenty-year-old officer, pale, poisoned by German
gas, who wore a turban and the Cross of St. George, with a sword
knot on his saber! Her silvery voice soared and soared, and she was
still the girl he had fallen in love with, and never have I seen a
more tremulous, living memory of a great writer than this! In love
with her tiny bell of a voice, I bowed and scraped, finding nothing
intelligible to say as I left this never-open museum, which was so
alive with her life that even Mikhail Mikhailovich remained alive:
he had gone out to the little garden or terrace, while we chattered
on, without wearying him . . . Descending by the same narrow
staircase, I bumped my forehead after all. I saw stars, and her
laughter spilled out: How could I, after Mikhail Mikhailovich himself had warned me . . . Deeply moved, I was leaving, trudging
along beside the blank green fence next door, I don't know who
might have been staying in the government dacha behind it . . .

and along that same fence, which endlessly protected the park's
marvelous birches from our gaze and which had "No Stopping"
signs everywhere, but the Japanese didn't understand, they wanted
to take pictures, they wanted to go "to Russian forest," they didn't
want to go to the museum, but we smiled kindly, more Japanese
than they, and kept on driving past the fence, on and on, reassuring
them, like small children, it won't be long now, we'll be there in
a minute . . . And indeed, our delegation's motorcade entered
between the two narrowing fences like cattle entering a pen, and
again we found ourselves where I had never expected—

a great expanse—sigh deeply, gaze wide—opens up at this
famed country estate, where nature, to the same extent as music,
is the work of man, or was, in that waistcoated century. Yes, the
estate belonged to an aristocrat then, not a poet, but poets often
came here, and one of their sweethearts is buried under this monument . . .

Somehow, in this palace, unimaginable wealth did not have
the effect of overwhelming you with luxury; rather, you were impressed by the life and intimacy of the space, by the exact feel of
the living man who had walked here and filled the palace with his

presence. Suppressing a nostalgic sigh, I heard in the adjacent salon the shuffle of my great-great-great-grandfather's embroidered slippers (I must admit I wrongfully claimed him as mine) . . . I don't know why, here at Arkhangelskoe, I got so upset about the Japanese, who smiled so much and so politely that I didn't want to believe them capable of even a shred of the emotion that every Russian is obliged to feel at this estate, or perhaps I resented their unobtainable photographic paraphernalia constantly flashing and clicking as they captured themselves on film, or perhaps . . . And yet, what made me think that I was going to be reduced to ashes by the sight of their Imperial Palace, or would be able to feel what they felt over a Japanese garden or vase, of which our palace here had quantities and to which they (with such emotion) were touching their Japanese fingers . . . what made me think I had the capacity? was it because I planned to go to their country and for this very reason—that I would soon be their guest—was giving my Japanese guests a tour of a place which I myself, by the way, was seeing for the first time in my life, just as they were . . . and what made me think that *I* was the true Russian, when, waxing especially indignant at the lively giggling behind me, I turned around and caught my film producer (no less Russian than I, a man from a northern village), who also planned to go to Japan with me, that is, he had come to Arkhangelskoe for a reason no less sacred . . . I caught the two of them, the Japanese and the Russian, inquisitively satisfying their philological needs in a gleeful attempt to find a common language: pointing at the marble body parts of a little Cupid, the Japanese was naming them in Russian, and our film producer apparently in Japanese. They were repeating these words, which sounded so unlike their native ones, and laughing with truly childish gaiety, utterly forgetting the Penates, the cultural monument, and so on. At the time I was horrendously indignant,

now I think they were nice fellows, basically . . . it's better than making war . . . nice fellows! But why did I start sobbing so hard, for no reason at all, at the exit that time? . . . I had found myself there by chance, after failing several times to get in: first with my daughter, then with a Georgian friend, then with a foreigner . . . it had always been closed to us, that charming little house, that diminutive, even tiny, detached residence, whose narrow red side faces the Garden Parkway . . . first it was the lunch hour, then the day off, then the cleaning day . . . but here I was, walking along, no intention of going there, an hour with nothing to do (this in Moscow!), and the house was open! I considered going in. Too unexpected—I decided not to go after all. Chekhov evokes such emotion that you're somehow uncomfortable, or embarrassed in front of people, and now ashamed to face Chekhov himself, who portrayed this shame with such miraculous force . . . I won't go, I thought—but I had already entered, I was climbing the stairs, disdainfully avoiding the tour group, preserving my own incognito, humble as it was . . . them, explain Chekhov to me? My countenance expressing modesty and greatness, I was sauntering through the exhibit: Beautifully planned if I do say so, I'm fond of Chekhov, empathize with him to the full extent of my knowledge and insight, I penetrate his mind, so to speak . . .

and right at the end, suddenly on a small cushion, under glass, in a tiny, typewriter-sized display case, suddenly, on a small cushion, all alone, with no explanation . . . on a velvet . . . under unsmudged glass . . . the pince-nez and calling card of "Doctor Chekhov." For a moment, and another moment, I stood over them benumbed, and when I snapped awake (already there was an old lady at my shoulder, suspicious of me), I decided that I could look at nothing more and had to leave. I decided, but it so happened that there really wasn't anything more: To Exit. So I walked out, mentally praising the curators' tact and taste, went outdoors . . . and for another instant or so I smiled at the sudden outdoor light, a satisfied, relaxed smile, and for some reason I kept squinting, squinting, just couldn't adapt, squinting, the Garden Parkway, my eyes stinging, the cars, the cars, stinging worse, today!! now . . . and the sobs, with no thought, no idea, merely this mute emotion, began to "choke" me, as people wrote once upon a time. No strength to understand this or restrain it or conceal it or disappear . . . No place for me to hide in the middle of this snarling, fuming, treeless Parkway, leafless Garden, someone I know might . . . next door . . . what's next door? next door is the Writers' Union . . . Forty years old, father of three, I stood in the middle, and the tears— senseless, unruly, though certainly not drunken, because I hadn't had anything to drink—were not just flowing but pouring. Whence so many? and why? I have no words to explain them, even today. It was just me, now, in our time, on the Garden Parkway, in Moscow, with all my . . . all my . . . how could it be?

That is what happened. But why did they have to run dry,

how could they have ended? I can't understand it. No, I will never go to Mikhailovskoe! I don't want to see the oak around which the cat walked, don't want to see Arina Rodionovna's spinning wheel, don't want to go to the non-functioning church so wonderfully restored for visitors . . . That is roughly what was said to me by a monk to whom I gave a lift from the village of Nebyloe, in Vladimir Province. We were driving along, speeding. "Highway patrol!" warned the considerate priest. The car sat back from a hundred and twenty to sixty, right under the nose of the policeman ensconced in the bushes, and as I braked I had time to read the implausibly sudden sign for the village of Boldino. What made my heart leap so? Fear of a fine? That tremendous autumn of Pushkin's? . . . The policeman did not stop me, for some reason. Nor did I stop myself. I realized this only as I crossed the opposite border, like the finish line, and read the word *Boldino* in the rearview mirror . . . No, I couldn't stop here! and I didn't. With what eyes I stared at the landscape as it sped past, sped away from me. What clouds drifted above! the very same as above him! Had I known that this was another Boldino, of another province, a namesake village . . . I raced past, avoiding it as if I were my own namesake. Thus I make myself up to play Hamlet, but it's already time I rehearsed Lear. And no sooner had we gotten past the highway patrolman,

no sooner had my friend slammed on the brakes in front of him, shaking us all up like piglets in a sack, than we found ourselves at our destination—there we were at Saguramo. Immediately my pictures of the unseen evaporated, so that everything reverted to the state of happiness in which one has no preconceptions. No tour groups were here, we were first and alone; there was no exaggerated superstructure over the sacred spot; there remained neither sister nor widow . . . Everything here was quite normal—not dilapidated and not renovated, normal enough that one could even have carried on life as they had lived it. For us alone did the watchdogs come running out, purebreds unexpectedly fine for such a remote place; from us alone did the black swan turn away on the small pond; for us alone were the admission tickets torn from a fresh, untouched pad. But the ticket lady, of course, was not alone. Several women sat in a cozy, idle circle on the museum porch, bringing it to life. Who were they? Employees, relatives, or maybe both . . . One of the women was twirling a coffee cup in her hands; she had obviously been interrupted in midsentence. A second woman hadn't yet lost the intensely interested expression worn by everyone whose fortune is being told. Another cup, upside down, awaited its turn on the ticket lady's desk . . . We went on in.

It was quiet and clean inside. The floor, in the peasant manner, was scrubbed in some places, rough in others, with country-style wicker mats, rag rugs . . . It felt cozy, as though we were planning to stay a few days, perhaps, or perhaps to drive on after all, or perhaps they had invited us but our host had waited and waited and then gone out literally just before we walked in, and as always, being a stranger here, I felt unclear: our host? was he coming right back, or in a week? Time has a different life here . . . The great man's memory had not cut short the life of those who lived here. This was another nice thing: I felt no trepidation before the great Ilya. My friend probably did, but I was not obliged to. I felt a sincere and fitting respect for him, but that was all. To me, he did not stand for the fate of my people. And thank heaven. We need a rest from that, too. Everything here was conducive to rest, with a kind of shadiness-in-principle, not merely the shade under the trees . . . Besides, he was a good man. That our host Ilya was a good man seemed very clear to me, even without my friend's passionate explanations. A man's way of life does not lie.

As we went up to the second floor, we saw personal belongings in a large display case on the stair landing: a walking stick, a valise, a white waistcoat—for a sizable, or, as people used to say, a stately man . . . as though he had returned after all, overtaken us, and hurried off just now to change his clothes . . . and in the meantime the servants had let us right into his study, as they hastily hid the crimson velvet barrier behind their backs. That was how the tour guide looked—she had caught up with us, and my friend was having a courteous talk with her, which I didn't understand—she looked like a distant relative, possibly a poor one, helping out around the house. Ilya had entrusted us to her for the moment . . . She hid behind her back the crimson anaconda with the hook at the end, and we walked into his study. It was as I had imagined it, both manly and cultured. We read the spines of the books on the shelf —not so very many, but all substantial. We saw a writing desk unwearied by excessive work, a well-worn carpet, and bolsters on a narrow divan for sudden drowsiness . . . We went out on the balcony:

a beautiful park sloped gently downhill. The trees were openly spaced, so that dappled sunlight flickered in a special way among their trunks and on the dry, dwarfish grass; the dapples played freely about the park, affording now shade, now light, so that the light was nowhere scorching and the shade nowhere dense . . . The trees were all as fine as the dogs that had run out to meet us at the entrance. "This," my friend explained to me, dreamily and tenderly, "is where they usually put the table . . ." His gaze traveled beyond the trees, as though following someone departing in the distance . . . Or perhaps someone was even now approaching, someone we expected? . . . "Like this," he was saying with gentle emphasis, a round gesture. "Right here where we're standing. One day, when they were conversing about fate, Ilya and Akaky didn't even notice that they had eaten a whole suckling pig . . ." And again his gaze went to meet someone, there in the distance.

Then we, too, ate what we had brought, there below the balcony in the shady golden park; we ate, and washed it down with water from the spring; we played badminton with little Levan, my friend's son; nobody lost to anybody . . . but the sun suddenly began to hurry toward sunset, and Ilya had not come back. What could have happened to him? . . .

THE POET'S TOMB

The question is why. Why Ilya? Why Galaktion? Alexander Sergeevich Pushkin—why??

"I felt worse about Alexander Sergeevich," a peasant said, on the death of Lev Tolstoy.

Why do they do this for us? Why do we do this to them? Why must they have this fate?

Where should a poet more properly be buried: where he was born? where he wrote? where he perished?

But where, for example, did he write? When did he have time? He had neither time nor place.

Now we erect for them the houses in which they lived. Temples. And we idolize them. In the icon cases are photographs, first editions, rough drafts . . . portraits of fathers and sons, of sweethearts . . . inkwells, chairs, umbrellas . . . seals, gloves, pistols . . . a tailcoat, a frock coat . . . A caftan!

A small boy's frock coat, with a stylish tuck. In the skirt of it a tiny hole, narrower than a finger. We looked through this hole at the light . . . Silence.

The belongings are proof that the poet existed. As if we didn't believe it, as if we were persuading ourselves. Only the exhibits are indisputable. As if the texts weren't enough for us . . . We need his biography, too. It's nice to have a fact you know for certain; it's nice to have a fact that's familiar to everyone . . .

. . . Born in the Ukraine. Lived in Petersburg and Italy. Never married. Traveled to Jerusalem. Received a letter from Belinsky. Requested that he not be buried. Was reburied.

. . . Born in Taganrog. Educated as a physician. Lived in Moscow, in Melikhovo, in Yalta. Traveled to Sakhalin. Died in Germany. Buried at Novodevichy . . .

Who are they? . . . All together: Pushkin! That's right, children. Gorky.

Let's fill in the blanks in the crossword, in one fell swoop:

Born 1796–1828 to a modest landowning family of ancient stock; died 1829–1910, having lived 26–82 years. Knew from two to six languages. Painted. Wrote waltzes. Served in the Ministry of Foreign Affairs. Waged war. Was reduced to the ranks, was exiled to the Caucasus, Siberia, and his family estate. Traveled, was denied permission to go abroad, lived for ten, twenty, thirty years in Italy, France, and England, where he died. Perished in a duel, was murdered, caught cold, perished . . . His body lies in his homeland, was transported from foreign soil, his grave is lost. Wrote *Woe from Wit, The Bronze Horseman, A Hero of Our Time, Dead Souls, War and Peace, The Idiot,* and several other works. A hundred volumes of letters.

Concerning recognition in their own lifetime, the situation wasn't so bad for Russian writers as it was, let's say, in America. Our country wasn't a hundred years behindhand in discovering a Stendhal, Poe, Potocki, or Melville. Both the readers and the authorities knew, more or less immediately, with whom they were dealing. Concerning their life stories the situation was somewhat worse, but nevertheless better than in the next century. What the poets kept was their exceptional patriotism.

Yes, we have the life story. But then where is the house we just visited? When did the poet live in it? He was born in it or he died in it. He came to visit. Only Lev Tolstoy . . . and even he, at the end, could not bear it and died on the road.

Soon the anxious day will end.
    The faithful traveler praises God.
The road is not illusion,
    Already the goal shines near.

He has no home—only the road. The journey. And if the start of the journey, his birthplace, had the smallest chance of being preserved for his grateful descendants—because a newborn genius looks like any other baby and you can't tell the difference (how astonishing the plaque on a Moscow high-rise: Lermontov was born here!)—then his grave and the place of his death must be far clearer, after the man has accomplished so much . . . Or so you'd think.

"These people won't remember me . . . These people will remember me . . ." Between these phrases lies the very generation that will forget everything.

And their wanderings do not cease beyond the grave.

How could it have happened that it started to rain, his wife took to her bed, only four men (one of them Salieri) followed the coffin and just one walked all the way to the cemetery, the grave was not ready, he was buried in a common grave for paupers, and when the widow came a day later the superintendent could not direct her to the grave? And this a man known since early childhood to the ruling personages of the major courts of Europe! Not to mention that he was a genius such as the earth had never seen, and moreover was recognized as a genius in his lifetime. "And Mozart in the chorus of the birds . . ." There, in the leaves, is his tomb.

And as often as we may cite the intrigues of the secret police, who feared popular disturbances, we will never fully understand why the sleigh with the poet's coffin had to be driven to Mikhailovskoe, in such secrecy, by night, with an escort of gendarmes. This time, it is true, the grave is known. But the site of the duel underwent mysterious shifts during the lifetime of the immediate witnesses and participants—twenty years later they couldn't even establish whether it had been on the left side of the road or the right. So that, when you stand by the obelisk at the site of the duel, quite possibly you are not on the site where Pushkin's blood was spilled.

And Gogol's restless remains? He pled so hard, tried so hard to prevent . . . But in the eyes of people who had no doubt they

were burying a genius, what did his last will and testament count
for? They took it for delirium.

> *And the road, the journey, stretches on.*
> *Though the world has many men,*
> *The road is not illusion,*
> *Already the goal shines near.*

A poet's remains are disturbed after hundreds of years; more
honorable or more symbolic burial places are found for him. Can't
the bones rest content? Can't we? Columbus's remains crossed the
ocean twice, even after his death; they simply drifted on the waves
for four hundred years. Chaplin's were stolen . . .

Khlebnikov, eternal pilgrim, was wandering the steppe with
his friend, and the friend began to die. Khlebnikov did not stay to
help. "The steppe will sing your funeral service," he told the dying
man. It sang Khlebnikov's own service, too. As the ice of the steppe
sang Tsvetaeva's, and Mandelstam's. And the rocks of the steppe
Pirosmani's. No, this isn't just a matter of our ingratitude! There
is something else here, we will never understand what.

The great exiles and wanderers whose birthplace equals their
place of death . . . Who are they? Where did they come from, and
where have they gone? What has left this trail across our earthly
life, as across the firmament? . . .

. . . I was still standing there, my back to the tourist center.
Vardzia had been plunged into night, as into silence. I couldn't
make it out any longer, but there was something growing heavier
and heavier in the gloom, something *present*. Behind me, a dance
was warming up at the tourist center. Neither the music nor the
light, though they were pounding at my back, reached across to
that other world. I was standing at the border between the two. A
star flared briefly and streaked past.

> *Were I to stay among the living,*
> *I must part with reason.*
> *Birds strive upward to their souls—*
> *So, too, the body waits the end.*

Rustaveli went away to Jerusalem. They have all gone to their
Jerusalems. And have not returned. When I gazed into the nocturnal

silence of Vardzia—this memorial to the bird-men who once peopled it—when I myself stood mute before this super-tomb of history and homeland, I believed all the more in Rustaveli himself, and all the less in his tomb. Not that it didn't exist or had never been found . . . But the very fact that he was in it, under a stone. His tomb was here. His homeland is his tomb. He is its star.

> *Life is but a fleeting instant.*
> *I can only loathe the world.*
> *For me, union with the earth.*
> *Heartache leads me into the night.*

Poets are everywhere the same. Centuries later, a Russian poet who did not know Rustaveli would repeat:

> *Not life do I mourn with tedious breath.*
> *What matter life and death? I mourn the fire*
> *That shone forth over all creation*
> *And departs, weeping, into the night.*

Scattered Light

---

*How unexpectedly they were plunged into ruin! were
destroyed, and perished from the horrors.*

To the memory of my father

So many times we have sighed and exclaimed as we came out to
the forest's edge, as we reached the mountaintop, as we rounded
the bend and spied the sea . . . Have a great many landscapes and
vistas been revealed to my gaze in my vagabond life? No. Not many.
The more I traveled, the fewer there were. The farther I went, the
more I kept seeing my worn-down shoes and the dust beneath my
feet. I kept trudging through a no longer distinguishable forest,
emerging from a garden, crossing the mountains, going deeper into
the thicket . . . I was guided by words from the most meager of
dictionaries.

I am left with what I had—the lake by the dacha in Toksovo,
and the Finnish pine grove at the Pioneer Camp, with their view
of the Peter and Paul Fortress. The fifty-kilometer distance between
them is immaterial, veiled by memory; they appear to be side by
side against the background, right in the same locale. Nowadays,
even this is considerable. The lake is overgrown, the woods are
denuded, and the view of the Neva has been sucked dry by postcards.
But this much is mine. Further, I have captured one or two places
in description, made them a fact of my life, assimilated them. They
are located there in my manuscripts—an Armenian monastery, a
Georgian town, a Tashkent bazaar . . . I am recorded as having
seen something.

Having seen my fill, I walk down a street, enter a house, and
sit down at a table, as before—and it's a generic street, a generic
house, a generic table. Which means it's not mine. As for what's

mine—this is it. It's all there is. I'm doing well if it's as much as it used to be.

I want to see it. I want nothing more. Or I'll see again . . .

This place clearly didn't belong to me. I won't name it. On the way from Tbilisi to my homeland . . . Its anonymity will be my excuse. The description, for fear of being inaccurate, will be minimal. May anyone who recognizes it forgive me.

It was unexpected, this place. Or had *become* unexpected. This had happened within our visible life span. Before, perhaps, the place had seemed to grow up from some broader locality, to crown it. Now it was strikingly incongruous—impossible—as if the enormous city that used to prop it up had wholly ceased to be. No, this isn't a description after an atomic attack . . . There is construction here, there is life; the avenue goes straight, always straight, and with no change at all becomes a highway; the same deadly white multistory boxes, occupied and unoccupied, finished and unfinished, all equally unlivable; no people can be seen going in or out of them; you feel as if you're driving through one and the same place, that is, standing still; and here, at the city limit, when the highway finally plunges back into the less developed space of Russia, you have to turn left, and your mind is so lulled by the monotony of the road that you are quite unprepared for perception.

For one thing, there are hills; for another, trees. As though the earth had started to breathe, its breast rising and falling—you, too, begin to breathe in rhythm with the crests and turns of the road, which by now is humanly narrow. Here, snaking along the hill, is the white stone wall of a citadel, and at last you come to its improbably thick and sturdy gates. Inside, on the grounds, everything is different: level lawns, old trees, a church of God . . . a museum and a nature preserve, a happy home for ravens. Space. First cultured, later a culture park. There are also ancient wooden buildings here, out of character, though very agreeable in themselves. They were moved here from the north of our boundless land. You visit the log cabin in which Peter the Great stayed in Arkhangelsk. You measure your height and palm against his (a notch on the door jamb, a cast of his handprint). Gradually you leave behind the section of the park that has been completely restored and rehearsed; increasingly often, you come across piles of building materials and trash, with a view of an astonishing bell tower, a masterpiece of Russian gothic: the peaked polyhedron of its hipped roof is inscribed in a similar polyhedron of construction scaffolding, and although the eye is unaccustomed to it, this multifaceted angularity somehow remains Russian. When you have seen your fill of all the restorations and restorations-in-progress, you may walk on . . .

Oh, this imperceptible transition, from the life-affirming ugliness of construction to desolation and incipient wildness! Weeds. Does the plantain have a unique power to triumph over being trampled? Or has it learned to enjoy being trampled, to prefer it? Burdock, thistle, dandelion . . . Their clean leaves are already coated with dust. Tin cans grow into the earth, turning rusty and red; the text in the scraps of newspaper fades; rags rot away, corpselike, pining for the body; the dusty thistle is replaced by leaves dusty since birth, so caressing to the touch. This is life taught by death. (Here I saw a toothwort that had finally poked up through a pile of trash. All my life I had carried the memory of this obscene weed as a childhood horror, like the words *war, Fascist, solitary confinement.* The only time I had seen it growing was in 1944, behind the mess hall of my first Pioneer Camp.)

How wonderful, the way nature struggles with the civilized layer! These trashy flowers and grasses are her infantry, winning back the earth for her, in order to restore their own culture. Wilderness is not this desolate. Nature is desolate only where there has previously *been* something, even if a beautiful park. The raspberry canes, now small and wild, had escaped into a gully, and I followed them. A festering brook flowed there, and a new board had been thrown across it.

Climbing uphill from the new board was a rotten staircase, steep and high, with one railing collapsed and the other crudely repaired. Up here it was shady and gray, with a dankness in the air. Everything still gave the appearance of having escaped from cultivation, especially the green leaves. The leaves weren't green, although they were no longer dusty. They were as tinny and colorless as the leaves of an artificial wreath at a neglected graveyard. But you had only to reach the top at last, climbing sideways up the clay to get past the missing steps, and there, indeed, was the graveyard, with its trashy wreath.

Culture, nature . . . tall weeds, fallen crosses. It was painful to imagine what it must have been like here some three or four centuries ago, when the builder first came. How graceful, finished, and exact it had been! The sumptuous skeleton could still be seen through the tattered rags of drapery: the bank was just as steep, the river just as wide, and just as unexpectedly the bank receded, leaving below it the soft green lake of a flooded meadow, and in the distance it turned suddenly as if at a shout, and froze in the far-off blue of the forest, as though the river had swerved and switched banks, the left becoming the right, and the right the left . . . the sky, too, probably remained as before, although perhaps just slightly faded. What lines there had been, if they still remained!—such lines that the abbot and the builder had sighed, deeply and in unison. Their doubts had vanished: Here!

Nature could offer nothing greater. The perfection of her offering was plain to see. Such places call for a temple, a citadel, a city. Within a century or so, people had mastered this space, made themselves a part of it, and it had become *civilized*. Now the finish and perfection of that civilized space could only be inferred—from the "entrance area" (no longer the entrance to a monastery, but to the "grounds"), where everything had been restored "as it used to be." In its newness and tidiness you could see the dispatch of the "plan." They had used whatever paint they had on hand, the lawn was somewhat less than a hundred years old, and the boards and logs still remembered the haste of the woodsman's ax. But never mind. Time (and not much of it!) will pass, and before everything here begins to fall apart again (this time even faster), there will indeed be an interval when it becomes almost "as it used to be." Time also labors, after all, like man: at first perfecting, and only later destroying. Such a curious quantity of boundaries! Wilderness bounded by a civilization returning to the wild; the wilding civilization, by civilized space; the civilized space, by ruins; the ruins, by wilding gardens; the wilding gardens, by wilderness . . . Everything here was in mutual transition, mutual schism.

I scrambled up the precipice. Never will you see such abomination of desolation—not even in a tangled windfall—as in a ruined cultivated space! Oh, how much wilder than wilderness is incipient wildness! The wind murmurs triumphantly in the garbage pit that was once a church and a graveyard. Wreaths toss, tin cans roll about, a newspaper gallops like tumbleweed. Piles of bricks and filth grow up. Ravens take wing, circling—over the past, not the present. And layer shows through layer, structure through structure.

Through the festive, fair-booth layer of restoration, you can
see the layer of destruction, shoddily painted over (the devil is no
craftsman); through the layer of ruin, the painstaking work of the
old master; and through the thinning corpus of his work, the primordial perfection of Creation. Now, skidding and detouring from
layer to layer, you find yourself at a sudden overlook. A sharp
whistling breath (by no means a sigh of relief) penetrates your smoke-
filled chest: you can see *everything* from here! Everything as it used
to be. My God! How does it always survive, this unique point of
origin, at which you wake up and recall—yes, *recall*—how the
world used to be?

But do not attempt even one step to the side! If you should
have the good fortune—no, the honor—of finding yourself at such
a point, it will be unique. One step to the left and a flock of tower
cranes has pecked apart the space on the horizon. One step to the
right and you plunge down the cliff, into the garbage pit and dump-
ing ground. One step back and you land on—or tear your trousers
on—barbed wire.

It remains in this world! Remains and will never abide in this
world. The blueprint—no, a fragment of it—no, the footprint—
no, the shadow—no . . . but the tread of the Creator. His net is
still cast. The framework, the construction scaffolding. Surer by far
than meridians and parallels is this net, this thread, which the
restorer can grasp. The memory is lost—the recollection remains.

I lurched and stood still, too anxious, or shy, or timid, to take
even a step. The unsteadiness of my pose can be explained by the
uniqueness of my standpoint: strolling on the dusty, musty back of
the canvas, I had fallen through a barbaric hole and landed in the
layer of paint . . .

I was trapped. Write another *Journey* . . . call it *Man in a
Landscape: New Information on Birds* . . .

No. Go home!

I return from Moscow, bringing a small anecdote. "They amputated the Shah's leg . . ."

As you get on the train, so shall you get off. If it weren't for
the sign saying LENINGRAD, there would be no difference. Someone's
ideal idea, to make the Moscow station equal the one in Leningrad:
identical platforms, identical waiting rooms, and an identical grave-
like flower bed at the beginning and end of the journey.

Without leaving the train station, I plunge into the Metro. I'm still in Moscow.

I come out at Petrogradskaya and . . . at last! home! and everything is understandable. Joyfully I tread the ground. Yes, the ground, because first there's a small park. This is the shortest route. I can't say "I recognize it"—I know it! And I can't even say "I see it." That's the point, I don't see it, I'm merely convinced it's there. Still there . . .

My route recalls Konrad Lorenz's experiment with the shrew. That backward little animal lays out her path just once. If you put some obstacle on the path that first time and later remove it, she will detour around the non-existent obstacle until the end of her days. Forty years ago I used to cross the Karpovka River on a wooden footbridge. About ten years ago a substantial stone bridge was built, fifty meters away; for a while the two of them stood side by side, and I still took the little wooden one. It was deteriorating rapidly, with daylight showing through the fallen boards, and a glint of shiny worn nailheads. Later it was demolished. But even now, taking the shortest route, I walk first to the wooden bridge, convince myself that it's gone, and then fumble my way to the new one. I make a detour. The shortest route is different now . . . Thus, I expressed it rather accurately: I don't see. I feel, but don't see . . . What is here that I haven't seen? I walk, squint as though looking at the sun, inhale as though even the air were different here; I almost have a smile playing on my face. If I saw myself from the outside, however, I might notice that I'm walking somewhat crabwise—walking one-eyed, so to speak—and not looking where I'm going.

I walk so that my field of vision encompasses only the things that were here before—"before" meaning before my time. If I don't look to the left, this works, more or less: the Karpovka, the Botanical Garden . . . At the Garden, though, I can also turn my head to the left, for that's where my house is. The house stands as it always has. But the river is clad in granite now. Its trees, planted along the bank after the war, look almost a century old. The century-old trees along the Botanical Garden fell quite some time ago; they kept leaning, leaning away from the bank, which wasn't yet granite, and they fell . . . and the Garden has a different railing around it now. There are no longer flagstones underfoot, of course, and the pavement is no longer cobblestones—everything is asphalt. But my house is its former self, unless I tip my head too far back: the slanted

garret windows at the top are gone, straightened into an extra story
. . . But the view from my house hasn't changed along the entire
length of my route: the same Electrotechnical Institute with its small
tower, the same clock on the tower, and the same two-hundred-
year-old wooden Elizabethan huts in the corner of the Botanical
Garden . . . All this selective vision comes easily, unconsciously,
of its own accord—I'm still in my unchanged, unchangeable former
space, and no time has passed. All my associations are as memorized
as my route.

Just as the shrew *sees* the obstacle in her path—which is why
she detours around it—I first see the man in long drawers . . . he
dangles his legs from the roof of a seven-story building and threatens
to jump if the firemen who are clambering up from below come
near him . . . there I am, down below, I can't see it all, from
behind the people's backs . . . the siege lasts three hours . . . When
I pass the place now, my heart habitually sinks just as it did then,
when I finally started home without waiting to see the end, afraid
that I would get scolded for being late, and instantly I heard the
crowd behind me cry out in unison. Turning around, I saw a body,
sleeplessly white and empty-looking, halted forever in flight . . .

On the other bank of the Karpovka, where the hospital is, I
see ahead of me the word *morgue*. No, there's no sign on the
morgue. Simply, I was always afraid to look in that direction and
didn't know which of those gloomy buildings was "it." So the word
itself was the thing located on the other bank. That is probably why
I chose this particular turn, from the Karpovka toward Apothecary
Island, to start a certain noteworthy conversation with my mother.
I was in first grade at the time. Mama did not understand what I
meant . . . and even today, no matter how often I pass this spot, I
always ask her the same question and again get no answer: "Mama,
when I die, will all of me die?" My mother is in a hurry, we must
exchange our ration coupons for food, she must feed me and run
to her second job. "I don't understand. What are you talking about?"
I ask the question a different way: "Well, who was I when I wasn't
here? After all, I existed . . ." My voice quavers. But Mama simply
does not understand that if I existed before, I might also exist *after*.
With my horrible tonsils, I can't talk much in the cold. My life is
of interest to my mother in exactly the interval from "before" to
"after." Each time I round this corner, I do not cry.

I am on Apothecary Island. The Karpovka is behind me; the

Garden on my right is immutably lovely, and I am blind on the left—a factory wall. Home is still a few steps away, but even at this distance there is an identifying mark: a puny little oak, laboriously gathering its life juices from under the factory wall. Trees have two unequal fates: across the street the oak can see a happy life, on the other side of the railing, in the Botanical Garden . . . Even the unlucky life of the little oak, however, had been rescued for it. It had become infested with bugs, and my father, when he still went outdoors, spent a lot of time scraping the filthy things from each leaf with a stick. Passersby stared at the old man in surprise. He was unembarrassed, and if anyone asked, he gave a willing and didactic explanation. How senseless that pastime seemed to me! Over the summer, however, one by one, my father vanquished the bugs. Yes, there's the tree. The factory apprentice, the stunted child of 1945. But it is sturdily leafed, there are no bugs. If I look back, I will see my father: with one hand he supports the other, lest it drop as he reaches for the next leaf. His expression is lucid and concentrated. He hasn't even noticed me go by, nor have I hailed him. There he stays, in the space behind me, the same space where the flying man in the white linen bubble will never finish falling, and where I will get no answer about "before" and "after."

And here is the Tree. The Tree means home. There are plenty of trees here, but just one Tree. It grows right by the house, and although it, too, is beyond the boundary of the botanical kingdom, it is of their stock, related to them, just as mighty and ancient, a patriarch of Empress Elizabeth's gardens. It used to hang all the way across the street; stretching its gigantic lower branch toward its fellows, it reached over the railing, if only with its very last leaf, to its own kind in the park . . . A truck with an outsize load broke the branch. The container that fell off the truck was something to see. And the branch blocked the whole street; it in itself was like a century-old tree. I felt very bad about that branch. But quite soon the next branch hung across the street, every bit as mighty and low. Remembering the accident, they sawed it off in time. Then the whole Tree began to stretch over toward the Garden. It simply grew at an angle . . . Driving up in a taxi, I used to enjoy saying, yet again, "Stop there, please, under the Tree." The driver never asked twice, "under the Tree" was so clear. The Tree has been gone three years now. And every time, my eye stumbles at that void, the disgraceful bald spot denuding our entrance. At night, driving up in a taxi, I still open my mouth to tell the driver where to stop, but I catch myself: the Tree is invisible to the driver. I have nothing to tell him now. We travel an extra twenty meters in the moment before I say rudely, "Stop here." All right, I walk back a little way.

They sawed the tree down—this was an *event*. The elephantine logs lay around the yard for a long time. We did not tell Father. Father no longer went outdoors, and he never did know about the tree. My fortieth birthday found me in Moscow. He had time to congratulate me by telephone . . . An hour later . . . When I arrived on the first flight, and began to dress my father, I thrust my hand under the small of his back . . . it was his last warmth.

From a vast bunch of keys to the houses of numerous other people, I take just one. Before turning it in the lock, I thrust my hand into the mailbox slot. Opening partway, the shutter clanks. This sound used to tell everyone that Father was home. I turn the key.

"Hello, Mama."

No matter how constantly and urgently we complain about life, at the present moment we will not admit how dreadful our situation is. We don't have cancer, we're not being shot at, we're all alive, thank God. The worse our situation, the more it's ours: we wouldn't change with anyone. Other people might be even worse off. What keeps us on guard is the sheer certainty that if it got any worse we could not bear it. Already, in this sense, it couldn't be any worse. But in general things aren't too bad yet. They're bearable. If it's not for too long.

But death was instantaneous. He never even suspected. And he had feared it so. The last day was even rather easy and pleasant. He even had an appetite, requested a cutlet. He telephoned his niece and a colleague. He hadn't made a telephone call in over a year, but today he did, and accepted their congratulations on my fortieth birthday.

His face was handsome, serene. The bruise on his forehead— he hit himself when he fell—was hardly noticeable. So it turned out he hadn't felt any pain after all, the doctor said; he was already dead when he fell. He died even before he stood up. Dead, he stood up and fell. And it's just as well that he was cremated. That was his wish. Besides, we managed to have him buried in our cemetery. Burials were already forbidden there. With a coffin, we wouldn't have succeeded.

An idea I can never think through: those two razors that severed Father's life. However faintly it glimmered within him, his life did not have time to fade to nothing, did not flicker out in a last point of light, but suddenly broke off—all the life that was in him. A cliff, a waterfall. Not his own existence but rather the whole world he saw before him collapsed into the abyss. Time and darkness have this peculiar quality, which I cannot comprehend: the world cloven like an apple. And then—the furnace . . . Where did his soul come to visit on the third day, the ninth, the fortieth?

But a year later he came in person, in a dream. We encountered him on the street. He was somehow shabby and gay. Lighthearted. His trousers were frayed. Mama was with me, but he was very glad to see me in particular. He patted my hand. Mama was even jealous: "What about me?" Then we had lunch at some sort of snack bar. Father ate greedily and youthfully; we watched him eat. Talking with his mouth full (the habit that used to irritate my mother so), he enthusiastically told my mother about my literary successes. This was so surprising, and so unlike him! Here was someone, I had thought, for whom it was a blessing he hadn't lived to see these "successes": he could not have borne them. But look at this—he was convincing Mother of the reverse . . . Cheered by his unexpected encouragement, I decided to take this opportunity to pump him about life "over there" (not in America, but beyond the grave). Chewing, he brushed the question aside: "But I'm seldom there." This odd phrase lodged on his fork like a piece of macaroni. His hunger and his vagabond appearance confirmed my Christian doubts about the modern rite . . . but then again, his restlessness seemed to be purely external; otherwise, whence this unconcern and freedom, which had never been characteristic of him? So I did not pause, but pressed him on the main issue. I leaned toward him, lest Mama hear, and asked man to man, "Well, how long do I have left?" Father looked at me and chewed more thoughtfully. I began trying to convince him that my need to know wasn't sheer curiosity, I was prepared for the worst, but in that event I had to *get things done.* By this I meant my Work (with a capital letter), which, as I now saw clearly (and, being his son, found flattering), he fully acknowledged. Father did not listen very closely. He weighed some idea thoroughly, and at last, without ceasing to chew, he carelessly—as if he did not share our idle and mortal interest in life—carelessly put up two fingers. On the hand unencumbered by his fork. Like two horns, or donkey ears. Or so that Mother wouldn't understand. Or was it a roman numeral V . . . Why roman? He could have put up all five fingers, in the Russian manner. Or did this mean the Latin V for Victory? Of course, it immediately struck me as not enough. Two. I had suspected it wouldn't be many, but not two. July 25, 1980 . . . it was easily calculated, then and there. But I failed to verify it. The dream disintegrated.

Still, I had at least two years ahead of me . . .

On one count, Father has already proved right: his evident disdain for my interest. In these two years I have done *nothing*! Life is life. It can't be hurried. I haven't fulfilled my five-year plan in two years. Even though warned, I have lived as though unwarned, and in this one respect I am satisfied with myself. In this respect I proved free—I did not let the burden hurry me to the grave. I have three months left.

Unless it meant Victory, of course . . .

So my situation doesn't strike me as bad. Because how could it be any worse? My friends are forsaking me . . . My girlfriend doesn't visit . . . Out of work, no money; divorced, no place to live. And I can't seem to write: the fruits are cemented together in my womb, and all my labors haven't brought forth a single one of them. Not even one . . . what was the point of interrogating Father? True, my children are a joy and delight. But my daughter didn't get into college, and my son has caught another cold. True, I'm coping with my responsibilities, so far: I've sold the car for food. And the children still live as though I existed. True, there are still a few defective readers for whom I'm a light in the window. Wretched defective readers, but I am needed by them. And as yet unacquainted with them, thank God. True, there are still a few women, of past or future beauty, who are kindly disposed toward me. But I'd rather they thought worse of me than I do. True, I have Mama—God grant her good health!

On the whole, I'm managing . . .

A prodigal son, I return home. Forty years ago they brought me here; some forty years go by, and here I am again! My stronghold! I still have "a place to go"—that's about the sum of it.

My mother is a young girl. She talks brightly and joyously,

never surrendering to either age or mood . . . talks, and seems to have two bouncing, schoolgirl braids down her back, or two quivering, dust-laden butterfly wings. She dusts me with all the family news—the absolute latest, the most minute details, as if I had left only yesterday and therefore still remembered and knew everything. Now I am covered with this pollen, I take back the form of a cocoon, I am swaddled, I am prepared never to be reborn but to abide here, with her, with Mama . . .

"And you know, we're being evicted!" my mother chirps gaily.

Our neighbor Nikonovich tells me the details. It's a bit of an exaggeration, I think, when he claims to be eighty-nine. But it's possible; he used to show me his passport. It's possible. Nikonovich is eternal. Not only hasn't he changed, he has definitely grown younger in the last forty years. The Gerontology Institute counts him among its research subjects. He is tall, well built, and light; his smooth-shaven cheeks have a brisk ruddiness; his hair is no grayer than mine. Four wars have strengthened his carriage and bearing, and deliberate bachelorhood has worked to his advantage. He started out as a non-commissioned officer; now, at the summons of LenFilm, he consents to appear in a uniform no lower than a colonel's, which places him practically in the tsar's family, at the level of Grand Prince. His dashing appearance used to be complemented by a resonant voice, a baritone with rolling French *r*'s. But his baritone was removed because of cancer of the larynx; the operation was a great success, so now he's a research subject for the oncologists, too. And it must be said that he was never so talkative as he has been since the operation. At first we could hardly understand him, and he wrote endless notes in a firm, schoolboy hand. By now, either he has learned, or we have. I cease to hear myself answering, and we converse like two fish in an aquarium.

Our apparently doomed house, by the way, does look a little like an aquarium. The turn of the century, the *style moderne*— there is something of the aquarium in its lines. Nikonovich opens and closes his mouth, and I get the facts: we are being evicted, it is certain now, since there has been a decision by the City Executive Committee. Now. Any moment. But most probably after the Olympics. "After the Olympics"—it's already a formula. Like "after the war." At six in the evening, most probably. After a rain shower, if it's a Thursday. Brief, and slightly radioactive . . . That is how I hear his tranquil, ashy whisper.

An aquarium, two large old fish, and now a rain shower from above. My blood pressure falls rapidly, my eardrums and temporal bones are drawn inward, as though I were sucking myself dry from within. He keeps talking and talking. INDCOMMENERGSUPPSALES-MAINTPUB: he writes on a scrap an acronym that I cannot understand in his pronunciation. This is what has bought us, what has gobbled us up. An arthropod. So everything that was our life and our death is HOPSKIPBONKKICKKAPUT. We are already gone, but it—having devoured half of Apothecary Island—*it* goes on and on, ONCO-BURPBONKKOMMISTDAS . . .

By now the room is rocking slightly before my eyes. Space, as is proper in an aquarium, is drifting and playing tricks, and at a certain angle it converts its thickness to a lens, now flattening my companion like a flounder, now elongating him like a needlefish . . . Finally I complain to Nikonovich of dizziness and low blood pressure. Better I hadn't. In the first place, I must follow his example and drink dry wine before dinner (we have a ten-minute digression, delving into the properties of vitamins and glucose), though not much (that is a tip), but always (this, too, is a tip), and here before you, in person, you see the results . . . In the second place, dried apricots (another five minutes on the properties and prices of dried apricots) . . . And in the seventh place, bouillon (but by now it's a joke—Nikonovich gurgles for a long time). The joke is this: Descartes (he will show me the book) advised Pascal, who suffered from anemia and similar indispositions, to drink very strong bouillon (but what about cholesterol and sclerosis! . . . better I hadn't asked) . . . All right then, bouillon, and in the second place, to stay in bed in the morning for as long as possible, until he felt utterly fatigued by repose . . . Ha-ha-ha! Really? Descartes? . . . I'll fetch you the book right now . . . Oh, no, no, I believe you. Good night, Nikonovich.

In the morning, for a long time, I don't want to wake up. Inaudible, with the whisper of a night moth, my mother keeps flying into my room from the kitchen. I don't want to wake up, and then I don't want to be awake. I don't remember—don't want to recall —why I don't want this. I was supposed to be wakened by a telephone call. If I dangle my hand down, it will land on the telephone receiver. Perhaps my mother took out the phone? Without opening my eyes, I let my hand drop—the receiver rests securely on the cradle, it hasn't been knocked off . . . She didn't call! I turn my face to the wall, away from life. But sleep no longer comes. Inwardly I am conserving this last opportunity of the morning to think about nothing. Strange exertion! What, exactly, am I not thinking about? I can't seem to remember . . . The clock strikes once. What time is that? Half past what? If I could recall even a detail of my last dream, I might try to work back into the dream, recapture it . . . But it's gone, evidently forever. The pathetic attempt to fashion my own dream resembles the nauseating effort of writing . . . The clock strikes—again, only once. Which means I've had my face to the wall for half an hour, resisting . . . Relieved, I turn over on my back. What time is it, really? Either one or one-thirty. My resurrected capacity for logic delights me. If she had called, it would be no later than twelve, adjusting for all the geographical complications, all the connections from their Leningrad to mine . . . she has already failed to get through . . . And already this is something, that she has *already* . . . My head is absolutely empty. And now —the sun.

The sun reached me. It didn't care about me, of course, any more than did time, which I had been lying there trying to outwait. Meanwhile, everything had continued. I must open my eyes to this.

I did. What I saw was worth the effort. Filled with the empty-headedness and inner immobility I had amassed by diligent repose, I lay and observed a well-known phenomenon—specks of dust in a shaft of sunlight. How many years since I had seen this? Ten? Twenty? All of thirty? The shaft was a tall rectangular prism, beating between the window frame and the curtain; it was cut off from below by the high shoulder of my luxurious writing desk, at which my grandfather, too, wrote not one line, though the desk was custom-made to his own design. The truncated prism of light rested on the parquet and dug one of its facets into my pillow. But what an abundance of dust. Rising and settling, twisting into galactic spirals, the dust swirled and even sparkled, deftly discovering its facets, admiring the secret matter within it. It rose up from earth, demonstrating the cosmic solidarity of matter. Earth, dust, speck, particle, body . . . An inscrutable miracle. Yes, if this were the seventeenth century, Descartes's advice would be apropos. I would lie on my side, in the pose of an integral, and discover two or three classical laws—were I Pascal, of course. Something about air streams, or the dispersion of particles, or an opaque body . . . The

integral calculus, if not yet discovered, hung in the air of its own
accord . . . A triumphant vortex—a victory of regularities—was
being created in the shaft of sunlight. It was even exulting in its
own inscrutability: the laws weren't hiding, they were demonstrating
themselves to my feeble mind, with essentially no risk that I could
understand so much as a tendril of Creation. And how clearly I
saw that it wasn't worth straining the poor thing (my mind); this
dust contained, not only all the laws that constituted the glory of
classical mechanics and mathematics, but absolutely all the laws—
all that had followed, and all that were yet to be discovered—and
all of them would be as nothing compared to what was happening
in this shaft of light. This demonstrative dance—because by now I
seemed to hear both rhythm and music—also implied that it wasn't
intended for me at all, or even for Pascal, lying in my pose three
centuries ago on Descartes's advice . . . "Triumphing regularity,"
I repeated to myself, and the thought slipped away from me, in a
whirl of other thoughts beyond my grasp. It filled me with joy. This
triumph was not a triumph over me and my beggarly consciousness
(which had ended with a passionate desire never to lift my head
from this pillow), or even over human consciousness in general
(which I represented at the given moment, not fully, but as best I
could) . . . the triumph lay in the constancy and interminability of
its own lastingness: lasting and lasting, it, she, and he, something
and someone. So we need not strain our minds: any law we might
detect not only would be an insignificant part of the universal system
that embraces all time and swallows up all things but would also
vanish outright, our wretched little law, the moment it was captured
and formulated; along with our consciousness of it, it would even
disappear from the universe, as a dead and needless thing which
the universe, in its own everlasting lastingness, would continue to
do without, since the law hadn't even existed, and we had been
going backward with it, applying it to a universe that had flown
away from us during our absurd cerebral pause, flown away to a
distance incommensurable with its distance from us during the
intoxicating moment when we thought we had understood and
discovered something about something . . . An inspired joy gripped
me at the sight of this earthly dust swirling before my eyes—the
inspired joy of my own insignificance. On which of these specks,
rushing past myriads of others, was I? If I had to name my newfound
land, I would name it Hecuba . . . (What land could I, as a scribe,

enter without quotations?) Scattered light! The light had scattered on the glimmering specks—it had settled these worlds. Or did it lie between them? Had they been scattered in the light? Had I once more had the honor of falling prostrate, only to lose all this, yet again, by thriftily brushing the dust from my knees? Had I seen the light, had the light shone on me, so that my dusty facet could sparkle as I rushed past forever? It's really not scary that God exists. Thou art welcome to exist, Lord—I don't mind. Such exultation, that I've been granted a ride on Thy carousel! Scattered light . . . Where did it scatter to? and when? What has it forgotten, or lost, in being scattered? And yet, however scattered, it's still light! And light, however faint—oh! light is always *whole*. A particle of it is a part of all light. By no means too small. Scattered light—it still reaches us. And we still exist. For where can we hide, if the light has not been scattered utterly? And perhaps the sun is not setting but dawning . . .

The shaft of light moved on, leaving beneath it, to my surprise, an unusually clean and polished parquet, without a speck of dust . . . and shone on Mama. She seemed to have been woven of that magical dust, with a trace of light still shining through her. The ray was refracted by her, but she merely absorbed the light, like an opaque body, as if ray had struck ray . . . interference, perhaps? . . . generating her airy, sacred shadow, so that my eye could distinguish her in the scattered light. Mama! . . .

"You're awake! What would you like for breakfast . . ."

"I'd have some bouillon."

Oh, why bring Pascal into it! No one knows whether he tried Descartes's advice . . . The bouillon burned my mouth. The persistent taste of it poisoned my first cigarette and all the hard-earned inspiration of repose.

———

I so wanted to continue, and was so unable . . .

The deadline passed. I survived . . . Scattered light! Where has everything scattered to? What have we done! . . . Everything is thickening around us. Narrowing. A gorge, a tunnel. The light has been scattered and absorbed, but there's something growing . . . a little patch of some sort . . . up ahead. Ahead, or at the end? That is where the light comes from. The next world.

Someday I'll get this book written! In it, time will go in its true direction—backward! But no flashbacks! Simply, at the beginning, our House will drive out the eerie institution that has swallowed it. Then, first of all, Father will be resurrected, and next his illness will recede into the distant future, the Tree will rise up and the branch grow back on it, and even the suicide will fly back up to the roof from the asphalt, in his linen shirt; my mother will grow young . . . Quickly, in a speeded-up film, the bombs will fly up into the sky, the ice of the blockade will melt, and the war will fail to begin. The leaves will sparkle more caressingly—as in childhood, as after tears, when you have been spanked unfairly. And now you haven't even been spanked yet . . . Grandmother will come back to life. The sky will look down with a gaze increasingly untroubled, suddenly I will cry out at the first spank, and—the storyteller isn't yet born. How will the world be changed by my not being in it yet? With what unknown hues of envy, hope, and expectation will it be tinted in my absence? . . . How it will splash and play in happiness!

And lo—literally nothing has happened. All has been swept away into the future.

A carriage will come clattering over the cobblestones. A lady with a parasol will spring lightly from the running board, her elbow supported by a gentleman in whom I don't immediately recognize my grandfather—I guess only later . . . Below the ruche of her slightly raised skirt the lady will bare, above her slipper . . . what a pretty little ankle! What a beautiful, what a young grandmother I have in 1910! And what is this rattle of commands? A thick-lipped little boy, with fair curls and a sailor shirt, is hugging a glass jar that contains a preserved raven—my uncle felt his calling before anyone else . . . And here's my aunt, too, I recognize her by her nose, but she isn't even two years old—there's not much to say about her . . . and I'm not actually so eager to inspect them individually. My gaze is riveted on another little girl: only she is capable of being so astonished by everything, only she could have eyes so round with ecstatic horror . . . Mama! Little Mama . . . Don't be afraid, you don't know me . . . But what an interesting day for you . . . They're carrying in the trunks, cartons, boxes, valises . . . How new the house is! How big! Is it really true that you're going to live in it, little girl of mine?

And what an entertaining house, really, not like the others! No one knows yet that you're in the style of the turn of the century, you are *moderne*, you are *art nouveau* . . . You are simply new, and convenient for my living family to live in . . . Now they, too, walk away from me into the indiscernible distance of the future, and for some reason this concerns me less and less . . . Isn't that the question I asked my mother some day later? Whether I had existed? But lo—I, too, am gone.

What a book this will be one day! Oh, I must hurry . . . Perhaps it's still not too late? . . . Perhaps it's still not too . . .

1970–73, 1980–83

From the Translator

I had never before broken free from the confines of boundless Russia. Gaily I rode into the long-dreamt-of river, and my good steed carried me out on the Turkish bank. But that bank had already been won: I was still in Russia.

PUSHKIN, *Journey to Arzrum*

THE LITERARY CAPTIVE

Andrei Bitov has remarked that Russians visit the Caucasus with a sense of homecoming: they have returned. Most are returning to a realm of courage and beauty, familiar from their reading of Pushkin, Lermontov, and Tolstoy; some, like the poet Mandelstam, are communing with ancient Christian cultures and world history; Bitov himself finds in Armenia a promised land of "real ideals." These are glad homecomings, and yet they imply a degree of estrangement from the everyday reality of the traveler's own homeland.

Lessons of Armenia is subtitled *Journey out of Russia*. Although written as a highly personal travel memoir, a thoughtful and entertaining account of Bitov's experiences in Armenia, it is more than that. It may be read as the journey of a man who repeatedly breaks free "from the confines of boundless Russia," only to discover that in some sense he is still in Russia. Bitov is, after all, an alien "agent of empire"—and, at the same time, an alienated captive of his own beloved homeland.

This realization leads to a journey of another kind: *Choosing a Location* is Bitov's quest for his own place and time. If, when abroad, he is still in Russia, and if, when in Russia, he is oppressed by a cultural nostalgia, an obscure homesickness, then where is his true home, the true locus of his nature as a Russian?

His dilemma reflects the contradictions of his society. Writing in the years just before *glasnost*, he feels that Soviet reality has shifted in such a way that Russian words no longer hit their targets; at its heart there is a silence that resists articulation. Bitov's effort to penetrate the truth, therefore, becomes a duel with silence. For this, no setting could be more appropriate than the Caucasus— scene of so many famous duels in Russian literature—and specifically Georgia, a nation still struggling with its identity as the homeland of Stalin.

By calling his book A *Captive of the Caucasus*, Bitov places it in a long Russian tradition of Caucasian writings. The title was originally Pushkin's: in 1820, after a period of exile in the Caucasus, he wrote a romantic poem in which a highland maiden falls in love with a captive Russian officer and helps him escape. So popular was this poem that the young Lermontov, and later even Tolstoy, adopted the title for their own variations on the same plot.

Nineteenth-century interest in the Caucasus was high, because the Russian Empire was engaged in a long drive to acquire and pacify the exotic lands south of the mountains. Georgia was annexed in 1801, portions of Armenia in 1829. Pushkin and Lermontov went on to write many other poems of love and valor in southern settings. The continuing struggles with Turks, Persians, and proud highland tribesmen inspired a variety of prose works, among them Lermontov's romantic novel A *Hero of Our Time* (1840) and Tolstoy's realistic tales of war. By the turn of the century the territory was firmly under Russian control; the "Caucasian tradition" ended, in effect, with Tolstoy's last story, *Hadji Murad* (1904).

This literature served as a kind of proving ground for an important figure in Russian novels, the wandering "superfluous man." Pushkin, soon after completing his *Captive of the Caucasus*, decided that its Byronic hero—disillusioned with Russian society, coldly moralistic in his rejection of the highland maiden's love—was unsuccessfully portrayed. He planned his novel-in-verse *Eugene Onegin* as an attempt to develop the character further. Onegin became the prototype of the alienated Russian hero who stands apart from his time, unable to serve.

Pushkin himself—and many a writer after him, chafing under the tsar's censorship—identified with this aspect of his hero. Always under suspicion because of his liberal views, Pushkin was never allowed to travel abroad or even to serve in the army. In 1829, he did make an impulsive, unauthorized trip to observe a military campaign against the Turks in western Armenia, which he recounted in *Journey to Arzrum*. But, like Onegin (whose European adventures were never published, presumably because of the censor), Pushkin went no farther than the Caucasus.

Bitov, in turn, galled by pre-*glasnost* Soviet constraints, feels a poignant kinship with Pushkin. He draws his epigraph for *Lessons of Armenia* from Pushkin's travel notes. At the same time, he hints at the contemporary relevance of his book by giving it the subtitle *Journey out of Russia*—taken from his own novel, *Pushkin House* (on which he was working when he went to Armenia, though it could not be published in the Soviet Union for another twenty years). At the end of that novel, when the hero realizes with despair that he has betrayed his conscience for the privilege of a trip to Paris, he conceives of a brilliantly ironic article on the subject of Pushkin and travel abroad. The title will be "Journey out of Russia," he decides, and the epigraph will be Pushkin's anecdote—quoted above, as the epigraph to these notes—about crossing into Turkish territory and finding himself still in Russia.

When *Lessons of Armenia* first appeared in the Soviet Union, in 1969, it was shorn of its subtitle. The censors had made numerous other small cuts. More recent editions, since *glasnost*, have included much, but not all, of the deleted material, which is restored in this translation at Bitov's request. *Choosing a Location*, as published in 1973, was an essay on contemporary Georgian filmmakers; it has evolved into an "album" in which Bitov's impressions of Georgia alternate with thoughts of home.

In his travels, Bitov is always conscious of the companionship of writers who have preceded him. Although the point of his allusions will generally be quite clear to Western readers from the context, major literary landmarks are identified in the notes that follow.

I am forever grateful for the advice and encouragement of Rima Zolina, Boris Hoffman, Professor Michael Connolly of Boston College, and the kind friends who read my manuscript. I would especially like to thank Diana Der Hovanessian for providing translations of lines from Osip Mandelstam's *Armenia*.

NOTES

PAGE 13 / *"The Armenian language is a wildcat," Mandelstam said* During a visit to the Caucasus in 1930, Osip Mandelstam wrote a group of poems about Armenia. For Mandelstam, as for Bitov, Armenia was a promised land where he sought to overcome his alienation from the present. His sojourn there restored the gift of poetry to him, according to his wife. (For the circumstances of his trip, see note to page 213.)

PAGE 53 / *Saryan* Martiros Saryan (1880–1972), a well-known Armenian painter. He is the subject of the chapter "The Patriarch" (page 127).

PAGE 75 / *Aelita of Aparan* Aelita, or The Decline of Mars (1922) is an intensely romantic science-fiction novel by Alexei Tolstoy (a distant relative of the great Lev Tolstoy). The heroine is a delicate, blue-skinned Martian princess. In a twentieth-century variation on the captive-of-the-Caucasus theme, Aelita falls in love with a captured Soviet space explorer and helps him escape.

PAGE 146 / *Bored with posing as a Melmoth . . .* These lines are from a draft of the chapter that Pushkin had planned to write about Onegin's travels. Experimenting with various poses of alienation, Onegin imitates, among others, the gloomy hero of Maturin's *Melmoth the Wanderer* (1820).

PAGE 151 / *I traveled by post-chaise from Tiflis . . .* The opening of Lermontov's novel *A Hero of Our Time*. Declaring that he has lost most of his own travel notes, the narrator substitutes anecdotes about Pechorin, an enigmatic traveler he has met in Georgia, and concludes with passages from Pechorin's diary. A high point of the diary is one of literature's most memorable duels, fought on a cliff above a ravine.

Lermontov, a member of the Life Guard Hussars, was twice assigned to duty in the Caucasus as punishment: once for writing an angry poem about Pushkin's tragic, untimely death in a duel (1837), and once for participating in a duel himself. Lermontov, too, died young, in yet another duel, at a North Caucasian spa in 1841.

PAGE 183 / *two rubles eighty-seven kopecks* The price of a half liter of vodka.

PAGE 186 / *an ascension from lush and blooming Dilizhan, or is it Borzhomi* Ascension Day, the fortieth day after Easter, commemorates the ascension of Christ (who died at the age of thirty-three) to Heaven. Dilizhan and Borzhomi are resorts in Armenia and Georgia, respectively.

PAGE 198 / *To the memory of Nikolai Rubtsov* The poet Nikolai Rubtsov (1936–71) is said to have been murdered by his wife.

PAGE 213 / *a Gogol's Overcoat complex* "The Overcoat" (1841) is Gogol's story of a humble Petersburg clerk named Akaky Akakievich. After much sacrifice, he finally acquires a new overcoat, only to have it stolen the first time he wears it. As an account of the plight of the "little man," the story is commonly taken to be a forerunner of Russian realism. The remark "We have all come out of Gogol's *Overcoat*" has often (although erroneously) been attributed to Dostoevsky.

PAGE 213 / *Mandelstam "in a fur coat too lordly for his station" . . .* The phrase is from Osip Mandelstam's own description of his high-school literature teacher, in *The Hum of Time* (1923), an account of his childhood in Petersburg.

Bitov, however, is applying the phrase to a complicated incident later in the poet's life. As recounted by Nadezhda Mandelstam in *Hope against Hope*, her husband had once bought a wretched secondhand raccoon coat at a southern bazaar, simply to keep him warm in Moscow. In the late 1920s, his enemies recalled his "magnificent fur coat" and cited it as evidence of his "bourgeois ideology." At this time Mandelstam was fighting a false charge of plagiarism. Critics accused him, in effect, of stealing the fur coat of Russian literature from Akaky Akakievich. The affair was a protracted, ugly "Dreyfus case." A high official finally put a stop to it in 1930 and sent the Mandelstams on an eight-month visit to Armenia to recuperate. In a furious polemic titled "Fourth Prose," written toward the end of the trip, Mandelstam rejected the tribe of professional writers by rhetorically stripping off his "literary fur coat" and trampling on it.

P A G E   213 / *my city ("familiar to the point of tears")*   When Mandelstam arrived home from the Caucasus in December of 1930, he wrote a poem called "Leningrad": "I have returned to my city, familiar to the point of tears." He wrote steadily thereafter until his arrest in 1937 (he died in a transit camp in 1938), but his work went unpublished in the Soviet Union until the 1970s.

P A G E   230 / *the* Petersburg *in which "I, too, was born, perhaps" . . . and in which "you, too, were wont to shine."*   Bitov is adapting lines from *Eugene Onegin*, in which Pushkin introduces his hero as an old friend, born in Petersburg, "where you, too, were born, perhaps, or were wont to shine, my reader."

P A G E   230 / *Yevgeny and Akaky Akakievich*   The humble heroes of, respectively, Pushkin's poem *The Bronze Horseman* and Gogol's story "The Overcoat." Both men are depicted as oppressed by the inhumane city of Petersburg.

P A G E   240 / *the Larins*   The heroine's hospitable, provincial Russian parents in Pushkin's *Eugene Onegin*.

P A G E   242 / *the tomb of Griboedov*   Alexander Griboedov (1795–1829) is beloved as the author of the comedy *Woe from Wit*, and is also remembered as the composer of some charming waltzes. While in the Russian foreign service, he was stationed in the Caucasus and married the Georgian princess Nina Chavchavadze. Shortly afterward, he was murdered by religious fanatics in Teheran. (As every Russian reader knows, Pushkin, on his way to Arzrum, encountered the ox-cart bearing Griboedov's body home to Tiflis.)

P A G E   250 / *Serov*   Valentin Serov (1865–1911), a well-known portrait painter who enriched traditional realism with an impressionist's use of light.

P A G E   273 / *Pomyalovsky . . . Tolstoy . . . Goncharov . . . Kuprin*   Pomyalovsky's collected works fill two volumes; Tolstoy's, ninety volumes; Goncharov's, eight; and Kuprin's, nine.

P A G E   287 / *Kazbegi's house, and Pshavela's house, and also to Gori*   Kazbegi and Pshavela were nineteenth-century Georgian writers. Gori was the birthplace of Joseph Stalin.

P A G E   296 / *and Ilya had not come back. What could have happened to him? . . .*   The eminent writer Ilya Chavchavadze (1837–1907) and his friend Akaky Tsereteli were leaders of the Georgian nationalist liberation movement. On a journey from Tiflis to his estate in Saguramo, Chavchavadze was murdered by the secret police.